EVERYTHING WE LOST

KATE SMITH

COPYRIGHT © 2018 KATE SMITH

This book is a work of fiction. Names, characters, places, and incidents are either the product of the author's imagination or are used fictitiously, and any resemblance to actual persons, living or dead, business establishments, events, or locales is entirely coincidental.

All rights reserved. No part of this book may be reproduced, scanned, or distributed in any printed or electronic form without permission. Please do not participate in or encourage piracy of copyrighted material in violation of the author's rights.

KateSmithAuthor.com

Paperback ISBN: 978-1-9993893-1-4
E-book ISBN-13: 978-1-9993893-3-8
Cover credit: Ana Chabrand Design House

for my daughters

Chapter 1

Savannah

The O'Hare air terminal bustled with activity, the volume of passengers causing Savannah's eyes to widen. She dodged through the crowded concourse clutching her small blue backpack, the sheer number of faces blurring her vision.

"Vanna." Leanne cut into her thoughts. "Hurry up. If we miss the next train, Ms. McGillis will be pissed."

"Coming." Savannah hurried after her best friend and joined the queue of luggage-toting teenagers. She bounced on her toes, peering around the platform, her gaze drawn to a blonde woman with a toddler in tow.

Leanne nudged her with an elbow. "Her nose is too pointy, Vanna. She looks nothing like you."

Savannah glanced at her friend, a rueful smile appearing. "Yeah, maybe."

"Keep together." Ms. McGillis handed out the tickets and ushered the group toward the train. "I don't want to make phone calls to parents about missing kids." The teacher focused her attention on Savannah. "Ms. Phillips. Get your head out of the clouds. We're on a tight schedule."

An excited buzz rose in the car as the doors slid shut and the train pulled away from the platform.

The city flashed by, and she grinned at Leanne. "This is so awe—"

A horrendous bang echoed through the carriage, followed by the screeching sound of tearing metal. The car lurched and pitched sideways, screams and cries filling the air as it twisted and rolled, bags and suitcases tumbling onto the frightened passengers.

Savannah clung to the metal bar and crouched with her eyes clenched shut, pain lancing through her as a piece of flying luggage struck her shoulder.

Leanne's shriek rang in her ears. Shattered glass rained over them, a blast of cold air rushing in as windows disintegrated under the assault.

Tears streaked down her face, her sobs mingling with Leanne's frightened squeals. Her knuckles whitened and her fingers ached as she struggled to hold on. Her chest constricted and burned as she gasped for air, still clinging to her backpack.

The motion stopped with a jolt, followed by a moment of heavy silence before pandemonium erupted. Loud moans and cries, along with panicked voices, and an incessant screaming reverberated through the train.

Savannah forced her eyes open and focused on her best friend, wishing she could block out the mayhem, the blood, and the crying. She felt lightheaded and nauseous, sucking in deep breaths and hoping she wouldn't pass out.

A red patch stained Leanne's jeans, growing larger every second. The girl's face paled and contorted, tears flooding her eyes. "It hurts so bad. What happened?"

Savannah wheezed through a parched throat. "I don't know." She brushed at her cheek as something warm and sticky trickled into her eyes, blurring her vision.

"You're bleeding." Leanne pointed with a trembling finger, her voice dropping into a low flat monotone.

Savannah squeezed Leanne's hand, fighting the urge to curl into a ball and weep. The distant wailing of sirens calmed the worst of her fears. "They're coming." Her voice sounded strange and hoarse. She cleared her throat. "Help is coming, Leanne."

"We're going to die." Leanne's ashen, tear-streaked face lifted toward her.

"We'll be okay. It's over." Her limbs refused to obey her command to move as she stared at the odd lump forming along the top of her friend's leg. A shiver ran down her spine as she closed her eyes in order to get her bearings, desperate to shut out the living nightmare surrounding her. Frantic screams for help emanated from all around.

The two girls huddled among the debris, clinging to each other as red and blue lights flickered through the shattered glass.

Chapter 2

Aiden

Icy bits of snow danced in the air as the helicopter touched down with a bump. Flashes of bright red and blue washed over the chaotic scene. A multitude of ambulances and fire trucks had arrived, and paramedics, police, and firemen dodged scattered luggage, briefcases, bags, and shattered glass.

"What a mess." Aiden surveyed the twisted wreckage before looking at his colleague. "Ready, Em?"

Emily nodded. "Let's do this."

Aiden slung one medical bag over his shoulder, grabbing his second case of supplies before hopping to the ground. He shivered in the biting wind, drawing the collar of the heavy flight jacket up to his chin and tugging the black wool beanie over his ears.

Their boots pounded on the pavement as they bent low to avoid wash from the spinning rotors.

Emily motioned toward one of the overturned cars.

Aiden caught her hand, leaning in close, hoping she could hear him over the drone of emergency helicopters. "Take care, Em."

She raised her brows. "You too," she mouthed. After a quick squeeze to his fingers, she dashed to the closest unattended casualty.

Aiden stared after her for a moment before turning in the opposite direction. Emily was an experienced emergency physician so he shouldn't worry, but he did. Over the years he'd become close to his colleague. Or as close as he ever let himself get to a woman.

"Hey, Doc." A fireman waved before pressing gloved hands to the bloody sleeve of the man stretched out on the pavement.

Aiden rushed through the light snow, hopping over bits of debris, assessing the situation with a practiced eye. He kneeled and listened for breath sounds and a heartbeat. "Keep the pressure while I establish an airway." He stripped the wrapping from an intubation tube, taking a steadying breath before tipping the man's head and sliding it in.

A paramedic arrived and attached an Ambu bag. "Got it, Doc."

"Thanks." Aiden sliced the bloody sleeve and applied a pressure dressing before performing another check on the man's vitals and assessing his other injuries. "He's ready for transport. Let's get him on the backboard."

Once they'd secured the man, Aiden made a final assessment, and the paramedics loaded the patient into an ambulance.

"Doc." Another firefighter flagged him down and pointed to the wreckage. "We have a passenger in there with a serious leg injury."

Aiden nodded and hauled himself up, peeking through the window they'd cleared of shattered glass. He wiggled through the opening and dropped inside the car, picking his way through the debris and crouching in front of the teenager. "I've got her." He nodded to the fireman sitting with her. "We'll need a backboard."

"I'll be right back."

"Hi, I'm Dr. Hamilton. What's your name?" He noted the blood and odd angle of her leg. "Let me look."

Her fearful face lifted. "Savannah?" she whispered, her dark hair falling across her pallid cheeks as she clutched a blanket around her shoulders.

"Is that your name? Savannah?" He pulled shears from his bag and slit her pant leg.

The girl's entire body quivered as her head tilted, and she focused a blank stare on her leg.

"Don't worry, Savannah, we'll take good care of you." Aiden checked for other injuries and peered into her eyes before running his fingers over her scalp. "A small bump. Do you have any allergies, Savannah?"

The teen gave him a puzzled look before shaking her head, fresh tears dribbling down her face. "No."

"You'll feel a small pinch." Aiden injected morphine before he dressed and splinted her leg to stabilize it for transport. "They'll x-ray your leg at the hospital."

"They took her." Her voice shook as her gaze darted around the now empty train car. "Where'd she go?"

"Took who?" Aiden looked around. Judging by her odd behavior, she'd sunk into deep shock. "We'll get you out, okay?"

A paramedic slid through the window with a backboard. He helped Aiden transfer and strap their patient onto it.

"I can't leave her." The girl clutched his arm. "Where's Vanna?"

He squeezed her hand. "Everyone's evacuated. We'll find Vanna." With the help of the paramedic, he lifted her into the waiting hands of the firefighters.

Aiden accepted a helping hand from a fireman and dropped to the ground outside as paramedics placed the girl on a gurney.

A blonde teenager rushed toward them clutching a small blue backpack to her chest, the blanket wrapped around her slim body billowing in the wind. "Oh, no, Leanne."

"Are you Vanna?" Aiden wrapped an extra blanket around the girl and seated her on an empty gurney.

She nodded. "That's Leanne." The girl trembled, her gaze locking onto her friend. "They made me leave her on the train. So much blood." She huddled under the blanket, her teeth chattering.

"Leanne's okay. She'll be on her way to the hospital in a minute," he said. "Let's check you over. You're freezing."

Savannah nodded as tears streaked down her reddened cheeks. "We've been here forever."

Aiden swept off his beanie and tugged it onto her head. The poor thing needed it more than he did. "Which hospital are you taking Leanne to?" he asked the paramedic.

"Yours," the man said before he wheeled the gurney away.

"Can I go with her?" Savannah's gaze flitted around as they took her friend toward the waiting ambulance.

"I'll make you a deal. Let me dress these cuts and examine you, and we'll send you to the same hospital." He disengaged her icy grip from the backpack.

"No!" Her eyes widened. "I need that."

"Don't worry. It'll be safe." Aiden helped her lay back and tucked the small bag beside her. He noticed how she winced and clutched her arm against her chest. "Does your shoulder hurt?"

She blinked at him, a small frown creasing her forehead as he cleaned her cuts. "A little."

Aiden performed a quick exam before flagging down a paramedic he recognized. "Ben, can you take Vanna to my ER? Ask them to order an x-ray of her shoulder. Tell them I triaged her."

"You got it, Aiden."

"Thanks." He tucked another blanket around Vanna. "I'll check on you when I get to the hospital. Ben will take excellent care of you until then."

The teenager nodded and clenched her eyes shut as Ben wheeled her away.

Aiden watched as the paramedic loaded the gurney into the ambulance. Savannah possessed an eerie familiarity, though he couldn't place when or where they'd met.

~

Two hours later, Aiden and Emily arrived at the hospital on the chopper and passed their patient to a surgical team.

Aiden slumped against the wall of the elevator as it descended, swiping a hand through his short dark hair. "I'm beat."

"My fingers are numb." Emily rubbed her hands together and blew on them. "I'm chilled to the bone."

Aiden brushed a smudge of dirt from her cheek with one thumb before pressing her icy hands between his palms. "A coffee will warm you up."

"That feels amazing." Emily smiled, leaning toward him as if trying to absorb the warmth of his body. "How are your hands not freezing?"

A shiver ran through him as their gazes met. A frisson of attraction rose as it always did when they were together, but the moment evaporated when the elevator doors slid open, revealing the bustling ER. Gurneys littered the hallway, nurses ran back and forth, machines beeped, and the buzz of conversation filled the air.

Aiden claimed Emily's medical bags and pushed her gently toward the lounge. "Warm up before Dragon Lady drags you into the fray."

Emily offered a grateful smile before hurrying down the hallway.

As he placed the bags on the counter of the front desk, Dana, Chief of the ER—AKA Dragon Lady to him and Emily—spotted him.

"Dr. Hamilton. Glad to have my chief resident back." Dana snapped up the gurney's rail before the surgical team wheeled her patient toward the elevators. "How bad was it?"

He shrugged off the grimy flight jacket and slung it over the counter by the kits. "A total nightmare."

"Fatalities?"

Aiden set his lips in a grim line. "Several. The crew was transporting the last minor injuries when we left."

Dana sighed. "We're buried and have several minors from the train accident, plus the waiting room's overflowing. I need you to stay and help."

Aiden nodded. He suspected it would be a long shift.

"Ben said you triaged this patient." The desk clerk pushed a tablet and an envelope into his hands. "Exam 2."

"Thank you." Aiden pulled out the x-ray and peered at it before he started toward the exam room.

"Dr. Hamilton? Can you check this x-ray? Broken, right?" A medical student motioned to a spot on the film mounted on the light board.

Aiden scanned it. "Call for a consult. The patient might need surgery." After making a note for the chart, he turned to run the gauntlet, fielding a barrage of questions from both residents and medical students. He smiled as he finally entered the exam room. "How are you feeling, Savannah?"

The blonde teenager rubbed her arm. "Okay."

"You're a long way from Portland. No parents or chaperones here yet, Rosa?"

"Parents are being contacted now." The nurse checked the IV. "Someone should be here soon."

"How's Leanne?" Savannah tipped up her ashen face, her eyes shiny with tears.

"Let's find out. What's her last name?"

"Billings."

Aiden nodded at Rosa, who dialed an extension and murmured into the receiver. "While Rosa checks on Leanne, let's take a look at you." Aiden began his exam. "Any more pain?"

"I have a headache and the cuts sting." She grimaced. "My shoulder aches. Things were flying all over the place."

"We'll give you something to relieve the pain." He slid her gown down to view her shoulder. "You'll have quite the bruise, but it's not dislocated." Rosa handed him a fresh ice pack, which he placed on the girl's shoulder. "You'll need a few stitches. Any allergies?"

"No." She stared wide-eyed as he prepared the needle. "Will it hurt?"

"Just a small pinch while I numb the area." He injected the local. "Done. Not so awful, right?"

"It wasn't too bad," she whispered, averting her eyes from the suture kit he'd opened.

"Dr. Hamilton's a pro at stitches." The nurse patted Savannah's arm. "Leanne's fine. Her surgery went well and she's on the way to recovery."

The girl let out a rush of air. "Leanne's all right?"

"She's being well taken care of. Take a deep breath and close your eyes. I promise I'll be quick with the stitches." Aiden sutured as the girl exhaled a long slow breath.

Emily stuck her head in the door. "I need your assistance, Aiden. Will you be long?"

Savannah tensed, sitting ramrod straight.

"Relax, Savannah." He glanced at his dark-haired colleague. "Can it wait five minutes?"

"It's not urgent. Exam 4." The door swished shut as she backed out of the room.

"I'll dress this, Rosa. You probably have patients waiting."

The nurse swept out, leaving the sterile dressings on a tray within easy reach.

"How old are you?" Savannah asked.

"Mmm, what?" Déjà vu overtook him as he studied his patient's deep brown eyes.

"A weird question, right?" Her voice quivered.

He shook off the odd feeling as he inspected his handiwork, taking extra care with the sutures. This one was on her forehead, and he wanted to prevent scarring.

"Dr. Hamilton?"

Aiden cleared his throat. "I'm thirty. How old are you?"

"Fourteen." She seemed to relax, and a touch of color returned to her face.

"What grade are you in?" He pressed a dressing onto her wound.

"Ten." She stared at him. "Could I come back and ask you some questions? You know, about being a doctor?"

Aiden pushed back his stool. "Sure. If you call the front desk, we can work out a time. Leave a number if I'm busy." He selected a card from the small stack on the counter. "This is the direct number for the ER. Rosa will be in with care instructions, and she'll arrange for you to see Leanne."

"Thank you … Dr. Hamilton."

"You're welcome, Savannah." As he added notes to her chart, he observed the girl from the corner of his eye. His heart skipped a beat as he realized he was also under intense scrutiny. Those soulful brown eyes held a hint of curiosity, tinged with something he couldn't name. "Are you all right?"

"I'm fine." She continued staring at him in a most unsettling way.

"Have Rosa find me if you need anything." His breath caught in his chest and pain lanced through his heart as the faintest of smiles crossed her face. This girl reminded him of someone he used to know. "Rosa?" He waved down the nurse. "Can you keep an eye on Savannah? She'll need care instructions for those stitches."

"Social Services will be in to see her," Rosa said. "My break is coming up, so I'll take her upstairs to see Leanne."

"You're a sweetheart, Rosa." Aiden smiled at this motherly woman and his favorite nurse at work.

"Anytime, Aiden." She patted his arm before heading in to check on Savannah.

Aiden shook his head. Impossible. His imagination had veered off on a tangent at the mention of Portland. He strode toward Exam 4, pushing the thoughts of Savannah from his mind.

Chapter 3

Savannah

Savannah tapped her pencil against her notebook and glanced at the clock which now showed ten past one. Her knee bounced as she fidgeted and tucked a lock of wavy honey-blonde hair behind her ear. Every ounce of courage had poured into making the call, her heart pounding and palms sweating as she requested the meeting with the enigmatic young doctor.

She shifted on the red upholstered bench, refocusing on the open page. The words blurred and she rubbed her eyes.

Her shoulders sagged as the door opened, revealing a young couple who chose a table by the window. The door opened yet again.

At the sight of the tall dark-haired man approaching her booth, Savannah exhaled a long slow breath.

"I hope you haven't been waiting long." He shrugged out of his wool overcoat and hung it neatly, tucking leather gloves and a cashmere scarf in the pocket before sliding into the opposite seat. "I got held up at the hospital." He ran slim fingers through his dark brown hair, settling the disarray caused by the icy wind. "How are you feeling today? How's your shoulder?"

"Sore." She rubbed her arm. "I have a huge bruise, but it's much better."

"Keep icing it. It'll take a few days to heal," he said. "I checked on Leanne. She's doing well, but not ready to fly. Are you planning to see her today?"

"I visited this morning and promised I'd go back this afternoon. She needed to sleep so they kicked me out." Her mouth went dry, and she took another sip of water before clearing her throat. "I have some questions."

"Would you like to eat while we talk? My treat." Aiden perused the menu. "The food's decent, or so I've heard."

Savannah opened her menu, even though she wasn't sure she could eat. Her stomach had been flip-flopping all morning. She wiggled her shoulders in a futile attempt to release the tension from her body.

Aiden motioned for the waitress, who arrived at the table sporting a bright smile. "Coffee, please. Savannah? Would you like a drink?"

"Coke?" She fought the urge to roll her eyes at the woman who'd ignored her when she'd first entered the café. The waitress had eventually poured Savannah a glass of water, but the arrival of this handsome doctor apparently warranted five-star service, complete with simpering smile and fluttering eyelashes.

The waitress trotted off but soon reappeared with their drinks. "What can I get you?" She poised her pencil over a small notepad, her gaze locking onto the young doctor.

"Savannah?"

"Chicken burger with fries." Savannah closed her menu.

"And I'll have a bacon cheeseburger with the garden salad. Thanks," Aiden said with an easy smile as he set his menu aside.

"Right away." The waitress beamed before heading off to place their orders.

"Have you always lived here?" Savannah frowned at the woman who kept peering their way, though she couldn't really blame her.

The guy seemed blessed with a genuine, classy charm. His deep brown eyes lit up when he smiled and he was decidedly good-looking and well-dressed. Leanne had already labeled the man a chick-magnet which made Savannah squirm, considering the circumstances.

"I was born here, though I lived in Philadelphia during medical school. Have you always lived in Portland?"

Savannah nodded. "I was born at University Medical. My mom taught fifth grade and my dad worked for a bank, but," she said, studying the man closely, "they're not my real parents."

"Oh?"

"They adopted me when I was an hour old." She pushed the ice around her soda with her straw. "My mom died a year ago. My dad is retired."

"I'm sorry about your mom, Savannah. You must miss her," he said softly. "How'd it happen?"

"A drunk driver." She sucked in a deep breath to combat the sudden pang. Her stomach clenched every time she thought of the needless and sudden way her mom had died. Even worse, the man who'd destroyed her life had yet to atone for his actions.

"It's okay to be sad and cry." Aiden's gaze never left hers.

"Here you go." The waitress placed food-laden plates in front of them.

"I'm starving. I never seem to have time for lunch." Aiden bit into his burger. After a sip of coffee, he motioned toward her. "Shoot."

Savannah ate a bite of her chicken burger to stall the conversation. Forever she had waited for this moment. Now it was here, she was afraid to hope this meeting would have a happy ending. That she'd finally found what she'd been seeking. It couldn't be this easy. Could it?

The man across from her continued eating, so she assumed he remained oblivious to her turmoil and doubts. Then she caught his swift glance and realized he'd been observing her the entire time. It unnerved her. *Does he know what I want?* She wavered, almost losing courage under his intense scrutiny.

"Dr. Hamilton?" Savannah drew in a deep breath. "I don't want to be a doctor."

"Oh?" He set his burger on his plate. "So why …?"

"Please don't be angry." It took massive effort to look his way.

"I'm not." He leveled his gaze at her. "What's on your mind?"

She twisted her napkin in her hands, summoning the courage for the next step.

"What's bothering you, Savannah?"

Savannah's heart pounded in her chest, and her hands grew clammy. She dug into her worse-for-wear backpack, removed the plain brown manila envelope, and held it out, willing him to take it.

Aiden eyed the package before plucking it from her trembling fingertips. He stared at it without so much as twitching.

"Open it." She forced out the words in a tiny voice. "Please?"

It seemed to take forever for him to extract the contents. The swift intake of breath was audible. He stared at the photo, at her, then back to the picture in his hands.

Savannah's knees shook, and a shiver ran down her spine, goose bumps rising on her arms. "Look at the back." She held her breath as he turned the photo. After spending hours inspecting the name written in flowing script inside the faded red ink heart, she could imagine it in her mind.

His hand passed across his jaw, his fingertips rubbing the rough stubble before he inspected the second document. "You were born on January fifth." He set the birth certificate on top of the envelope.

"Yes." Savannah shifted.

"Where did you get this picture?"

"My mom."

"How …? Where did she get it?"

A thrill ran through her. This man sitting across from her bore a striking resemblance to the smiling teenager with his arms wrapped around the beautiful blonde girl.

"She found the picture tucked inside my baby blanket. Along with …" She pulled up her sleeve and unhooked the ornate gold watch before dangling it over the table.

He retrieved the timepiece from her fingers and stared at it for the longest time before he turned it, surely seeking the inscription: *forever in my heart*.

"You've seen it before."

"Yes." He swept his fingers through his hair before he drummed them against the wooden table. "How's this possible?" Aiden shook his head and rubbed the back of his neck.

"Are you my Aiden Hamilton?" Tears burned her eyes as she searched his expression for a sign. "Say something, please?" She reached out, grasping his hand.

He wrapped his warm fingers around hers, squeezing gently. "I think so." His voice shook as recognition dawned in his eyes. "But … wow, this is crazy."

It seemed surreal, sitting here across from this man who'd just admitted he could be her father. "Who is my mother?" Savannah whispered.

"Oh, Savannah." He shook his head. "I can't tell you."

"What do you mean?" Disappointment flooded through her as she sniffled, fighting the overwhelming urge to burst into tears. "How can you not know?"

"It's complicated," he said. "I'd need to talk to her. And …"

"What?" Her heart sank at the realization he might not divulge the information she sought.

Aiden took several deep breaths. "I can't drop this on her without proof. We need to be absolutely sure."

"I have the picture, the watch, and my birth certificate. That's not enough?"

He rubbed at the light stubble on his jaw. "I'm … I never thought … the adoption was closed and sealed. Where to even start?"

"Can you start by telling me about my mother?" Savannah had spent hours imagining every possible reaction if she ever found Aiden Hamilton. She hadn't bargained for this confusing and hopeless situation.

"Savannah." Her name rolled off his tongue softly. "We never talked about you finding us. I never thought it possible."

"How do I prove it? I have all this." She motioned to the items on the table, swiping at her damp eyes with the back of one hand. "Why'd you give me away? Who'd do that?"

"Hey." He grasped her hands. "It's nowhere near simple. We were kids. I never even got to see her … you."

"Did you love my mother?"

"Yes." He hesitated. "I've always wondered what happened to our baby girl. If she was happy and had good parents. I can't quite wrap my mind around the fact you're sitting here after years of wishing for answers."

"Now what?"

"Without access to legal files, which we're unlikely to get, we'd need DNA testing." His gaze held hers.

She shuddered, wondering what testing involved. "Does it hurt?"

Aiden shook his head. "It's a big cotton swab they rub on the inside of your mouth."

"Let's do it. I want to know."

"It's not that easy. You're fourteen. Your adoptive father is your legal guardian and needs to provide permission."

Tears brimmed in her eyes. "I want to know if you're my father."

"I would too, believe me."

She nibbled at her lip, unsure of what to do next. Even with Aiden Hamilton sitting right in front of her, she wasn't any closer to finding answers.

He studied her, his eyes narrowing. "Does your dad know you're asking these questions?"

Savannah bowed her head, picking at the pink polish on her fingernail.

"Oh boy." He pinched the bridge of his nose. "This is beyond complicated."

"He knows I have questions about my parents," she whispered.

Aiden emitted a long sigh. "Does he know you're searching? You brought this," he said, pointing at items in front of him, "from Portland, but you didn't know I was here, did you?"

"It's silly, but I … like to look at the photo, so I keep it with me. I wear the watch every day."

"Nothing you've said is silly, Savannah." The corners of his mouth turned down. "Adoption is both a blessing and a curse. It leaves a lot of unanswered questions."

Savannah tilted her head. This man succinctly voiced something she'd never had the courage to express out loud. She loved her mom and dad, but she also had a gaping hole in her life. A missing piece she felt compelled to seek.

"There's no way around it. I can't cross that ethical or legal boundary, so you have no choice but to talk to your dad or you'll have to wait until you're eighteen."

"That's another three years."

"I'm sorry," he said. "More than you know. Giving up a child for adoption isn't easy. Having answers would be amazing."

Savannah faced the inevitable truth. Without her dad's blessing, the truth would be impossible to learn. "He won't be happy, but I'll talk to him when I get home."

Aiden pulled a card from his wallet. "These are my personal numbers. He can contact me." He squeezed her hand and smiled. "How about we finish lunch? You can tell me what you really want to do as doctor is off the table."

Savannah nodded. This hadn't turned out as she'd hoped, and she wasn't sure her dad would agree to DNA testing. She feared his reaction.

"Savannah?" Aiden dangled the watch. "Why don't you keep this?" He caught her fingers in his warm hand and fastening the sparkling jewelry around her wrist.

"You don't think she'll want it back?"

"She clearly wanted you to have it, and I bought it for her, so ..." He turned her arm. "It suits you. You need to keep this too." He handed her the envelope but tucked the picture in his pocket.

She almost protested, but maybe he needed it more than she did.

Chapter 4

Aiden

Those useless words echoed in his ears—*I'm sorry*—as he awoke bathed in a cold sweat, struggling against the sheets and blankets tangled around him. His heart pounded, his chest constricted, and the lingering pain curled deep in his gut.

Old ghosts flashed through his mind as he rubbed trembling hands across his face, shaking off the sound of her hysterical voice still ringing in his ears. It had been years since he'd had this nightmare, but now ancient memories stirred along with deep regrets. Seeing that picture left him breathless. He'd been sucker-punched by the reminder of *her*. Savannah's deep brown eyes misled him.

Four in the morning was too damn early, but nothing would be gained by tossing and turning. He shucked his damp shirt and sleep pants and tossed them into the hamper before attempting to wash it all away in a blasting hot shower.

He armed himself with an extra-large coffee and arrived at work two hours early, diving straight into the backlog of patients.

Emily caught up with him at the front desk as he signed discharge orders. "You're a keener. It's"—she glanced at the clock—"six and you've seen five patients. Working on that promotion?"

"Hmmm, what?" He stared at her.

"The attending job?" She raised an eyebrow.

He blinked, forcing his focus on Emily and the lovely green eyes reflecting concern. Normally he'd have a comeback, but his mind remained a complete blank.

"What's with you?"

He shrugged.

"Pull it together before the Dragon Lady cometh. She's on the warpath."

"I'm fine." He smiled faintly, taking in the sweet smile of his favorite colleague.

"Spill, Aiden." She rested a hand on his arm.

"It's personal."

"Is that my cue to butt out?"

"I'm not up for sharing." He attempted another smile.

"Is this about Tara?" Emily's cheeky grin faded quickly and her lips settled into a flat line.

Aiden sighed. "Why would it? She's only a friend."

"Me thinks you doth protest too much whenever it comes to the nurse."

"And me thinks I'm sick of hearing about this fictional connection." Aiden bowed his head, scrolling through the patient record while picturing the devastated look on Savannah's face. That sad, betrayed, and disappointed way her eyes had pleaded with him to reveal the truth.

Complicated was an understatement. How could he approach Tiffany? Or tell his family about the daughter he'd given up? Best to be armed before exposing the unsuspecting kid to shark-infested waters. Solid irrefutable proof would be the first thing they'd want.

"You haven't heard a word I've said." Emily smacked his arm, her annoyed tone dragging him into the present.

"Sorry, I've got a million things on my mind. My grandmother misses my grandfather and calls constantly. Work's been crazy and chart reviews are stacking up. I'm overwhelmed."

"Want to grab dinner after our shift?"

"I'd be terrible company. Another night?" He rarely refused her invitations as he enjoyed spending time with his dark-haired colleague. Today though, he was preoccupied and afraid she'd pry the information out of him. Nothing got by her, and he hated the idea of lying to Emily.

"Suit yourself." She eyed him before picking up the next chart in the queue.

It turned into a long, busy day, and he regretted his decision to come in early. The sole bright spot appeared when Emily handed him an extra-large, extra-hot latte from the coffee shop across the street.

"I thought I'd save you from that toxic sludge in the lounge." She graced him with a radiant smile.

"Thanks, Em." Aiden savored his first sip, admiring the soft sway of her hips as she sauntered toward Exam 4. A glance toward the admission desk told him he wasn't the only one noticing the lovely doctor. Tara's narrowed gaze followed Emily's progress as well.

At six, he gave a grateful sigh and signed off on the last of his patients. He stretched, ready to disappear before something else happened. The hiss of the sliding glass doors made him glance up, expecting a rush of paramedics wheeling a gurney.

To his surprise, Savannah appeared, sending him a hesitant smile as she approached the desk. "Dr. Hamilton?"

"Savannah. Everything okay?"

"You know her?" One of the residents eyed the teenager.

Savannah sized up the resident warily before looking at Aiden. "Could you check my stitches? They're a little red."

"Sure. In there." He pointed, circling around the desk.

"I'll do it." The resident studied the teenager.

"She's my patient." Aiden waved the resident away. "Find something useful to do, like tackling the full waiting room." He lowered his voice. "Quit ogling the patients, especially the underage ones." Once the over-eager young doctor picked up a chart, Aiden entered the exam room, snapping on gloves.

"The cuts are fine." Her cheeks reddened as she peered through the glass. "Those guys made me nervous, so I said the first stupid thing that came to my mind." She bowed her head. "I fly home tomorrow morning."

"Quick thinking. It reminds me of ..." *Tiffany at fourteen.* Savannah must be his daughter. Or did he simply want it to be true? He gave her a reassuring smile, ignoring her curious look as he removed the dressings. "I'd love to talk before you go. Do you have time for dinner? There are some great little restaurants around here."

"I'd like that."

"I'll check these cuts." He winked as he located some fresh gauze. "They're healing well, and you shouldn't have any scars. Follow up with your family doctor in a week, okay?"

The girl nodded.

"Meet me inside the double doors on the P2 level as I'm in the doctor's lot. I should be done in ten minutes."

"It's a plan." Savannah smiled, sliding her coat on. "Thanks."

Aiden headed for the lounge the moment she disappeared out the door, determined to escape.

Emily appeared moments later, opening her locker and reaching for her coat. "Long one, wasn't it?"

"Better than being on scene like the other day. I'm beat. Thanks again for the coffee."

"You haven't changed your mind about dinner? We could talk about whatever's bothering you. You were off your game today."

"Not tonight. I have a hot date with my pillow." He leaned in and gave her a hug. "Night, Em." Once out of the lounge, he loped down the stairs, concerned the girl would leave if he took too long. He paused at the bottom as he spotted her shuffling her feet in the frigid confines of the parking lot. Her wavy honey-blonde hair was unmistakable and so much like *hers* his heart skipped a beat.

Savannah turned, an uncertain smile appearing. "You came."

"I didn't realize how cold it was tonight." He hit the remote starter and led her toward his black Lexus SUV. After getting her settled, he slid into the driver's seat and adjusted the heat to maximum. "What kind of food do you like? Italian? Chinese?"

"Maybe chicken or noodles or something?"

Aiden pulled out of the lot. "I know the perfect place."

Savannah fiddled with her seat adjustment. "This thing has more buttons and screens than a spaceship, and it's as big as a tank."

He laughed at her expression. "I suppose, but we have to stay safe on the nasty winter roads."

Being mid-week, the restaurant was quiet, and they were immediately seated in a cozy booth. This place was one of his favorite little hideaways, known mainly to the locals. It had some of the best food in town and the tables were suitable for private conversation.

"Dr. Hamilton?" She spoke as soon as the server left with their drink orders.

"Call me Aiden when we're away from the hospital. Dr. Hamilton is too formal." He opened his menu but looked at Savannah rather than reading the selections.

"Aiden." She studied him with wide brown eyes. "It's strange. You could be my father. I never thought I'd find you. It's like we were fated to meet."

Aiden acknowledged the comment with a small nod. Similar thoughts raced through his head. Not only the randomness of her appearance but how she'd found him. People had died in the train accident, and she'd walked away with minor injuries. To him, it was a miracle. "It's unexpected."

He observed her with covert glances as they perused the dinner selections, fighting a grin when he realized the girl was doing exactly the same thing; her subtle and silent looks and the twitch of her lips reminded him of Tiffany during her days as a mischievous teenager. The only thing missing were those captivating crystal blue eyes.

"Are you married?" she asked after the waitress left with their order. "You're not wearing a ring."

He shook his head.

"Kids?" A small frown appeared. "Besides ... me, maybe?"

"No."

"Does ... she?"

He allowed another small shake of his head.

"Oh." Her bottom lip jutted out. "Why not? You're thirty."

He lifted one shoulder. "Residency doesn't leave much free time for a social life."

"You want to get married?"

"Sure, one day."

"Sorry, too nosy, right? My dad says I ask too many questions."

"I don't mind. It's natural to want answers."

"What about ... her?" She clamped her teeth onto her bottom lip. "Sorry," she muttered.

"You've done the math and understand we were fifteen, right? Hardly ready for marriage."

"Or raising a kid?"

"That either." Aiden wasn't prepared to dig into the mess of his past or the dynamics of his family. Part of him worried this girl might run, and he wanted the chance to talk to her a while longer. It might be his only opportunity. "Tell me what you like to do."

"Hang out with my friends? And I like art. I sketch and sometimes paint, but my favorite thing is writing."

Aiden digested the information. As a teenager, Tiffany had carried a sketchbook everywhere and covered her assignments in doodles. It had driven the teachers crazy.

"What do you like?"

"Lately it seems to be all about work, but I love to be outdoors. You know, skiing, sailing, and I've traveled all over the world."

Her eyes lit up. Savannah spent the majority of their meal asking rapid-fire questions about the places he'd visited. "You've been everywhere." She let out a small laugh. "This is the farthest I've ever been from home."

"How did you end up in Chicago?" Aiden sipped his coffee while Savannah nibbled at a piece of chocolate cake.

"Leanne and I volunteer at a Community Center that provides after-school care for low-income families. We help the kids with homework, read, play games, and take them to the playground." Savannah blushed. "The supervisor submitted our names for this trip. We were supposed to go to a convention and tour Chicago, but we missed it."

"I'm sorry." Aiden nodded. "But good for you, I wish we had more of those programs in Chicago." He felt proud of the girl and her accomplishments even if he had nothing to do with how she'd turned out.

"I'm sad, but I'm doing better than poor Leanne who's stuck in the hospital. She'll be alone because I have to go home, and her mom's not here yet."

"Don't worry about Leanne. I'll check on her until she's released."

Savannah blinked at him, her eyes tearing up. "You'd do that?"

"I might even be persuaded to sneak in some decent food if you tell me what she likes."

"Are you kidding? She loves burgers and fries, and she adores chocolate milkshakes. Oh, and Hawaiian pizza." The girl grimaced. "She detests hospital food."

"I hate the food too." Already he was forming a plan so Savannah could relax about her friend. "Let's get you back to the hotel. I don't want to get either of us in trouble."

As Aiden walked Savannah to her door, he wondered if testing was necessary. She was so similar to Tiffany as a teenager, and unless he was imagining it, she had his eyes.

"You have my number, so call me once you talk to your dad."

"I will. Tonight was fun. Thanks for dinner."

"You're welcome. I'll keep an eye on Leanne. Don't worry, okay?"

"I feel better knowing she won't be alone. Aiden?" She fiddled with her key. "Do you think I'm your daughter?"

He'd been sure she'd come back to this discussion. "I know you want answers, but don't get your hopes up. Talk to your dad, and if he's willing, we can find out for sure."

"Okay." Savannah stared at him, tilting her head before she threw her arms around him.

He gave her a squeeze, wishing with every fiber of his being that it was true. "Go in before your chaperone sends a search party. Goodnight, Savannah. Lock up."

"Night, Aiden." She stepped into her room, shutting the door.

Aiden waited until the lock clicked before he wandered down the hallway, marveling at the fate that had brought them together. As much as she seemed like Tiffany, he couldn't let himself get too excited. It all seemed too good to be true.

Aiden waved at the triage nurse behind the desk. "Morning."

The glass doors slid open, and he sauntered toward the doctor's lounge. He'd come in early, sneaking in a burger, fries, and a milkshake to a depressed Leanne. The girl didn't have much to do aside from sleep and watch television.

Even the few minutes of company he'd provided cheered her immensely. He'd promised to drop by again when he had a break.

As he opened his locker, he reviewed the events from last night. The more he thought about it, the more he hoped Savannah's father would allow testing and confirm her as his long-lost daughter. He found himself liking her sweet disposition, and she was smart and funny, even if he was biased in his assessment.

The lounge door opened behind him, and he glanced over his shoulder. "Good morning, Em. Sorry about last night."

She leaned against a locker, a frown marring her features.

"What?"

"You know what."

"I'm sorry?" He lifted a brow. "Are you upset about dinner? How about tonight?"

Emily crossed her arms. "Tell me about the teenager."

"Teenager?"

"You've taken an interest in Savannah and her friend."

"They were my patients at the derailment and I treated her in the ER. What else is there to know?"

"Did you drive her somewhere last night?"

"She's fourteen. Wandering around alone at night in Chicago is hardly recommended, and she's a teenage girl who's unfamiliar with the city."

Emily raised a brow. "Being a good Samaritan?"

"They're kids let loose in Chicago. Someone needs to watch out for them. Clearly, the chaperones aren't."

"People could read things into it." She held up a hand. "I'm an attending and someone commented about seeing you with the girl, so I had to bring it up."

"Perhaps that someone should mind their own business." He folded his arms over his chest.

"You're right, but you know that will never happen in this hospital." She slung her stethoscope around her neck. "Even I noticed there's something about Savannah. Be careful, Aiden."

"She only asked about a career in medicine."

"A mentoring thing?"

"Don't worry, Savannah's on her way home." He didn't like evading her questions, but he couldn't disclose the real conversation.

"Fine. For the record, I'm not concerned. I know you better than that, but ..." She shrugged.

"I get it." He waved a hand at her. "Let's get out there before Dragon Lady appears. I still want that attending job." He pushed his locker shut as the lounge door opened.

"Aiden?" The dark-haired women peeked inside, a smile brightening her face as she skipped toward him, throwing her arms around him. "It's a boy."

"And you're not at all excited." Aiden grinned as he lifted her in a hug. "Congratulations, Lex. Everything looks good?" He set her on her feet.

She rubbed a hand over her belly. "Our little guy is perfect, so we are planning to tell everyone." Alexis assessed Emily with a keen gaze. A smile twitched her lips. "Sorry, I didn't mean to interrupt, but I had to share the good news." She stuck out her hand. "I'm Alex Nichols."

"Emily Anderson." She accepted the woman's hand, shooting a glance at Aiden. "You've been in before."

"Mmhm, but this guy," Alex said as she nudged Aiden with her elbow, "has never properly introduced us." She glanced at her phone. "My husband's waiting in the car, so I have to run. Bye, honey." She pressed a kiss to his cheek. "Call me later."

Emily raised a brow at Aiden as Alex disappeared out the door. "She's … energetic."

"Yeah, and today it's warranted. She and Joel have been wanting a baby ever since they married."

"How long have they been trying?"

"Six years, give or take. It's been a bumpy ride, but they're optimistically hopeful this one will stick."

"Miscarriages?"

"Several. After the first two, they stopped telling people, so it's excellent news that they're ready for the reveal."

"But they told you?" Emily studied him. "The doctor thing in action."

He shrugged. "That's part of it, but Alex and I have been friends forever, so she shares more."

"Friends, huh?"

He rolled his eyes. "Did I mentioned I've been friends with her husband since we were twelve and that he's been in love with Alex as long as I've known him?"

"Ahh." Emily headed toward the door. "Better get out there if you want that attending job."

Chapter 5

Savannah

Savannah sprawled across her bed, capturing her thoughts on Chicago in the battered notebook she carried everywhere. Today, she'd spent the entire time writing about Aiden while debating how to broach the subject with her dad.

Her fingertips brushed the black beanie hiding under her pillow. She pulled it out and traced the lettering. Just by looking at it and touching the soft wool, she could tell it was expensive, yet he had placed it on her head without a second thought and never reclaimed it. "Aiden Hamilton." The sound of his name made her smile. The rattle of her door handle made her jump, and she'd only crammed the hat under her pillow when her door opened.

Her dad peeked into her room, looking hopeful. "You've been cooped up all weekend. Why don't we go for pizza?"

"Yum." She closed her notebook and tucked it into her bag. "Let me change." Savannah motioned to her worn sweatpants.

"I'll warm up the car. Five minutes?" He ruffled a hand through the thick hair that had changed from salt and pepper to gray since his beloved Jayde had died.

"Okay, Daddy." As soon as her door closed, Savannah dragged a brush through the tangled mess of hair and changed into dark wash jeans along with a faded pink sweater. With a sigh, she peered at the dark circles under her eyes, taking a moment to dab on a light covering of foundation before checking her bag to ensure the business card was tucked safely inside.

After a deep calming breath, she slung her bag across her shoulders and headed out the front door.

As soon as she was buckled into the passenger seat, her dad backed out of the driveway onto the quiet tree-lined street. "Everything good?"

"Why wouldn't it be?"

"You've been quiet since you got home. That's to be expected, as I'm sure the accident was quite the ordeal. I'm thankful they located all the students and chaperones and everyone is coming home safely." Her dad drummed his fingers on the steering wheel. The familiar sound comforted her. "Is Leanne back yet?"

"Tomorrow." Savannah had reluctantly said goodbye to her friend before she flew home to Portland, but at least Aiden had provided Leanne some company. Though she wasn't supposed to know, Leanne's parents had been stressing over gathering funds for the flight. They'd pulled the funds together somehow, and Leanne's mom was now in Chicago.

Half an hour later, they pulled into the parking lot of their favorite little pizzeria. Savannah closed her eyes and inhaled the fragrant aroma of homemade tomato sauce and fresh-baked ciabatta. She loved the cozy and welcoming atmosphere. It always reminded her of better times. Before her mom died, they would eat here at least once per month. Tonight, as like many nights before, they settled into one of the booths and ordered their favorite home-style pizza.

Her dad gave her a long searching look before resting his chin on his folded hands. "The school has arranged counseling. Maybe you should talk to someone? You haven't been eating much, and you've holed up in your room."

Savannah smoothed her napkin in her lap before peering at him across the table. "Daddy? I do need to talk about something. It's kind of a big deal."

Concern reflected in his eyes. "What's wrong, Savannah?"

"I met someone unexpected." She focused on her hands.

"A boy? Is that where you kept disappearing to? Chasing boys wasn't the point of the trip."

"It's nothing like that." She gave a small shake of her head. "Remember the picture Mom left me in her letter?"

"How could I forget?" Her dad sighed. "I loved your mother with all my heart, but I wish she hadn't encouraged that nonsense." The ever-present gold watch on her wrist seemed to have caught his attention. After a moment, he lifted his gaze to meet hers. "The adoption records were sealed for a reason. No good can come from you pining for the woman who gave you up. It's unlikely you'll ever find her."

"It's not nonsense."

"Oh, honey. I'm so sorry, but already this search is creating issues. I wish things were different, but the chance you'll ever locate either of your birth parents is slim. What if they don't want to be found?"

"What if they do?" In her opinion, Aiden seemed more hopeful than upset that she'd approached him, but she wasn't sure her dad would feel the same. "It doesn't mean I love you or Mom any less. It just feels like a piece of me is missing." She drew in a breath. "I-I found Aiden Hamilton."

"What do you mean?" A deep frown appeared as his lips tugged downward.

"Aiden's a doctor. My doctor. The one who helped me and Leanne at the derailment."

"Your doctor was Aiden Hamilton?" Her dad paled. "How do you know he can help? Were you spending time with this man? That's where you were when the chaperone couldn't find you?"

Savannah bit her lip and nodded. "He bought me lunch."

The quick and audible inhale of breath combined with his eyes widening a touch.

"I pretended I was interested in being a doctor. Aiden mentors students and allows them to job shadow. He agreed to answer questions. When I showed him the picture, he admitted it was him."

"How can you know for sure? Perhaps he agreed to gain your trust. I thought I'd taught you better. Meeting strange men in secret is dangerous."

Savannah cringed at the stern tone and concentrated on folding her napkin neatly into thirds. Anything to avoid direct eye contact. "We met in public. I didn't go anywhere with him alone." Except for the ride to dinner. And he'd accompanied her to the hotel room, even if he hadn't come inside. She wouldn't mention those minor details to her dad. It hadn't been an inspired choice, and if he'd been lying, she could have found herself in a serious predicament. It had all turned out well …

"Savannah Jayde Phillips." Her dad's eyes locked on her, accusing laser beams burning a hole into her forehead. "Look at me, young lady."

She clamped her teeth onto her lower lip, forcing herself to do as he demanded.

"You took a huge risk meeting a grown man in a strange city." A deep red flush colored her father's face. "You can't say for sure who he is."

"He helps people. He's chief resident in the ER." She dug her nails into her palms. If she backed down now, she'd never know the truth. "Aiden said he'd do DNA testing if you gave your permission."

"He's encouraging this foolish behavior? Helping you to sneak around and aiding you? He should know better. How old is he?"

"He's thirty," she whispered.

"It's a bad idea, for so many reasons. You have your hopes up. What if he's not your father? Or what if he is? What happens then?"

"He can help me find my mother."

The slap of his flattened palm against the table made her jump. "This is unreal." Her dad shook his head before resting it into his hands. "Please tell me you didn't ask him about her."

This couldn't end well. Her confessions were only upsetting him further, but she trusted her instincts. Aiden wasn't dangerous. Nothing about what he'd done seemed contrived or planned.

"Don't be mad," Savannah said as she sneaked a look at his florid face and narrowed eyes, "but shouldn't this be about what I want?"

A sad look appeared on his face. "I only want what's best for you, honey," he said softly. "This has the potential to be …"

Damaging. The word popped into her head. But it had an upside too. All the "what ifs" played through her mind.

"It's a chance I need to take," she said. "Aiden gave up a baby girl for adoption who was born in the same hospital on the same day, but he doesn't have access to the legal records to prove it was me."

"What if he's some kind of whack job who's only telling you what you want to hear?" He lifted his hands.

"He's not. If you met him, Daddy, you'd see."

"You want me to meet him?"

She allowed a tiny nod.

"If I agree, who'd pay for the testing? What if you find out he's not your father? How are you going to feel? You can't chase after every Aiden Hamilton in the country until you find the right one."

"I'll pay for it from my savings." She used her best puppy dog eyes on him, widening them and batting her lashes. "Will you meet him? Please?"

"It doesn't mean he's not a crazy wing-nut." He exuded a long sigh and lifted his brows, signaling he knew her game in using her doe-eyed look. "Why would he agree to DNA testing? He gave you up when you were a baby which terminates his legal rights. Or any other rights for that matter. Does he think he can waltz into our lives fifteen years later?"

"This was my idea, not his." A frown knit her brow as she folded her arms across her chest. "He doesn't want to take me away. He agreed so I can find out where I came from. You'll always be my dad."

"Understand, Savannah, this has serious implications. What part will these people play in your life if we confirm the relationship?"

"He's not *these* people. He's one man who can tell me about my mother. Let him visit and you can ask him whatever questions you want." She took his hand, blinking at him. "For me, please?"

"Are you sure you know what you're asking? Is he truly okay with submitting to testing and answering a million questions?"

"He said it was up to you, and he'd understand if you didn't want to do any of it," she said. "Can you at least phone him?"

"You'll never let up on this idea?"

She shook her head. "If you don't allow me to do it now, I'll contact him when I'm eighteen. It would be so much better if I found out now. Please, Daddy? Please?" Savannah's eyes filled with tears. This wasn't a whim, but something she'd wished for with all her heart. Hopefully, her dad would see that.

"It's against my better judgment, but I'll talk to the man. No promises beyond that, okay?"

"Thank you." Savannah bounced from her seat, rounding the table to hug him. "You won't regret it."

"I sure hope not, honey." Her dad squeezed her tight. "This better be the right decision, for all our sakes. Give me his number when we get home and I'll have a conversation with the man." His lips set into a grim line. "Don't assume there are no consequences for your actions, young lady."

Savannah nodded as she took her seat on the bench.

"You took a huge risk. For the next two weeks, you're grounded."

She opened her mouth intending to argue but snapped it shut at his stern look.

"No phone. No friends. To school and right back home." His gaze softened, as did his tone. "I love you, Vanna. I only want to keep you safe. Always."

Chapter 6

Aiden

AIDEN CONTEMPLATED THE QUIET SUBURBAN setting from the seat of the rental car. The modest home sat on an idyllic tree-lined street and appeared homey and comfortable compared to the massive houses and boarding schools he'd lived in as a teenager. It appeared Savannah had grown up in an environment opposite to his. Maybe Thomas Hamilton had done the girl a favor, even if Aiden hated to acknowledge it.

He found himself on the steps without consciously arriving there. The faint chime of the doorbell sounded through the simple metal door, followed by heavy footsteps. Moments later, he faced an older gray-haired man who he guessed was much the same age as his own father. It felt odd knowing this man might have raised his daughter.

"Dr. Hamilton," the man said, holding out his hand, "I'm Ross."

Aiden straightened and shook the offered hand. "Please, call me Aiden." He followed Ross inside, noting the comfortable, though slightly worn, furniture. The homey feel to the tiny living room was reassuring.

A smile lit Savannah's face before she threw her arms around him. "You actually came," she whispered.

Emotions threatened to overwhelm him as he returned the embrace. "You look great. Your cuts healed up nicely."

"I had an amazing doctor." She dropped to the couch, tugging on his hand.

He sat, angling toward her. "You were a brave patient. Leanne told me how great you were at the accident scene." Aiden leveled his gaze at Ross.

"I appreciate you allowing this visit. Savannah finding me was completely unexpected. I had no idea about the picture."

"I can imagine, given the adoption was closed." Ross scanned Aiden, his concern reflected in his eyes. "I'm sure you understand my hesitation."

Aiden nodded, giving the teen a gentle smile. "I can't say I wouldn't feel the same in your position."

"Thank you for making the trip all the way across the country. This is a huge imposition on your time, but my daughter wouldn't relent until I agreed to meet you."

So much like Tiffany. He squeezed the girl's hand. "I saw how much it meant to her."

Savannah barely moved but her own grip tightened as she blinked hard.

Having those shimmering brown eyes fixed on him was nerve-wracking, but he'd learned the art of keeping his emotions under tight control at an early age. "You have questions?" he asked with a calmness he didn't feel.

"I'm sure you can appreciate how unsettling this is." Ross slid forward on his chair. "You're willing to submit to DNA testing? Savannah mentioned you wanted it?"

"Unless you have paperwork confirming the relationship, it seems the best option." Aiden shifted in his seat. "I don't want to stir up anyone's life without irrefutable proof."

"If you are her biological father, what then?" Ross raised his brows.

Aiden let out a long breath. He'd been debating the same question for the past several days. It would be tough to confirm Savannah as his daughter and then walk away when he hoped for the chance to know her, but this wasn't about him. "Savannah should decide what involvement she's looking for."

"If we don't test? Then what?"

A wave of sadness washed over him. "I hope we do. If Savannah's my daughter, I'd like to get to know her, but I won't interfere."

"Maybe we should start with more about you."

"Go ahead."

"Why adoption?"

"Daddy. I already told you."

"I'm sure Dr. Hamilton can speak for himself." Ross shot her a warning glance.

Aiden took a long breath. There'd be some tough questions coming. "My grandfather and ... my girlfriend's parents, decided adoption would be in everyone's best interest."

"You were fifteen?"

He nodded. "My grandfather was a strong-willed man. We couldn't say no."

"What did he do? For a living, I mean."

Aiden had expected questions about his family. Savannah had shown more interest in his personal life, and she hadn't delved into his background aside from asking if he had a wife and children. Now the truth would be uncovered, and he was glad he'd had a chance to visit with her, however briefly. "My grandfather was a criminal trial lawyer."

"What about your parents? Didn't they have any say in the matter?" The man's brows rose, though his voice remained level.

"I'm not sure they knew."

A frown formed on the older man's face. "How could they not know?"

"They'd already moved to New York." There was no point in hiding anything. He owed this man complete honesty if he wanted to be allowed in to their lives, even if the complete package wasn't so attractive. "I attended a boarding school and spent most of my time in Chicago with my grandparents or traveling during the school breaks." Aiden worried revealing the dysfunction of his family would sway the man's decision. Vowing that he'd work hard to create balance if he ever had his own family meant little when by his own admission, work was all he really had in his life.

The man's lips flattened into a straight line. "What does your father do?"

"He's an ADA in New York. He started out as a trial lawyer in Chicago."

"Hamilton." Ross narrowed his eyes. "James Hamilton? The one trying the capital murder case that's all over the news?"

"Mmhm."

"What's an ADA?" Savannah asked.

"Assistant District Attorney. He prosecutes criminals on behalf of the City of New York," Aiden said. "My father has political aspirations. I figure my grandfather was going for plausible deniability so my father could say he had no idea."

"Would you have kept your baby?"

Aiden met the man's gaze. "Yes." His family was no exception to the deceptions and cover-ups in politics. Aiden didn't even want to get into the story of Tiffany's family. "I did what I had to do at the time, and part of it was to protect ... her."

"Vanna's ... mother? Where does she fit in?"

Aiden shrugged. "We haven't been together for years. It was stressful and difficult, and we broke up. I haven't told her about this visit and I won't unless we verify the relationship through DNA testing."

"You're a doctor in the ER."

"I'm chief resident. I have a job offer for an attending position starting in July."

"You aren't married, and you don't have other kids?"

"Not yet. Medicine is a demanding career, but perhaps one day."

"So this is totally your decision, and you're willing to put yourself through the testing?"

"It's a simple, noninvasive procedure. A quick swab and it's done."

"Simple, but not. It has repercussions and it's expensive."

"Once we have the results, we can figure it out." To him, the cost of testing seemed reasonable, but maybe to Ross it was a lot of money. "I'll pay for the testing."

Ross shook his head. "I can't ask it after you've gone to the expense of flying out here."

"I get benefit out of the procedure." Aiden met the man's gaze. "I'm fine with covering the cost."

"If she's not your daughter? Then you're out of pocket."

"I'm willing to take that chance."

Ross looked at Savannah's anxious face, and then back at Aiden, who met his gaze without flinching. The man heaved a sigh. "I made an appointment for tomorrow at a lab to collect the samples. It should be done with all of us present so there's no question on the results."

"I'd prefer that too." Aiden nodded. "It'll only take a few minutes. What time?"

"Ten tomorrow morning?"

Savannah jumped up and hugged Ross. "Thanks for agreeing."

"Don't thank me yet. Promise not to get your hopes up, young lady," Ross said in a stern tone, even as his lips twitched. "What do you say to Dr. Hamilton?"

"Thank you for coming out here." Savannah smiled. "And for agreeing to be tested."

"You're welcome." Aiden let out a long breath, feeling a sense of relief. He'd been tense and worried, but this was the best he could hope for; a chance to discover the truth.

Chapter 7

Savannah

A disappointed huff escaped as Savannah peered into the empty mailbox. It had been seven long days since they'd visited the lab. Every day, she checked the mail after school, but each day, nothing.

She combed her fingers through her hair and peered down the street, hoping to spot the mail carrier. How long did a simple, teeny, tiny DNA test take? The gathering of the sample had been quick and painless, even if it felt awkward being there with both her dad and the man who was in all likelihood her father. She yanked open the front door, letting it swing shut with a bang as she entered the house.

"Easy there." Her dad looked up from his task of sorting paperwork, his eyebrows rising as she stomped into the room.

"The results aren't here." Savannah dropped onto the chair across from her dad with a grimace, pushing a pile of paper out of the way. "They're taking forever." She drummed her fingers against the tabletop.

Her dad held up an envelope and waved it in the air. "I was tempted to open it, but perhaps you want the honors?"

"Finally." Savannah grabbed at the piece of mail.

Ross pulled his hand back, keeping it out of her reach. "Remember, if the results aren't what you hoped, you need to stop searching and wait until you're eighteen. You promised, right?"

"Cross my heart." She swept her finger across her chest. "I won't search anymore. It's just he was right there and so easy to talk to." She stared at the envelope as he placed it on the table, keeping his hand on top. Her knee bounced and her fingers twitched as she resisted the urge to lunge across the table and grab it.

"Well, he's very straightforward and seems a good person. I suppose he's not a crazy person or a stalker." He extended the envelope.

Savannah snatched it from his fingertips, holding it close to her chest while she took a deep breath. After ripping it open, she unfolded the enclosed papers. Her hand rose, and she pressed her fingertips to her mouth, tears brimming in her eyes.

Conclusive, 99.99%, Aiden James Thomas Franklin Hamilton is not excluded as the biological parent of Savannah Jayde Phillips.

"I'm sorry, honey." Her dad's voice cut into her thoughts. "It was a long shot, right? Now you can put it to rest."

"No. Look." Vanna leaped from the chair, swiping at the tears. "He's my father." She shoved the papers at him, bouncing on her toes as her dad inspected them. "Aiden explained this while we were waiting at the lab. This is a positive result."

It seemed forever before he looked at her. "Wow."

Savannah smiled widely, her tears drying as the initial shock passed. She reclaimed the papers and examined them again, looking at the number in case she'd misread it. *99.99%.* There was absolutely no doubt. "I found him. I can't believe it. Aiden's my father." Her hand went to her lips and she nibbled on her nails. "I wonder if he knows. Can I phone him?"

"He said you could call anytime. I'm sure he'll have the results by now. It's surreal you found him on your trip." Her dad's head bobbed as he mumbled, "What are the odds?"

Savannah pretended she hadn't heard the last part. "I was pretty sure. How many baby girls could be put up for adoption on the same day in one hospital?"

"Hard to say. The information's private."

"That was rhetorical, Daddy. We can't know definitively. Logically, even if half of the babies born were girls, there couldn't have been more than one or two babies given up for adoption that same day."

Ross rolled his eyes. "You spend too much time on Google."

Maybe she had spent too much time analyzing the situation. She'd thought of nothing else since Aiden had visited Portland, but she didn't care. The final goal was in sight and she'd found *the* Aiden Hamilton.

"You're a touch scary some days, but intelligence is supposed to be hereditary. You could have done worse in the genetic lottery of life."

Genetic lottery? Savannah wrinkled her nose. Sometimes her dad was so weird. "I'm phoning Aiden." She covered the shorts steps to the fridge, snagging the card with his contact information and dialing. As it rang, she paced and twirled a strand of hair around her fingertip.

"Aiden?" Her voice shook as his greeting flowed down the line. *Breathe. Breathe.*

"Savannah. How are you?"

"Incredible. I got the results. Did you?"

"Yup. How are you feeling?"

"It's amazing, Aiden," she said and pursed her lips. "Do I still call you Aiden?"

"Sure." His voice sounded calm. "Now we have the results, I'd like to see you again so we can discuss things. Maybe? I don't quite know what you want to do next."

"Yes. Come see me. I have so many questions." Savannah continued to pace and fiddle with her hair. "When can you visit?" She glanced at her dad, who looked up from where he'd been pretending to be engrossed in his paperwork.

"What does your dad think?" Aiden asked. "It's okay with him if I visit again?"

"He's surprised I found you, but how could he refuse?"

"He doesn't have to let me visit you."

"He will, though," Savannah said. "I have tons of things to ask you about my mother. I mean, how you met ..." She rambled on for another minute before pausing to take a deep breath.

"All in good time. Can I talk to Ross?"

"Yeah." Savannah thrust the phone at her dad, almost dropping it in her haste.

Her dad managed to rescue it before it fell, indicating she should calm down with a small downward motion of his hand.

She paced to the fridge, poured some juice and then tidied the stack of mail on the counter. Anything to occupy herself. She gnawed on a fingernail as she half-listened to her dad talking to Aiden.

"Yes, that'll be fine." Her dad frowned, staring at her hand as he held out the phone.

She yanked her finger from her mouth. "Hello?"

"Savannah? All set. I'll fly out on Wednesday. It'll be better to talk in person. I have to get back to work, but I'll see you soon."

"Yes. I'll see you then. Bye." Her heart sang with joy, knowing she'd see him in a few days. She bounced down the hallway to her room and flopped onto her bed, flutter-kicking her feet against the mattress. At long last, she'd found Aiden Hamilton. She lay there for a full minute, savoring the moment before she dug out her dog-eared journal. This day would remain etched in her memory forever.

Savannah stared at the trail of red ink as her pen weaved across the paper. She tilted her head, considering the flowing script along the edge of the notebook. *Aiden Hamilton.* Her father.

"Earth to Vanna."

The sharp poke of a fingertip against her shoulder made her jump. "What?" She offered her friend a blank stare as she flipped her book closed.

"Could you help with my stuff?" Leanne leaned on her crutches and tapped the cast encasing her leg.

As they were in most of their classes together, Savannah had been elected to carry Leanne's book bag. Not that she minded. Her friend would do it for her if the situation was reversed. "Oh right. Sorry. Must have drifted into a coma due to the riveting subject matter." Savannah forced a giggle as she rose from the hard plastic chair, stuffing her notebook and pens in her own bag before grabbing her friend's pack.

"You're in luck." Leanne grinned. "It's time for our favorite subject."

"Lunch?" She rolled her eyes, but followed her friend as she maneuvered through the crowded hallway toward the cafeteria.

"You're lost in space. What's up?" The other girl asked as they claimed seats on one of the benches and opened their lunch bags. "You've been grouchy and moody all week."

Savannah snorted. "It's only Tuesday."

"Your grouchiness makes it feel like Thursday. Are you upset about Justin?" Leanne motioned toward the other side of the cafeteria where the aforementioned boy goofed around with his friends.

"No." Savannah bit into her ham and cheese sandwich, spying on Justin from the corner of her eye. Before she left for Chicago, she'd hoped the guy would ask her out, but now her thoughts were elsewhere.

"It doesn't bother you he's flirting with Christina? They've been hanging out a lot."

"Well, it does. He's changed so much, and I wish ..." She sighed. The scrawny, short boy who followed her like a puppy last year was gone. Over the summer, he'd developed into a tall, acne-free, buff, undeniably hot guy who now seemed interested in Christina, the girl whose family had money and bought her everything she'd ever wished or dreamed of having.

"He'd ask you out? Last year he tried, Vanna."

"Last year I was sad about my mom, and I didn't want to date. My dad would never let me anyway. He says no dating until I'm sixteen, which is another year away. What would be the point?"

"Believe me, I get it. Your dad is bad, but my mom is worse. And how do we compete with perky, perfect Christina?"

"We don't." Savannah shrugged before taking another bite.

Tall, beautiful, blonde Christina dressed in the latest trendy fashions and was blessed with an appealing and smiley personality. Savannah's dad never bought her those kinds of clothes, nor did they have the money for them.

"So what? If it's not Justin ..." A sassy grin appeared. "I bet," Leanne whispered, "it's about your mad crush on my hottie doctor in Chicago. He's a touch old, don't you think?"

Savannah's stomach lurched as she stared wide-eyed at her friend. "Ewww, no. I'm not ..." She shook her head. "Bite your tongue. I am not crushing on Aiden."

"Aiden, huh." Leanne snickered. "Denial. If you're not madly in love, how do you know his first name? It's a sexy name. Doctor ... Aiden ... Hamilton ..." Her friend wiggled her brows as she enunciated each syllable in a sing-song voice. "Even the nurses drooled over him. Admit it. He's hot."

She cringed. "Don't say hot and definitely stop with the *s* word. Not about him. It's ... disturbing."

"What's with you?" Her friend's brows shot upward. "He is though, and he's sooo nice. Thanks to him, I ate burgers with fries and milkshakes while the other patients suffered with mystery meat." A giggle escaped, but her excitement faded at the dark look from Savannah. "Seriously. What's the issue?"

"His name is ... Aiden ... Hamilton," Savannah said in a low voice. "Doesn't that sound the tiniest bit familiar?"

Leanne tilted her head, her brow furrowing in concentration before her eyes widened. "Wait. Isn't Hamilton the name on the back of ...?" She slapped her hands over her mouth. "No. No ... no way." Her head wagged back and forth. "Do you think he's related to the guy in the photo? Maybe he's your uncle."

"Shh." Vanna pressed a finger to her lips. "He's not my uncle. It's him. Dr. Hamilton is my father."

Leanne giggled. "Are you sure? How would you know it's him in the picture?"

She sucked in a breath. "Because we did DNA testing. Aiden's my biological father."

Leanne's mouth dropped open and she stared at Savannah.

"Say something," Savannah muttered.

"You. Are. Kidding." Leanne maneuvered her good leg over the bench so she faced her friend. "You are kidding. Aren't you?"

"No. It's really him." She dug in her bag and pulled out the slightly tattered envelope. "My father is a thirty-year-old doctor in Chicago."

Leanne snatched it from her fingers. "You're serious." Her eyes widened as she read the enclosed paper. "He was fifteen when you were born?"

"Uh-huh." She sucked up the last of her juice.

"I don't know what to say. This is incredible news."

"I never thought it would happen for real. I had no idea who he was until another doctor called him Aiden and it clicked." Savannah frowned at the recollection, the details of the lovely dark-haired woman saying his name in that soft voice becoming clear in her mind. "She flirted with him. After that, he looked like he knew I was inspecting him."

"What does your dad think?"

"My dad freaked when he found out I'd gone for lunch with Aiden. Imagine how long I'd be grounded if he knew Aiden took me to dinner and I rode in his car."

"You went for dinner with him? You didn't tell me any of this. How could you not tell me?"

"I'm sorry." Savannah furrowed her brow. "I didn't know what to do. Aiden said I shouldn't say anything to anyone until I talked to my dad. He didn't want it to become a big deal, you know? In case he wasn't my father."

"Well, my parents would be pissed. Meeting a stranger in a big city and sneaking around?" Leanne's head bobbed. "Wow. He's your father. That still freaks me out."

"You don't have to tell me."

"He asked if we were good friends, and I told him yes. When the accident happened, I was terrified, but you were there and made me feel better. The nurses said how lucky I was to have such a great doctor. They were gaga over him," Leanne said. "What about your mother? He's not married, is he? I never saw a wedding ring."

"They're not together, but that's all I know. He's single. No other kids." The corners of her mouth turned down. The news she didn't have siblings disappointed her. She'd always wanted a sister or brother. "Aiden's coming for another visit." A frisson of excitement built inside. By tomorrow night, she hoped to have answers.

"So you'll meet her?" A smile appeared.

"I hope so." Vanna wrapped her arms around herself, fighting the smile. Finding her mother was something she wished for with her entire heart.

"Was she fifteen too?"

"Aiden said they were both teenagers and too young. Can you imagine?"

"Nope. My parents would freak if I had a baby. I don't even know how I'd tell them. Your dad would flip out. I don't even like to think about it."

"He'd probably chain me in the basement and never let me leave the house ever again. Being grounded for two weeks is bad enough."

"But he's still allowing you to see Aiden? That's not so bad."

"You're right." Savannah consoled herself with the thought that it was a small price to pay for finding Aiden Hamilton, and she'd do it all again if it led to realizing her precious dream. To know her mother.

Chapter 8

Aiden

Aiden tapped the edge of the envelope against the back of his hand. It had taken forever to pluck up the courage to open it. Days of anxiety and several sleepless nights preceded its arrival, and he almost hadn't broken the seal.

"Will it bite?"

Startled at the voice, he looked up. He hadn't heard the nurse enter the room. "Hey, Tara, I haven't seen you around for a few days." Worried she might catch a glimpse of the return address or recognize the lab's logo, he flipped the envelope. Silly perhaps, as it could be for a patient, but he didn't want to deal with her questions.

"I visited my brother. He's getting married." Tara poured some coffee, sniffing before taking a tiny sip. "Yuck. When did they make this? Two years ago? It tastes like stale dirty dishwater."

"Joe made it."

"That explains it." She grimaced and tipped her cup into the sink.

He stood and stretched. "Grant's engaged? How do you feel about that?"

"Fine. My mom's bugging me though. He's three years younger, so the pressure's on."

"My family nags me too. It's annoying, but so far I've escaped."

"You can run, but only so far." She eyed him and bit her lip. "One day, some girl will catch you." Tara's comment hung for a moment before she cleared her throat. "I should get back to work. Are you on shift?"

"I have a couple more hours." He looked away. The woman made comments all the time, and he knew what she wanted, but he couldn't force a connection he wasn't feeling. Besides, dating coworkers inevitably became messy. Best to stay away from complications; he already had enough of those in his life.

"See you out there." Tara spun and rushed through the door.

Aiden scanned the results for the hundredth time, the turmoil in his mind making it almost impossible to think. He knew what came next, but he dreaded her reaction. Facing her after all this time would be the hardest part.

***

Three hours later, he stared at the sign over the gallery. After straightening his shoulders and taking a deep breath, he stepped through the door.

A dark-haired young woman approached. "Can I help you, sir?"

"Is Tiffany in today?"

The woman had an eye for detail, and this impressive space was no exception. The muted and subtle decor showcased vivid paintings and several stands displayed sculptures. She'd put her artistic talent to good use and fulfilled her dream of breaking into the art world.

"May I tell her who's asking?"

"Aiden Hamilton." The clear cool voice echoed down the length of the room. "Thanks, Isla. I've got this."

Isla nodded and strode toward the back.

Tiffany stared at him, her icy gaze traveling over him from head to toe. "To what do I owe the honor of a visit?" Her cold tone suggested she wished he'd just disappear.

"It's been a long time," he said. "How are you?"

"Fantastic. You?" Her voice had a sharp edge to it, but the curiosity reflected in her eyes gave it away. Her interest was piqued.

"Can we talk? Privately?"

"Is there anything to be said?"

"There is."

Her vivid crystal eyes always reminded him of a clear blue sky, though now perhaps an iceberg was more fitting. At one time, she'd have thrown herself into his arms and covered him with kisses. Today, she regarded him like a bug she longed to pulverize with a shoe.

If only I could return to better days and erase the angry words between us.

"I can't imagine you'd say anything of interest." A huge sigh escaped her pursed lips. The stiffness of her body and the set of her shoulders told him he'd be lucky if she agreed, however, she fluttered a hand toward the back of the gallery. Without a word she spun, her heels clicking on the polished floor as she marched toward the offices.

He followed her into the largest of the three and pushed the door shut behind him.

"I thought we'd finished this years ago." Her perfect brows lifted and she crossed her arms, one foot tapping as she surveyed him.

"It's important."

"Then say it and get out of my life."

Was it wise to open this particular issue? The revelation would introduce a pile of problems into her world, but an image of Savannah's hopeful face flashed through his mind. This conversation was unavoidable. Their families had denied them the right to keep their daughter, and he couldn't compound the injustice.

Her foot continued to tap a staccato beat. "Are you planning on letting me in on whatever this is about?"

Aiden cleared his throat and rubbed the back of his neck, already defeated by her stony silence. "You're happy?"

"Of course, I'm happy. I'm marrying a wonderful man, and I'll have everything I ever dreamed of." The venomous glare accompanying this statement struck an arrow through his heart. It screamed: *everything you couldn't give.* "I'm engaged. Don't mess that up."

Aiden longed to bolt, but he stood firm. He owed it to Savannah to see this through. "I heard." *Engaged to a slimy, slithering snake.* He closed his eyes, refocusing his mind. Not his place. Not anymore. "The last thing I want to do is interfere."

"Then walk away. Whatever it is, I don't want to hear it." She stalked toward the office door. "We're done."

He stepped in front of her to block her progress. "She's fourteen."

She bowed her head, the sharp inhale sounding like a hissing cat. "You think I don't know that? I was there, or don't you remember? Oh. Of course, you don't. I was alone." Tiffany's voice choked up. "Why bring this up? I've done everything to get past it, to move on, yet you do this now? What's the point? I don't want to talk about it. Ever again." She pointed at the door. "Get out."

"Savannah," he said.

"What?" Her head snapped up, tears brimming in her eyes.

"Her name. It's Savannah." He sucked in a breath. "She lives in Portland."

"How do you know?" Her eyes widened. "You found her?"

"She found me. She wants to meet you."

"You told her about me?" Her voice shook as she placed her flattened palms against her desk, her entire body trembling.

"I didn't reveal your identity." He cocked his head. "You left a picture. And the watch I gave you."

She snatched a tissue from the box on her credenza and dabbed her eyes. "I never told anyone."

"Was I just *anyone*?"

She clamped her bottom lip between her teeth and looked away.

Right.

"You're certain it's her?"

"I wouldn't disrupt your life otherwise." He reached into his jacket for the envelope, failing to control the shake of his hand. "She's a carbon copy of you." *Except for those deep brown eyes.*

Tiffany snatched the envelope and scanned the enclosed document before tossing it onto her desk. She sank onto the couch, pressing a fresh tissue to her eyes and shaking her head. "I can't."

"Can't?" Aiden's heart sank. "Or won't?"

"My life is perfect. It'll ruin all that I've built. It could destroy Harrison's career. Don't you dare tell her who I am."

"So he's like your dad? More worried about his damn career than you? Or," he said, shaking his head, "I guess you're just worried about you."

"That's not fair." She glowered.

"It's fair and accurate, but it's your life." He refused to flinch. To reveal his devastation. "Haven't you always wondered?"

Tiffany dragged in a long breath, a moment of silence hanging between them before she broke eye contact. "We were fifteen. Why do you think our families covered it all up? To protect me." She bounced off the couch, throwing her hands into the air. "Harrison is running for Governor. I'll be a wife in politics, so acknowledging an illegitimate child …" She wagged her head back and forth. "No. The paparazzi would love it. Cut it off. Now. Before you ruin my life."

"After fifteen years of wondering, I shouldn't see my daughter?" His stomach clenched. "I refuse to ignore her. You're making a huge mistake, Tiff."

Her lip curled. "And if someone finds out?"

"So what? I'm done with the politically correct, self-serving bullshit our families forced on us." He turned away, bowing his head to hide his rampaging emotions. "I regret what it put you through. What it did to us."

"Don't do this. I've put this all behind me, and now you're here like my worst nightmare, bringing it all up again."

The words sliced through his soul. "Well, that puts our entire relationship in perspective." The picture he'd reclaimed from Savannah rested in his pocket, an unwelcome memory of happier times. With a shrug, he tugged it free and held it up, waving it before tearing it straight down the middle. "All your deep dark secrets are safe." The two halves drifted to the floor. "Marry Harrison. Pretend we don't exist. I'll never bother you again."

He yanked open the office door and stalked through the gallery, straight out the front door. Pain blossomed in his chest as his heart broke all over again. That sweet, wonderful woman he'd once loved had vanished without a single trace.

Aiden touched down in Portland for the second time in two weeks and headed to pick up his rental car. He stared into space as the couple in front of him bickered over the insurance.

He'd struggled with his emotions the entire trip, wondering how Savannah would take the news. He resented Tiffany's refusal to acknowledge her daughter, or to have anything to do with this entire situation.

Situation. That's what his grandfather had called it so many years ago when he'd found out.

He shuffled his feet, staring at the baby the young woman in front of him bounced on her shoulder. The tiny soul crammed a fist into her mouth, gnawing at it, her wide blue eyes staring.

Just like the baby on that poster so long ago in the clinic. A baby with bright blue eyes, so much like *hers.*

Aiden shivered at the memory of the hard plastic chair and stark white walls. If he closed his eyes, he could picture the pleading look in Tiffany's red-rimmed eyes as the nurse ushered her toward the exam room, leaving him helpless in the waiting room.

Worst of all were the promises made that day, all of them now broken. *"I'll love you forever. I won't abandon you. I'll take care of you always. Both of you."*

"Sir?" The young man lifted a hand. "Can I help you?"

"Oh, sorry." He stepped forward and handed the clerk his confirmation number, grateful for the distraction. Now he had to face what came next.

By the time he reached the middle-class neighborhood, he still wasn't ready. What to say to this lovely girl he'd let down in so many ways?

Before Aiden emerged from the car, she vaulted across the driveway, her blonde hair streaming behind her. The sight of her and how much she resembled her mother pained his heart.

"Aiden." She threw her arms around him, but the hug was far too brief. Moments later, she stretched on tiptoes, peering over his shoulder, looking for someone who wasn't and would never be there for her.

"How are you?" He forced a smile, wishing he was anywhere but standing in this icy driveway in the middle of November, about to break his daughter's heart.

"You came alone?" Her voice trembled and she blinked hard.

"Yes?"

"Oh." The smile that appeared didn't reach those shimmering eyes and the corners of her mouth twitched.

And he knew. He read her as easily as he'd read Tiffany the many times—too many times—she'd been disappointed and about to dissolve into tears.

"Come in." Ross appeared on the steps, beckoning them inside the cozy house, straight into the living room. "It's good of you to make the time to come all this way."

"Can I get you something to drink?" Savannah leaped off the couch. "I made iced tea."

Before he even opened his mouth, the girl hurried into the adjoining room, followed by the sound of ice tinkling against a glass.

"She's," Ross said, peering toward the kitchen, "a little high-strung today." A rueful smile appeared. "She's talked non-stop about this—"

"I made cookies. Do you like chocolate chip?" Savannah balanced three glasses on a tray along with a plate of the home-made treats.

"They're my favorite." He accepted one of the glasses and took a sip, grateful for the cool liquid soothing his throat.

She perched on the arm of the couch, looking at him expectantly.

The last thing he wanted to do at this moment was eat, but he retrieved a cookie, savoring the chewiness. "Mmm. This is about the best cookie I've ever had." He bit off another chunk and nodded. Despite his lack of appetite, he appreciated her effort.

"I have a secret ingredient," she said. "My mom …" Her chin dropped and she glanced toward her dad.

Ross helped himself to a cookie. "You've outdone yourself, honey."

Clearly, the man loved this girl, and given the tender smile she sent in return, he sensed Ross was a good father. Along with the relief that his daughter had been welcomed into a loving home was a surge of loss and pain that it hadn't been his.

This man had enjoyed the happiness and love of raising this girl as part of his family, where Aiden had only experienced the agony of never knowing her. As he sucked in a breath, he looked away, swallowing hard to loosen the lump in his throat.

"Aiden?" she whispered. "Did you find my mother?"

Time to pull it together. Pretend it's a family who has lost a loved one. Say it. No prevaricating. He cleared his throat and shuttered his emotions. Whatever happened next, he had to stay strong or he'd dissolve. He stared at his hands, blinking hard before he lifted his chin.

"You couldn't find her?" Her disappointment projected clearly in her voice.

"I've always known where she lives." He took her hands in his and tugged her onto the couch beside him. "I'm sorry, but I can't tell you anything."

"You won't?" Savannah's face crumpled as pools of tears gathered in the corners of her eyes. "She doesn't want me?"

"I'm really sorry." He met her tearful gaze. "If there was anything—"

"That's it? I have no say in this?" Her voice rose as she sniffled. She fixed an accusing stare on him, but at the same time, her eyes begged him to say it was all a mistake.

"It doesn't seem fair." Aiden ran a hand through his hair. "She needs time, Savannah. This was so unexpected."

A single tear tracked down her cheek. "You said neither of you wanted to give me away. How can she not want me?" Her shoulders slumped.

"We didn't. It took years to get past it." *Not that I ever really recovered…* "I have to respect her wishes. I'm sorry. I can't give you what you want."

"What about me? If you cared, you'd make her see me." She pulled away from him and burst into tears. "If you cared at all, you'd tell me."

Ross pushed tissues into her hand, and Savannah blotted her face. She jerked back as Aiden reached toward her, turning her head aside.

"I do care," he whispered, "but I can't break that confidence and you need to understand—"

"Those are just lousy excuses. How can my m-mother not w-w-ant me?" Choked sobs wrenched from her and her entire body shuddered.

"Savannah—"

"Go home. You didn't want me, and I don't want you." Savannah bolted from the room. The reverberation from the slamming door echoed down the hallway, leaving an awkward silence in its wake.

The ache in Aiden's heart weighed him down. The sting of rejection after having so much hope was unimaginable. The torment sank so deep he could barely breathe. After a moment of tense silence, he sneaked a look at Ross.

The man's beet-red face exhibited an intensely sorrowful expression. His eyebrows knit together as he perched on the edge of his chair. "I'm sorry. She's not usually …" The silence grew again before he said, "This news about her mother is a huge disappointment. It's not you, Aiden."

Ironic. He'd been about to say the same thing to Savannah. That it wasn't her. "I knew it wouldn't be easy, and she wouldn't understand. Who would?" He cleared his throat, gathering the courage to look up. "I don't blame her for being angry and emotional. I'm angry too, but it's beyond my control."

The older man's eyes were on him. He could feel it.

"You do keep it controlled, though," Ross said in a low and even voice.

"Yeah, well." Aiden clasped his hands together in an effort to stop the shaking. "Occupational hazard."

"This is different." A warm hand came down on Aiden's shoulder and squeezed.

"You're right. That was especially difficult and I … I—" His throat closed, choking off any further words.

Ross sat on the couch beside him. "I've been afraid of this happening. Vanna had high expectations. She expected you'd show up with her mother in tow."

"I figured, from the reception in the driveway. Growing up without a mom is a tough gig. From what I've seen, she's a great kid." Aiden sipped some iced tea, which eased his dry, constricted throat. At least now he wouldn't break down. Or so he hoped. "She wants me to go, but do you mind if I talk to her before I do?"

"Be warned, you might not get far. She's obstinate."

"Understood, but I can't leave it like that." Aiden rose and walked down the hall. After tapping on her door, he waited several interminable seconds before opening it. "Savannah?"

"Go away." Her muffled voice came from under a large pillow. "Leave me alone."

The words struck his heart. "I will. But first, I need to say something." He stared at the unmoving figure on the bed and hoped she'd listen. "I'm sorry, but don't judge too harshly. She was a kid facing enormous pressure. I wish I could tell you, but she's had too much imposed on her already. It's hard to understand if you haven't lived it, but she's scared," he said. "If you don't want to see me again, then that's your decision, but I'd like to see you. I've wanted the chance for fifteen years."

Savannah barely moved, only burrowing further under her pillow.

"If you change your mind, you have my number. Goodbye, Savannah." He closed the door and retreated down the hall.

"She say anything?" Ross asked from his position by the window.

"No, but I think she listened." Aiden rubbed the back of his neck, wishing for the ache to dissipate.

"I'll talk to her. She needs time to process the news." Ross cleared his throat. "Can she call when she's ready?"

Aiden shoved his hands into his pockets, inspecting the floor. He doubted it would happen. "I'd love it if she did. I'm sorry. This is causing major issues, but now she's found me … Anyway, she can contact me anytime."

"You haven't had it easy. It's hard to believe your parents don't know. Are you planning on telling them?"

"Only if Savannah decides to see me again." He kept his eyes trained on a small worn spot in the linoleum. If he looked into the man's eyes, he'd lose the small measure of control he had left. As it was, he was forcing himself to take long steady breaths. "We had a huge decision forced upon us, and we were powerless to change it. Her mother is scared of the implications in her life." He sighed. Even to his own ears, it sounded like a lame excuse. "It's hard to explain."

"I get the picture, and I'll try to help her see it. I've dreaded this day for a long time. She's been obsessed over that photo and finding her mother. To be so close but have her mother out of reach, well, she wasn't prepared for that eventuality."

"Perhaps it would be better if I bowed out. I wanted to know she was okay. Now I do. Perhaps it's a mistake to try fitting into her life when she only wants her mother. Tell her I'm sorry." He turned, ready to walk out of the door without another word. To drive away without looking back.

"Aiden." Ross grabbed his arm. The older man exhaled in a rush. "Are you staying in Portland overnight?"

Aiden shook his head. "I have a shift tomorrow at noon."

The man released his hold. "You flew here for one day?"

"Thank you, Ross, for letting us find the answer. The last thing I wanted was to make life difficult." He shook the older man's hand.

"Don't give up," Ross whispered as he pulled Aiden into a warm hug. "Please, Aiden. She's confused and angry, but that won't last forever. She has a good heart and I think you do too."

He couldn't speak so he squeezed the man's arm before he exited the house. The journey to the car seemed to take forever. His feet didn't want to carry him away, but he had to face the facts. Savannah's mother was missing from her life, not her father. She wanted Tiffany, not him, and he was kidding himself if he thought he could mean anything to the girl. He was simply the guy who gave her away.

He should have told her he didn't recognize the picture. Selfishness allowed him to carry it this far. His little girl had a good life without him and it would only cause trouble and heartache for everyone if he interfered.

Nothing could ever fix what happened to them or their daughter. He'd promised to protect them, and be there for them, and he'd failed. Nothing could ever make that right.

Chapter 9

Savannah

Savannah paced her room, sniffling and dabbing at her red-rimmed eyes. She dropped onto her bed, pounding her fists against the pillow before launching it across the room. It bounced off the wall and fell to the floor with an unsatisfying plop.

She snatched yet another tissue from the box and rubbed her damp cheeks before blowing her nose. The soggy tissue dropped into the growing heap on her bedside table before she flopped against her last surviving pillow. The pile drew her attention, and she finally heaved a sigh and stomped across her room to sweep them into the garbage can.

Done. Over. Final. Kaput. Things were falling apart. What to do next?

It seemed so silly. How she'd obsessed about cleaning the house, making cookies, and changing her outfit five times before hovering in front of the picture window. Her eager sprint through the front door. All to find him alone.

"Why don't you want me?" she whispered.

The photo on the bedside table caught her eye. A fresh wave of tears streamed down her face as she traced her mom's face.

How unfair. In her short lifetime, she'd lost not one, but two mothers. "I miss you." She set the silver frame in its place before yanking the last tissue from the box.

Nothing made sense, but she should have expected something would go wrong. The dread built as Aiden avoided her gaze and then her worst fear came true. How could a mother abandon her child? Aiden had said her mother had been devastated. So why would she refuse?

She tossed the last pillow from her bed and flung open her door, listening for any sounds. Nothing. Not even the usual small noises as her dad made dinner or the rattle of his newspaper broke the silence. She tiptoed down the hall, stopping for a sweater before she opened the door.

A few fluffy flakes of snow were falling, creating a light dusting of snow over the front walk which her dad was busy sweeping. After being cooped up in her room, the crisp air was refreshing.

She lowered herself onto the top step, observing as her dad concentrated on his task of keeping the yard perfect. The familiar pang hit as she thought about her mom.

Another injustice. The man who'd killed her in his drunken stupor was free. His children still had him, while her mom was gone forever.

"Where's Aiden?" she asked.

"He left."

"Where'd he go?" She huffed under her breath. Of course, he'd gone. *He gave me away before. Why wouldn't he do it again?* Even as the thought invaded, a small piece of her fought discouragement. He'd given up so easily, which meant one thing.

"Chicago, I imagine." Her dad stretched his arms above his head before bringing a hand down to rub his lower back.

"You're angry." Savannah hung her head.

"You seem angry enough for both of us." He leaned on the broom. "I'm sad and a little worried."

"Why? You should be thrilled he's out of our lives. He didn't fight it, and you never wanted me to see him to begin with."

"I wish your mom had burned that damn photo the minute we got home from the hospital. You've been obsessed with this quest. Now it's not happening and you're grouchy and disillusioned. Even worse, you're taking it out on someone who doesn't deserve it."

"I'm sorry, Daddy."

"I'm not the one who deserves the apology, Savannah." He wagged his index finger. "You've put Aiden in a tough spot. Maybe you'll see that someday."

"He's protecting her. I'm his child. It should be me he protects."

"Ask yourself how you'd feel in his position. This situation creates new issues in both of their lives. Can't you see?"

She brushed the back of her hand across her cheeks.

"Don't cry." He handed her a tissue and sat, wrapping an arm around her shoulders. "I'll always love you, no matter what. So will Aiden."

"How? I only met him a few weeks ago."

"You're his daughter." Ross sighed. "This isn't some abstract notion or a game. You've been so focused on finding your mother, you're missing the fact you've dropped into Aiden's life like a ticking time bomb. You're demanding something beyond his power to control. He can't make your mother see you or accept you into her life."

"Why not? He knows her."

"Just because you know someone doesn't mean you can or should bend them to your own will. He said quite plainly, she's endured enough abuse from her family. They took you. Not only from her but from him. I respect his decision to not push her into another situation she can't control or handle."

"I don't have a right to be upset my mother won't see me?"

"Nobody can dictate how you feel, but you don't have the right to take your anger and frustration out on Aiden. He went to a lot of trouble and expense to see you. The DNA testing, taking time from his work, and he's flown across the country twice. People count on him being there when they come through the door of that ER."

"Why did he bother?"

"That young man cares a great deal, but he's been forced into an untenable situation."

"I'll pay him back."

Her dad patted her knee. "You're missing the point. Is this only about finding your mother? Is knowing your father irrelevant? Do you even care whether you see him again?"

An ache grew in her heart. In focusing solely on the woman who'd given her birth, she hadn't considered the alternative. Now she'd refused to talk to Aiden and told him to leave, it probably didn't matter anyway.

"Savannah?"

"I don't know," she whispered. "I pictured this ending differently."

"Your expectations were set at an unattainable level. That happens when you truly want something." Her dad shook his head. "Consider how Aiden feels about how this ended." He rubbed her shoulder, sighing again. "Adoption is a heart-wrenching decision, even when you make that choice yourself. What happens when your child is taken away?"

Now she understood why her dad looked concerned. "You like him. You don't think he's irresponsible?"

"Why would I think that?"

"I'm a teenage mistake."

"It must have been difficult without the support of his family." He squeezed her shoulders. "Accept that your mother won't be part of your life, but Aiden would like to be. Maybe you should give him the chance."

Her dream had evaporated right as it was all within her grasp, leaving nothing but a dull sting. More hot tears trickled down her face.

"Oh, honey, this is what I was afraid of, except it isn't only you who's getting hurt, or has conflicting and painful emotions." Her dad turned her head so she was looking directly at him. "You aren't the only one struggling. You're not alone. Aiden's doing the best he can under stressful circumstances."

Savannah nodded. Perhaps cutting Aiden out of her life wasn't the right decision, but would he ever forgive her behavior?

Savannah stared out the window, wrapping a strand of hair around her finger while the teacher droned in a never-ending stream about some distant event in history. A bird landed in the small tree, pecking at the feeder hung there for the winter.

Her fingers guided the pencil across her paper, a small doodle taking shape. Her mind wandered to Aiden and the long conversation with her dad, which had morphed into interminable silences over the past several days.

Her inability to take action and make amends with Aiden disappointed her dad, and she was suitably chagrined. She wasn't this unfeeling, selfish person, or in her heart, she didn't believe so. Maybe she'd been unfair, but she couldn't rewind and change how she reacted, no matter how much she wished it.

"You're off in dreamland again?" Leanne prodded her ribs. "Class is over and I need some help here."

"Give me a minute." Savannah brushed her friend's hand away, taking her time gathering her things. By the time she was done, the room had emptied.

"Why don't you just call him?"

"Why would I?" Savannah shrugged, hoping to appear nonchalant even as her gut twisted. Aiden would turn her away after how she'd behaved.

"Because he's your father?" Leanne stared at her. "You've wanted to know about your biological parents for years, but now you don't care?"

Savannah bowed her head, hiding the tears burning behind her eyes. "He doesn't want me," she whispered. "I told him to go away, so why would he want to hear from me?"

"Did he say he didn't want you to phone? Didn't he fly to Portland just to see you?"

"Yeah." Savannah held up two fingers. "Twice."

"I dunno, it sounds like he wants to see you. When I fight with my parents, I apologize and they forgive me. I might have to do some extra chores but they're still my mom and dad." Leanne sighed. "Give him a chance. He's really nice."

"I was horrible."

"So apologize. He's your father so he'll forgive you."

"He doesn't know me."

"But he could. I saw him tons of times as he checked on me every day until my mom arrived. You should have seen him with the kids on the ward. I bet he'd make a great dad." Leanne grinned. "Think of the fun trips to Chicago, the extra birthday and Christmas presents." Her friend tapped a finger against her pursed lips. "If you don't want him, I wouldn't mind having a fun dad."

"Was it wrong for me to search for my parents? Maybe that's why my dad is upset."

"I'd wonder if I was adopted, and now you've found them. Or at least one-half, anyway. Did Dr. Hamilton want to see you again?"

Savannah pushed her hair back, fiddling with the ends, ignoring Leanne's pointed stare. "I need a haircut."

"Vanna? Did he?"

"Yes, okay? He said he wants to get to know me. I'm not sure what I'd say to him. He's so young to be my father."

"My older brother is twenty, and we hang out and have fun. You could do that with Aiden."

"Should I call him? I have his number."

"Why not? If you don't like him, you could stop seeing him. He lives all the way across the country."

"I guess I could see what he says."

"Promise you'll phone tonight." Leanne extended her pinky toward Savannah.

"Fine, I promise." Vanna linked their fingers, giving them a small shake. Now she was committed.

As soon as school was over, Vanna collected her backpack, making her way through the crowded hallways to Leanne's locker. "Ready to go?"

"Am I ever. My mom is waiting in the car. I have a doctor's appointment." Her friend tapped on the cast. "Hopefully, they'll take this clunky thing off."

Savannah helped her friend outside and handed off her bag, waving at Leanne's mom before she turned toward home.

She sighed at the sight of Justin chatting with Christina on the front steps of the school. The girl was never more than three feet from him at any given time.

Christina's light laugh carried through the crisp air and she leaned in toward the boy, flattening a palm against his chest.

Savannah rolled her eyes and trudged down the sidewalk toward her neighborhood.

"Vanna. Wait up." Justin loped toward her. "Can I walk with you?"

"Sure." She tightened the scarf around her neck to block the biting wind and struggled to free the black wool hat from her bag.

"Here." He tucked her long blonde hair behind her ears and adjusted the hat to cover the tender exposed flesh. "Better?"

She nodded and smiled, dropping her chin to hide the blush she was sure colored her cheeks.

"Let me carry that." Justin scooped her pack from her shoulder and slung it over his own. "It's cold. I can't wait until I can get my license. Dad promised me a car."

"Nice." She peeked at him. No doubt Christina would be thrilled at the news her boyfriend had transportation.

"You don't say much, do you?" He smirked. "Used to be you'd never quit talking."

Her cheeks reddened. Once upon a time, she'd played in his kiddie pool. They were inseparable during the early years of school.

Thankfully, they reached the front of her house. "Thanks for walking me and carrying my bag." She offered a shy smile.

His gorgeous eyes and adorable grin practically dissolved her into a puddle. "See you tomorrow?"

Vanna bit her lip and nodded. "Night, Justin." She opened the front door. For some reason, he was still standing there, so she waved and stepped inside. She pressed her back against the wooden frame and closed her eyes. *Nope. Don't even think it. He had Christina, where she was just the little girl who never quit talking.*

Chapter 10

Aiden

Despite the sun peeking over the horizon, a cold numbness crept over him. Aiden never wanted to feel so alone and full of regrets, the guilt and grief eating at him. Not again. Especially not now, just when he'd pulled his life together.

He hadn't saved their baby girl back then, and now, Tiffany didn't even want it. Yet their child only wanted her. His dream of having any sort of relationship with his daughter vanished.

He dragged himself into the shower, the hot water beating down as he leaned against the cold tiles, head bowed, his tears mixing into the water.

Men never cry.

That lesson had been drilled into Aiden's consciousness until he wanted to scream. He'd spent most of his early life learning to shutter his emotions.

He avoided the mirror as he dressed, finally leaving his apartment in a rush. Time had drifted by and now he was late for work.

The short journey to the hospital rushed by in a blur as did the thoughts about where he'd gone wrong. The break up with Tiffany, the stupid fights, and how he hadn't invested in any relationship since.

"You're late, Dr. Hamilton." Dana tapped her watch as he checked in at the front desk twenty minutes later. "You'll make it up at the end of your shift."

"Five minutes, but fine, whatever," he said under his breath.

"You'll still make it up, doctor." Dana narrowed her eyes, then stalked toward the elevators.

Aiden adjusted his lab coat, coming face to face with Emily. He hadn't seen the lovely doctor since his return from Portland.

"You owe me in a big way." Emily rubbed her bleary eyes. "I should have traded three nights for your two."

"Sorry." He selected a tablet and they proceeded toward the exam rooms. "How about I treat you to dinner? That play you were talking about is in town."

"Trying to wriggle out of those night shifts?" Emily eyed him. "Won't work, Aiden. You owe me"—she held her fingers in front of his face—"two shifts. No renegotiations. Besides, the play sold out weeks ago. Good luck getting tickets."

"I bet a few are available." Aiden forced a cheerful smile. Exhaustion blurred the edges of his consciousness, allowing him the courage to step over the friendship line without considering the consequences. "Saturday night?"

"Is this an invitation to hang out?" she whispered as they reached the exam room. "Or a date?"

"No pizza or beer." His lips twitched. "I'll make reservations somewhere nice."

"Stop it." She wagged a finger. "Those charming little smiles only go so far. And what about Tara?"

"Tara can't come." He winked. "You'll have to ask her out another time."

She arched a brow, a smile flickering across her features.

"It's a simple question with a simple answer. If you say no, I won't bother you again."

Emily tilted her head, tapping her pursed lips. "So a cocktail dress for dinner?"

"Perfect. Pick you up at your place around six-thirty?"

"Dinner would be lovely. It's a date." She graced him with a radiant smile before strolling down the hall, the gentle sway of her hips drawing his attention.

Tara appeared beside him. "Quit flirting and peel your eyes from her ass. The women around here demand respect."

"The patient in Exam 3 needs an IV."

The nurse scoffed, but pasted on a cheery expression before she entered the exam room.

His conversation with Emily had gone far better than he'd hoped, and he allowed a real smile to emerge. Perhaps it was a sign. Time to get on with his life.

⌒⌒

Aiden issued a low whistle when Emily opened the door. "Stunning."

The cocktail length, form-fitting, red silk dress hugged her curves and accentuated her waist. She'd pinned up her dark hair, showing off her slim neck and the simple diamond pendant and earrings she wore. Her sparkling green eyes appeared even more vibrant than usual. She looked perfect. *Mouthwateringly sexy.*

"Thank you. These are beautiful." She accepted the colorful bouquet he presented, leaning in to give him a hug and kiss on the cheek. "You look pretty good yourself. What is this? Armani?" She straightened the burgundy silk tie which complimented his tailored suit.

"Are you ready?" He trailed her into the kitchen.

A smile appeared as she arranged the flowers in a vase she'd pulled from the cabinet. "I am."

He helped with her coat, then waited as she locked the door before escorting her downstairs to the limo waiting at the curb.

Her face lit up as the driver opened the door. "First time a guy's treated me to a limo." Emily sank into the plush leather seat.

"Maybe you've been dating the wrong guys."

She tilted her head. "Do you always pick up your dates in limos?"

"Only the special ones." The words came out automatically, but they were true. He'd waited far too long to ask this incredible woman for a date.

She raised a brow. "Should I be super impressed? Flowers, limo …" A smile twitched at the corners of her lips. "Theater tickets?"

He held back a grin as he pulled the slips of paper from the inner pocket of his suit jacket and waved them.

"You didn't. How did you get your hands on those?"

Aiden lifted a shoulder, but he didn't explain as the limo glided through traffic, finally coming to a halt in front of the theater.

The driver opened the door and Aiden helped Emily out, keeping hold of her small hand as he ushered her inside and led her to their seats.

"Amazing." She settled in the plush chair and angled toward him. "You've outdone yourself, Dr. Hamilton. Is there anything you can't do?"

"Plenty, I'm sure."

The lights dimmed and the curtains rose, saving him from making any further comments. The tickets hadn't been easy to procure, but the trouble was worth it.

Emily seemed entranced by the action on stage. Half an hour into the play, she reached for his hand, giving it a squeeze and bestowing a radiant smile on him before refocusing on the stage.

Aiden kept her soft hand enclosed in his. Clearly he wasn't the only one feeling their connection. Or maybe that was just more wishful thinking.

After the play, they enjoyed a late dinner at one of his favorite restaurants. The conversation flowed easily, as it always seemed to with Emily.

"I didn't know what to expect," she said, once they'd been served coffee. "We never really go out. It's always something quick after work, but I never considered them dates."

"Maybe we should do it more often."

"Perhaps we should." Emily contemplated him from across the table. "Why do I know so little about you? You're an only child, and you talk about your grandmother, but you never mention your parents."

"I can never get a word in about them." He grinned. "You're always telling me about your sisters and your niece."

"Ha ha. I don't talk about them that much." She wrinkled her nose. "Do I?"

"I'm kidding, Em." He shrugged. "I'm not close to my parents. They've lived in New York for over fifteen years. I went to boarding school," he said. "I spent summers at my grandparents' house in Martha's Vineyard until I was fifteen."

"Boarding school, huh." She tilted her head. "And when you were sixteen?"

"I lived in Europe until I turned eighteen. Oxford, remember?" His grandparents sent him away right after Savannah's birth, irrevocably altering his life. His family never wanted him around, and they certainly never spoke about the rift between them.

"I always forget you attended all the fancy schools." She smiled. "What do your parents do?"

"My father is a lawyer. My mother lunches at the Country Club."

Emily laughed. "Wasn't your grandfather some big Chicago criminal lawyer?"

"He was. I broke with tradition by becoming a doctor, which wasn't a popular decision." Aiden sipped his coffee. "You've met Tom. He's running the firm now, and he's careful about his clientele."

"Tom Grayson?" Emily frowned. "I've said hello to him once or twice, but that's it. I don't know much about him," she said. "We don't travel in the same social circles. But you …"

"Tom's one of my closest friends. I've known him my entire life."

"What's your full name?"

"Why?"

"I plan on taking advantage of this opportunity." Emily leaned forward and rested a warm hand over his. "We've worked together for years, but you never get into your personal life. I'm curious."

That fact was undeniable. He preferred to keep a low profile at work. With the exception of his closest friends, he never allowed anyone to get overly personal. Especially women. "Aiden James Thomas Franklin Hamilton. What's your middle name?"

"You have three middle names?" Emily tilted her head. "How do you fit them in those tiny boxes on forms?"

"It's not easy." Aiden caught her fingers, stroking them with his thumb. "My grandfather wanted to name me after his best friend and law partner, Aiden Grayson. My father wanted me named after him. They compromised, leaving me with so many names, I can barely keep track."

"If you have a kid, they'll have four middle names?"

Aiden's thoughts raced. *No, I can't tell her about my daughter. What would be the point?* "I'd never torture my child, so no. You haven't answered. Middle name?"

"Alejandra. My name is Emelia Alejandra Anderson." Her cheeks flushed. "My mom won in naming me. She's Spanish, but my dad's family is Scandinavian."

"Beautiful, Emelia." Aiden savored the sound of her elegant name on his lips. "It's much easier to fit on forms, too." He motioned to the attached lounge once he'd paid their bill. "They have live music. We could have a drink, or are you ready to head home?"

"It's almost midnight and I have an early shift tomorrow, so home. You?"

"Same shift as you." He hid his disappointment that the evening was ending, but he collected their coats and escorted her to the limo.

"Magical. We come out and the car is waiting. Thank you for tonight. This has been fun." She leaned against him as the limo turned toward home. Her eyes closed, a soft smile touching her lips.

"Tired?"

"A little." Her gaze met his as the limo stopped in front of her building. "Are you in a rush?" She nibbled her lip. "Stay for coffee?"

Would it be wise to accept? Probably not, yet he couldn't resist. "Sounds good." He slid out of the car behind her. "We can suffer together tomorrow."

After dismissing the driver, he allowed her to lead him upstairs to her apartment, enjoying the soft touch the fingers interlaced with his.

Emily kept her head bowed as she let them into her apartment and locked the door behind them. She removed her sexy heels, letting them hit the floor with a soft click. "Stay awhile?"

He slung his overcoat on the rack by the door. As he removed his tie and unbuttoned the top two buttons of his shirt, he wandered into the living room, pausing to inspect the photo of Emily with a small dark-haired girl. "Isa has grown. She's a cutie."

"Mmmhmm. Aiden?" She tugged her hairpins free and gave her head a small shake, her hair cascading in waves over her shoulders.

Aiden couldn't tear his eyes away, every move she made etching into his brain. He froze as she approached and lifted her chin.

"Is this for real?" One hand rose and caressed his cheek. "Or is it all in my head?" Her eyes widened, drawing him into their depths.

"Definitely real," he murmured as he curled a lock of silky hair around his fingertip. On impulse, he leaned in to kiss her luscious lips, enjoying the sweet taste lingering on her tongue. The light floral scent of her perfume enveloped him as he cupped her face between his palms, barely taking a breath before he captured her mouth again.

Instead of pushing him away as he feared, she wound an arm around his neck, one hand slipping into his hair as she pressed against him. Their kiss deepened, his heart thumping in time with hers. As he tangled a hand into her hair, he forgot everything and simply enjoyed holding the incredible woman close.

Emily buried her head against his neck. "Wow, Aiden," she whispered, her breath warm wisps against his skin. She placed soft kisses on his jawline as her hands slipped into his suit jacket, pushing it from his shoulders and allowing it to drop to the floor before she worked at the buttons on his shirt.

He ran his fingertips down her back, catching the bottom of her dress and peeling it over her head as she lifted her arms. Even as he tossed it aside, his shirt gave way, the last few buttons pattering against the hardwood as she yanked on the fabric.

He gazed into her hazy green eyes as her mouth parted in invitation. As he tasted her sweet lips again, he unhooked her lacy black bra while she tugged his belt free. It hit the floor with a clunk.

Her skin felt like satin, their hands and mouths exploring as they performed a slow sensual dance down the hall to her bedroom.

Emily wrapped her arms around him, drawing him into the soft sheets, her mouth tight against his.

"Emelia." He breathed her name into the crook of her neck as it all rushed over him.

They were about to take an irreversible step across the line, and he was powerless to resist.

Aiden opened his eyes, momentarily disoriented. Judging by the dim light filtering through a crack in the blinds, it was still early. Her warm body curled against him, her soft, rhythmic breathing tickling his neck. A smile twitched at the corners of his mouth as the memory flooded in on him.

The night had taken an unexpected turn, and he'd gone with it. The sudden transformation of sweet, unassuming, Emily into the dark-haired temptress, Emelia, had stunned and delighted him in equal measures. Resistance was futile, and he hadn't wanted to in any case. It had been amazing, with boundless passion and chemistry.

His eyes popped open sometime later, the clock now reading five thirty. Time to get up, though he could've stayed cocooned in bed all day if Emily were with him.

Aiden caressed her cheek, brushing her hair back as her eyes fluttered open. "Hey, sweetheart, we have work. I should go home and change."

"In a minute," she mumbled as her eyelids closed. A sleepy half-smile crossed her face as she buried her head in her pillow, winding an arm around him. "Don't go."

He kissed her gently. "We work at seven. I'll call in half an hour to make sure you're up. I had a great time last night." Aiden gave her lips one final long caress before he dressed, one piece at a time. He followed the trail of scattered clothing down the hallway, finally donning his button less dress shirt.

After quietly closing the door of her apartment, he bounded down the stairs, humming to himself. He walked at a steady pace, unable to stop smiling.

Once home he showered and hoped she'd gotten out of bed. He perused his wardrobe options as he dialed her number.

"Where'd you go?"

"Home. Time to get up."

"I'm too tired. Someone kept me up half the night."

"Didn't hear any complaints at the time." He laughed. "It's six-fifteen, Emelia."

"What? Oh crap, I need a shower. Catch you there. Gotta go." The line went dead.

He just had time to pick up breakfast if he hurried.

Emily arrived in the doctor's lounge at five to seven.

"Extra-hot latte with a touch of sugar and a breakfast sandwich." He offered the cup and bag. "Cutting it close this morning aren't we, Dr. Anderson?"

"Maybe a little. I only had time for a quick shower and some clothes." She'd pinned up her dark hair, highlighting her glowing skin and sparkling eyes.

He would never have guessed she'd gotten ready in less than half an hour after barely sleeping.

Dana stuck her head in the door. "It's seven and my chief and attending are loitering in the lounge? On the floor. Now." She scowled before retreating.

"Eat. I'll cover for five." Aiden leaned in and pressed a tender kiss to her lips.

"What if someone saw that?"

"They didn't." He winked and stole another kiss.

Emily pushed him toward the door. "Go before Dragon Lady attacks."

"I'll keep her at bay."

He hummed under his breath as he fielded questions and assigned patients to the students and residents on shift.

"You're in a good mood." Tara's brows rose. "Have fun last night?"

"What?" Aiden almost dumped his latte at her sly smile.

"Didn't Emily drag you to some stupid play last night? You must have owed her big for taking those shifts."

"Oh." Aiden smiled as his panic abated. It appeared Emily hadn't shared the fact it was an actual date, which was fine with him. He didn't need the aggravation of hospital gossip. "It was a good play."

"Good play is an oxymoron." She twirled her finger in her hair. "Image getting excited about dressing up. Figures. Emily seems the type."

"The type?"

"High maintenance? The nails, the hair, the clothes. Must take her hours a day to look like ... that." Tara motioned toward Emily, who was examining an x-ray. "I bet she's up three hours before each shift to fix her face."

The dark-haired doctor was gorgeous with her silky hair, olive skin, and those alluring green eyes, but he knew it hadn't taken hours to put herself together this morning. "Most women enjoy dressing up once in a while."

"I prefer movies or hanging out. Fussing over big social events and stuff isn't my thing." Tara's lip curled. "I'm not one of those overly needy types."

"She's never struck me as high maintenance or needy."

"Enough about her." Tara's lashes fluttered. "We should go to a movie tonight."

"I've got patients waiting." He chose another chart and headed down the hall, spotting Emily at the front desk. The bright smile she sent in his direction had him grinning. He hoped no one noticed, especially Tara, considering the issues she had with the doctor.

Emily caught up with him as he examined an x-ray at the light board a while later. "Thanks."

"For what?"

"I had a wonderful time at the play and dinner was lovely. Then there was the wake-up call this morning, without which I would have been late, and a yummy breakfast. Especially that latte, which I desperately needed." Her tone was light and teasing. "Did I miss anything?"

Aiden smiled. "I had a great time, and I'd like to do it again. Go on a date, I mean."

"I knew what you meant." She smirked, but it faded as she stared toward the front desk. "What was Tara on about earlier? She's glaring at us with her usual pouty look. Does she know that we ...?" Emily's eyes widened before she shot another look at the nurse. "It would explain her comment."

"What comment?"

"She'd happily claw my eyes out." Emily's brows rose. "Did you two ever …?"

He pulled her into the closest empty exam room and shut the door. "Are you asking if I slept with Tara?"

She shrugged and evaded his gaze.

"Not that I owe you details of past relationships, but no. She's not really my type."

"You seem to be hers." Emily looked away again, brushing at her eyes.

"Why the tears?" Aiden lifted her chin. "What did Tara say?"

"It's not important." She sniffled.

"You're … crying." He slid his arms around her. "Shh, sweetheart." Aiden pressed a kiss to her hair.

"I'm not that woman." She sobbed. "I don't sleep with guys on the first date, but we've been winding up to it for months. The sexual tension was overwhelming. Now that we … Am I the flavor of the week?"

Aiden released her and took a step back. "Flavor-of-the-fucking-week? Good one. Just fucking perfect."

"What am I then?"

"I thought … Yeah, never mind that because it's pretty damn clear what you're thinking." He crossed his arms. "You're acting bat-shit crazy. I don't kiss and tell, I don't have a flavor of the week, and I'm seriously pissed at the ridiculous assumption you're my plaything."

Emily peered at him through red shiny eyes, her head tilting. "You really want to go out again? On a date?"

"I rarely say things I don't mean." He grasped her shoulders. "You're right, I don't have an awesome track record of long meaningful relationships, but I thought we had something."

She stared at him, wide-eyed.

"If you aren't feeling it, so be it. Just don't play passive-aggressive mind games," he said. "Either way, I don't think less of you because of last night."

"You don't?"

"Do you think less of me?" He held up his hand before she could even open her mouth. "Stupid question. Obviously, you do. Even worse, you think less of yourself." After rubbing a hand over his face, he leaned back and crossed his arms. "Can I ask you something?"

She bowed her head and shrugged.

"What if I hadn't let it go any further so we could follow some stupid arbitrary dating rules?"

A frown fleeted across her features. "I'd feel … Undesirable."

"Huh. You are so far opposite, it's crazy." How could Emily not understand why Tara looked at her the way she did? "You're pretty great, Emelia Alejandra

Anderson. You're compassionate, warm, and brilliant, not to mention beautiful, sexy, and passionate. What guy wouldn't desire that?" He sighed. "We've been dancing around the attraction for months, but I wasn't ready. Now I am. Are you?"

A frown knitted her forehead.

"Right. Pretend it never happened." He stalked from the room. After last night he'd hoped, but she clearly didn't feel the same.

He avoided her for the remainder of the day, fearing the inevitable awkwardness would linger whenever they worked together. If only he'd listened to that little alarm in the back of his head and gone home.

Aiden hummed along with the music, pausing only to drain his second glass of Macallan before stowing the last of the groceries in the fridge. *Drinking alone.* Never the best idea, but after the week he'd had ... He refilled his glass but set it untouched on the counter and dialed as he wandered onto the deck, sucking in the frigid but refreshing salty air.

"Hey, where are you?" Ryan asked.

"The beach house." He stepped inside and closed the French doors against the chilly night.

"Oh-oh. I'm scared to ask about the play."

"It was great." Aiden sighed. "Thanks again for the tickets."

"Hmm, sounds like it was a bust," his friend said. "Emily wasn't impressed?"

"She loved it, and dinner, and ... everything."

"So what's the problem?"

"We connected, and—"

"Sex on the first date? Bad move, dude."

"Stupid me, thinking she wouldn't judge. Now I'm the asshole who played her which totally fucks up our friendship."

"Damn. This woman has you all turned around. My advice? Apologize."

Aiden stared at the tumbler of amber liquid on the counter. "For what? Wanting something more than a one night stand?"

"Not sure intent matters. You have to work with the woman."

"Don't remind me." He massaged his temple with one hand. The faint crunch of tires against gravel caught his attention. "Someone's here."

"At this time of night?"

The thud of a car door was followed by a light tap, then a heavier one. "Just a second." He opened the door, his breath catching at the sight of the woman before him. "Emily."

"She's there? Why are you still talking to me?" Ryan snickered and the line disconnected.

"It's freezing." Emily tugged her scarf around her reddened cheeks.

"How did you …?" He peered around her, spotting the old red pickup in the driveway. "Ahh, Hal." He waved at the man and beckoned Emily inside.

She set her handbag on a chair and rubbed her red-rimmed eyes. "I'm exhausted. Who knew it took so long to get to the Vineyard from Chicago?"

"Everyone?" He hung her coat and ushered her toward the living room. After a curious look in her direction, he lit a match, holding it under the pile of kindling in the stone fireplace until flames flickered into life.

"There were weather delays in Boston." Emily extended her hands toward the fire. "Ahh, that's good. The heater in Hal's truck doesn't work so well."

"What … what are you doing here? How did you know where to find me?"

"I called Tom."

"Tom … Grayson?" Aiden scrubbed a hand through his hair.

"Mmmm. Except Jenna answered his phone and told me you were here."

Aiden sank onto the arm of the couch. "You tracked me through my friends?"

She gnawed on her lip. "Sorry, too far?"

"How did you get my personal information out of Jenna?"

A delicate pink crept into her cheeks. "I might have inferred there was a situation with one of your patients."

A grin twitched the corner of his lips. "Impressively sneaky." His smile faded. "But why?"

She bowed her head, tugging at the sleeves of her silky blouse. "It works for guys, so why not me?"

He gave her a quizzical look.

"The grand gesture that ends in forgiveness for acting bat-shit crazy?" Her cheeks reddened. "Stupid me. Why would you even care?"

Aiden stepped closer. "You came to apologize?"

"Your doorman said you weren't home."

"You flew hundreds of miles to a tiny island in mid-November to say … I'm sorry? Most people would phone first."

"I pictured a different ending. I'd show up, and you'd be incredibly happy to see me, and …" Something akin to panic flitted across her features.

"And what?"

"I spent ten hours in crappy airports, arrived too late to get a rental car, and had to beg for a ride. I'm a complete mess." She cupped her hands over her face, smothering a ragged sob.

"Hey." He pulled her against his chest. "Why don't you have a hot shower while I make us something to eat?"

"You're n-not mad?"

"No." Aiden released her and motioned toward the stairs. "After you."

Her softly swaying jean-clad curves created a vivid image of their night together. He shut it down, clenching his hand to prevent himself from reaching out as he followed her. "End of the hall on the right."

She paused before stepping into the master bedroom.

"I'd bring your bag, but it seems you don't have one."

"The airline lost my luggage. Perfect way to top off my day." She tugged at her wrinkled blouse.

"Bathroom is through there." Aiden pointed. "Towels are in the cupboard, and," he said, motioning to his closet, "help yourself to some clothes."

A faint smile appeared. "Thanks for not freaking out."

"Never." He returned the smile. "Come down when you're ready."

A slight sound made him look up. "Feel better?" He closed his laptop and stood, smothering a yawn.

A hesitant smile appeared and she held out her arms and turned, her tiny frame engulfed by his sweatshirt. Her gaze met his as she completed the full circle. "It's like a dress." A crease appeared in her forehead. "Aiden?"

He forced a smile, fighting the tumultuous thoughts tumbling through his mind. "Hungry?"

"Starving." She trailed after him, eyeing the seafood chowder he ladled into bowls before setting a plate of fresh biscuits on the counter. "That smells amazing."

"Wine?"

Emily nodded, but her brows rose as she stared toward the decanter and full tumbler of Macallan on the counter. "Why did you come here in the middle of winter?" She scooped a spoonful of chowder into her mouth. "Mmmm. Delicious. Did you make this?"

"Mmhm." He selected a bottle of Pinot Grigio from the rack and popped the cork, pouring two glasses and setting one within her reach. "This is my favorite place to unwind, especially when the summer people are gone."

"It's definitely quiet. I hope the owner doesn't mind me stealing his clothes." She wrinkled her nose.

"I'm sure he won't mind in the least." He winked before settling on the stool beside her, letting silence fall while they ate.

"That was incredible." Emily slid her bowl away and cradled her wine glass. She took two generous sips, then sighed. "Better." Her gaze met his. "I'm sorry for acting crazy." She twirled the glass. "It's about me. I haven't had fantastic luck with men."

"That runs both ways."

She blinked hard. "So apology not accepted?"

"I'm sorry, Em. The last thing I wanted was this awkward mess."

"Made worse by me showing up unannounced."

"Or better." He caught her hand between his, rubbing the back with his thumbs. "Tell me why?"

"No guy ever goes over the top on a date without an ulterior motive."

An indescribable sadness crept over him. "Em—"

"Wait." She pressed a fingertip to his lips. "You're not some guy I picked up in a bar, but one I've respected and admired for years. You've never been involved with anyone at work. Have you?"

He shook his head.

"Then maybe it's you making the necessary effort to shake us from complacency and that comfortable friend zone."

"It wasn't that calculated, but yeah, a woman like you deserves ... better."

She pressed a hand to her chest, blinking rapidly. "You feel it?"

"Stay and find out." He leaned in, brushing her soft cheek with his lips.

Her hand crept around his neck, her fingers drifting through the hair at the nape of his neck. "I thought you'd never ask."

Aiden sank into her embrace, pulling her closer, enjoying the hot tingly rush. This woman had him, and no matter whether the entanglement was wise or not, it was already too late. They'd built a true connection. One he hadn't felt with any woman since Tiffany had broken him.

Chapter 11

Savannah

A week later, Savannah still hadn't gathered the courage to call Aiden. Every time Leanne brought it up, she changed to a new topic, not wanting to admit her own cowardice.

"How was school?" Her dad peered over the top of his paper as she let herself into the house.

"Good. I'm making a snack before I do my homework." She fluttered her fingers and dropped her backpack in her room before heading into the kitchen. The card stuck to the fridge taunted her as she poured a cold drink, fixed a plate of fruit and cheese, and shut herself in her room. The pile of homework kept her busy until dinner.

Her dad cast glances across the table during their silent meal. "You want to talk about it?"

Savannah shrugged, pushing the last of her mashed potatoes around her plate. "I told Leanne about Aiden."

"Oh?"

Tears pricked at her eyes. "I promised I'd call him, but how can I?"

Ross reached out to capture her hand. "Is that what's bothering you? You want to talk to Aiden?"

She hung her head, squishing her potatoes and inspecting the pattern left from the tines of her fork.

"Call him. If you want to see him, I'll fly you to Chicago."

She lifted her chin. "You will?"

"This is a difficult situation, and it's no secret I wished you'd never pursued it. Now you've involved Aiden." Her dad shrugged. "I like him. It's best you get to know him. You've had these burning questions about who would give up a child and some notions about why. Maybe this will set your mind at peace."

Her lips tugged downward. How would she make amends? Would Aiden even speak to her?

"He told me you should contact him when you're ready."

Savannah's frown deepened.

"You've been beating yourself up about how it all unfolded, but don't. He understands how hard it was for you to hear and he sure didn't want to be saying it. Don't discount how difficult that was for him, and remember, it changes nothing. You are and always will be his child. It wasn't his choice to walk away. Not when you were born, and not after his last visit. Don't back out now. I'm certain you'd regret it."

It was humbling to realize as hard as this was, her dad supported her, giving her the freedom and support to pursue the answers. Perhaps this call wouldn't be so bad, and she owed it to Aiden to make the effort. She had dragged him into the middle of her own personal drama without warning.

Her mind remained occupied for the rest of the evening, and finally, she summoned the courage to snatch the card off the fridge and take it to her room. With damp palms and a pounding heart, she dialed the number. When his voice mail answered, she choked up, unable to leave a message. After pacing back and forth several times, she redialed.

This time he answered on the first ring. "Savannah?"

"Do you have time to talk?"

"Everything okay?"

"Umm … are you sure it's okay I called? It's late, sorry."

"I'm glad you did."

"I'm sorry about my behavior on your last visit." She sucked in an audible breath. "I'm disappointed and angry because my mother doesn't want me but it was wrong to yell at you," she said as she sank onto her bed.

"I'm sorry too. You went through all of that, and you didn't get what you wanted."

"I shouldn't have blamed you. It's not your fault. I'll never know my mother, will I?"

"I wish it could be different, but there's nothing more I can do."

"Do you want to get to know me?"

"Yes, but maybe it's not what's best for you. You have a dad who loves you, and I don't want to interfere or create issues in your life. The selfish part of me would love to see you, but if it's not what you want, then I'll let it go."

"Just like that?"

He took a deep breath. "I got the impression you'd prefer I left you alone, but I'd love to see you."

"Even after I was so awful? I said things that weren't very nice."

"I'm sure I said many not-so-nice things when I was a teenager."

A hesitant laugh escaped as she closed her eyes, picturing the teenage boy in the photo.

"I can forgive a few angry words, especially considering this strange and emotional situation we find ourselves in."

"It is that." As much as it pained her, she wanted Aiden to understand why she'd reacted the way she had. "I assumed you'd show up with her. Not having her appear hurt, and I forgot that I found at least part of what I was searching for. I'd like to get to know you too."

"What does your dad say?"

"He wants me to see you," she said. "Can I visit you in Chicago sometime?" She wrapped a lock of hair around her finger. "Maybe I could come around Christmas, after my exams. What do you think?"

Aiden cleared his throat. "I'd like that. I have tons of room so you could stay here, rather than at a hotel."

Her heart lightened at the thought. "I'll check my school schedule and send you some dates."

"I'm glad you called. I look forward to seeing you."

"Me too. Goodnight, Aiden."

"Night, Savannah."

Savannah spent the next day contemplating her talk with Aiden and discussing the trip with Leanne. Now she needed to confirm her plans with her dad.

She threw chopped onions into the pan. They sizzled as she gave a quick stir. "Daddy?"

"Hmmm?" He looked up from his task of opening the can of tomato sauce. "Darn can opener. It's almost impossible. We need a new one."

Savannah took over, spinning the can and popping the top off.

Ross tipped the sauce into the pan with the diced vegetables, a slight grin turning up the corners of his mouth. "What would I do without you?"

"Starve?" She giggled as she stirred the contents of the pan. She loved these times with her dad, especially since they'd lost her mom.

Her dad gave her a quizzical look. "You had a question?" He filled the large pasta pot with water, dropping in a pinch of salt as it joined the sauté pan on the stove.

"I called Aiden."

"You did?" He leaned back against the table.

"Uh-huh." She scooped a spoonful of sauce and offered it to him.

"Needs basil, but it's good," he said. "What happened with Aiden?"

"I apologized." She brushed a strand of errant hair from her cheek before sprinkling more of the herb over top.

"What did he say?"

"He forgave me, and I asked to visit in December after my exams." Savannah opened the ravioli and poured it into the boiling water.

"You've decided to see him?"

"I can stay in his guest room if I go to Chicago. Is that okay?"

Her dad nodded. "Your mom would have liked Aiden a great deal, and she'd be happy you have the opportunity to know your father."

"I miss her."

"Me too." Her dad sighed. "Your mom said you were the best gift she ever received. It was right about this time of year when we got the news. Another couple backed out of adopting you at the last minute. We were next on the list."

Savannah had heard this story countless times. Her parents were pushing forty and about to resign themselves to being childless when they received the call. "Mom said I was her Christmas Angel." She hugged him, resting her head on his chest. "I can stay with Aiden?"

"I'd prefer it to you being alone in a hotel." Her dad pressed a kiss to her temple.

"Thank you." She pecked his cheek. "This means a lot to me."

After a subdued dinner, she returned to her room and called Aiden, happy that he answered right away. "I talked to my dad and texted you some dates."

"I'll book your flights. I'm more than happy to cover them." His tone became serious. "Have Ross call if it's a problem, okay?"

"I'll tell him." Savannah flopped on her back across the bed and nibbled at her nails. "Do you have a girlfriend?"

"Yes. Emily's a doctor who works with me at the hospital."

"Can I meet her?" Her inquiry was met with a deep silence. "Are you still there?"

"Sorry, can I give it some thought? She doesn't know about you yet."

"Why not?"

"Complicated." Aiden's laugh sounded nervous and Savannah let out a long sigh. "I keep saying it's complicated, don't I."

"Do you really like Emily? Do you think you'll date her for a while?"

"Yes. Which means I should introduce you, right?"

"Unless you don't really want to." Savannah plumped up her pillow and closed her eyes.

"I've waited a long time for a chance to know you. I hope you feel the same way. This will get easier, I'm sure."

"Why haven't you told Emily?"

"It's not that I don't want her to know, but it's so new. Both meeting you and dating her, and I didn't think you'd want to see me again. I've held off the big discussions with friends and family."

It seemed he harbored the same fears as she had. "If we're going to get to know each other, I want to meet the people who are important to you." Savannah twirled her hair around her finger. "I hope I meet her."

After they'd said goodnight, Savannah flopped out her arm, dropping the phone beside her on the bed. A small smile crept across her face. A couple weeks and she'd be in Chicago again. Curiosity burned. What was he really like? Where did he live? A million-and-one questions zipped through her brain.

It left her with mixed feelings. She turned her wrist, the light dance across the gold band of the watch. Her mom kept it safe for her, and it had belonged to the woman who'd given her life, but that woman wanted nothing to do with her. Suddenly, she couldn't bear looking at it. It was simply a reminder of everything she'd never have.

Savannah tucked the watch inside a jewelry box hidden in her dresser drawer. As she shoved it to the back, she vowed to move on, not wanting any further reminders of the mother who'd forsaken her.

Chapter 12

Aiden

Aside from Tiffany, Aiden hadn't told anyone about Savannah, and now he'd have to reveal her existence, at least to Emily. It had to be soon if he wanted to continue seeing her. How much could he divulge without her dashing for the door or breaking his promise to be discreet?

"Aiden?" Emily's voice rang through the apartment.

He shook off his thoughts, pulling on his sweater as she appeared in the bedroom. "How was work?" After a gentle kiss, he drew her in for a hug.

"Not bad, but I missed you. Do you think Dana would schedule us for the same shifts if we told her?"

"She'd have us on opposite schedules until the end of time. Dragon Lady loves to make everyone's lives as difficult as possible."

They'd been careful to keep their hands to themselves and arrive separately, even when Emily stayed overnight, preferring to allow their relationship to develop before they opened up at work.

"You're probably right." Emily grimaced as she tucked her overnight bag inside the closet. "Dragon Lady hates me."

"It's fear, not hate."

She arched her brows. "I'm so scary."

"On a professional level you are. You're a talented, amazing doctor with the education and ability, which means serious competition. She wants to be promoted, and you'll get in her way, so watch your back."

"I'm not that much of a threat."

"You most certainly are. The staff likes you more than they like her and you're qualified for management. The only thing she has over you is seniority."

"You're sweet." She pressed a kiss to his lips. "Ready to see that movie?"

Aiden tucked his wallet into an inner pocket and they headed toward the front door. "One day you'll kick Dragon Lady's ass, professionally speaking." Aiden fully believed Emily had the determination and drive. "Hey, you off Saturday night?"

"Were you planning a hot date?" Emily said in a teasing tone.

"Not hot, exactly. My grandmother invited me to a formal dinner party."

"Ahh, luring me into the lion's den, are you?"

"Something like that. I figured if my family scared you off, now would be better than waiting until we've been dating longer."

"Getting ahead of yourself there, Dr. Hamilton." She gave him a flirty smile. "Who says I'll be sticking around?"

The words stung. Especially after the unexpected and slightly magical visit to the Vineyard. "Nobody." He forced his lips into a flat line, hoping to hide his discouragement. "Is it too soon to meet my grandmother?"

"I'm kidding." Emily caught his arm as he turned away. "I'd love to come. We haven't been dating long, but it's great." She cupped his face between her palms. "You're too sensitive."

"Don't feel obligated. It's a formal dinner party so you'll have to dress up. There will be at least sixteen to twenty guests, and it'll be boring."

"You make it sound as appealing as a root canal."

"Root canals are more fun. This is familial duty, and I shouldn't subject you to my grandmother. If I do, you definitely won't stick around."

"Now I'm confused." She quirked her brow. "First you invite me then you talk me out of it."

"I don't want to rush things." Aiden frowned as a surge of panic flooded him. "Are we rushing this?" This invitation put extra pressure on them as a couple. He joked about his family, but having them interfere in his relationship with any woman he dated was a real, underlying fear. It wouldn't be the first time they'd ruined something special, and they wouldn't hesitate to do it again.

"Relax. I won't hold your family against you if you don't hold mine against me. My mother's hounding me about my new guy. Come with me to my mom's for dinner." Emily winked. "Then she can scare you with twenty questions and her million and one hugs. It's incredibly embarrassing."

"Are you actually hoping she'll frighten me away and save you the trouble?"

"You're impossible." She poked him in the ribs. "I could say the same thing about meeting your grandmother." Her expression turned serious. "My Spanish mamá is overprotective and will ask you all sorts of crazy things, but she and I are close."

"I'd love to meet your mom." Maybe this relationship was going in the right direction after all. "Do you have a formal dress for Saturday?"

"I'm sure I can manage to look presentable." Emily leaned in and gave him a kiss.

The jangle of nerves hit Aiden as the limo wound its way down the snowy roads of Lake Forest.

"You're jumpy." Emily squeezed his hand. "Haven't you ever taken a woman to meet your family?"

"Yes." Aiden entwined their fingers, taking a calming breath. "I hope the two of you will get along."

"I won't use the wrong fork." She patted his leg.

"It's not about which fork you use. My family makes me a touch crazy. It's not you, it's them." Aiden gave a helpless shrug. "You'll see what I mean." *In about three seconds.*

She smothered a gasp, her eyes widening as the limo crawled through imposing iron gates and rounded the wide circular drive.

The stately mansion sat on a huge tract of land, surrounded by an acre of manicured landscapes, flowerbeds, and a pond with a fountain. At the moment the ground was covered in snow, but the house looked magical. The soft snowflakes fluttering from the sky added to the ambiance of the elegant seasonal lights and decorations.

"This is insane," she said under her breath. "Are we the first ones here?"

"My grandmother requested we arrive early so she can meet you properly."

"Oh." Emily nodded at his words, her grip on his hand tightening.

He was confident his brilliant and articulate girlfriend would hold up to his grandmother's inquisition, as he always thought of these "meet the family" evenings. "Don't worry."

The front door swung open. "Good evening, Dr. Hamilton. Your grandmother is in the reading room." The butler took their coats, and Aiden led Emily into the large ornate room.

The petite and impeccably dressed gray-haired woman stood as they entered. She scanned Emily from head to toe with an approving nod, the slightest of smiles softening her features.

Aiden kissed the elderly woman's cheek. "This is Dr. Emelia Anderson. Emily, this is my grandmother, Grace Hamilton."

"Very nice to meet you, Mrs. Hamilton." Emily extended her hand.

"Please sit, Dr. Anderson. Aiden, would you mind doing the honors of pouring drinks?"

"The usual?" At his grandmother's nod, he turned to Emily. "Emily?"

"Red wine, please." She smiled warmly.

"You work with Aiden at the hospital?" Grace asked in the usual formal and almost regal tone reserved for new acquaintances.

"We've known each other for several years." Emily's voice was light and confident.

They chatted for several minutes, his grandmother shooting a continuous line of questions at Emily before the butler announced the first arrivals.

Grace rose. "I must attend to my guests, but I do hope you'll visit again."

"Thank you, Mrs. Hamilton."

"Please, call me Grace." The older woman smiled. "Truly a pleasure to meet you, Emily."

Aiden grinned as his grandmother exited the room to attend to her hostess duties.

Emily took his arm. "I've been sufficiently grilled."

"You did great. My grandmother liked you."

Emily allowed a small giggle. "I'd hate to see how she acts with the women she doesn't like."

"I doubt it, unless you're truly looking to run for the hills. But she invited you to visit, so you can relax."

She took his hand, tracing his fingers. "How can you tell she liked me?"

"If she didn't, it would be Mrs. Hamilton and Dr. Anderson, not Grace and Emily." A surge of relief ran through him. Not many women could take the heat or tolerate his family.

"You weren't kidding. This is a huge dinner party," Emily whispered, looking around the room as they joined the rest of the guests. "You know all these people?"

"Most of them. I've been attending her dinners since I was a kid."

They spent the next hour mingling, and Aiden introduced her to the other guests.

He placed his hand on the small of Emily's back as the lovely blonde approached them, bracing himself for the encounter. Not ideal, but he should have expected her attendance. "Tiffany. How are you?"

"Good, Aiden." Tiffany examined the dark-haired woman who'd linked her arm with Aiden's. "How are you?"

"Fine. Harrison." He nodded at the man on her arm. "This is Dr. Emily Anderson. Emily, Tiffany Baxter and Senator Harrison Taylor."

Emily greeted them both, and they exchanged small talk before Aiden could politely guide her away.

"Isn't he running for governor? She looks familiar too."

"That's him. Tiffany's picture is frequently in the paper. Her father was the Mayor a few years back, and being engaged to Harrison now, I'm sure there are plenty of photo ops."

"Ah, Mayor David Baxter. You know him?"

"Yes." *Unfortunately.* "I've known the family for years." Aiden figured he could tell her that much, but this wasn't the time or place to get into the details of his past romantic entanglement with Tiffany.

He snagged two glasses of champagne from a tray as the server wove through the guests and kept them moving and mingling until dinner was announced.

It pleased him how well Emily fit. He'd never loved these dinner parties, but having a date who was comfortable on his arm was a definite plus. The more time he spent with Emily, the more she charmed him.

Aiden stepped onto the patio and inhaled deeply, relieved to escape the stuffy and crowded room. The heaters threw off a pleasant glow, making the outdoors bearable, even though the night air was crisp and clear.

"New girlfriend?" The familiar voice came from behind him. "She's certainly beautiful, but does she have what it takes to charm Dr. Aiden Hamilton? I wonder."

He turned to contemplate the beautiful willowy blonde. Even as he reminded himself of the endless pain she'd inflicted, that familiar twinge hit, making him resent how she still affected him. The sad fact was, no matter how hard he tried, he'd never been able to reclaim that piece of his heart she'd stolen all those years ago. As much as he wanted to hate her, his soul betrayed him.

"How long have you been seeing Emily?"

"I thought we'd agreed to stay away from each other?"

"It would be rude not to speak at a dinner party. You're practically the host. It is your grandmother's house." She took a casual sip of her wine. "A doctor. You always went for the smart ones."

"You know me."

"I certainly do. Maybe too well." She tapped her glass with perfectly manicured nails, staring over the snowy landscape. "You've stopped seeing her, right?"

"Who's that?" He raised his brow. Part of him longed to see her squirm and make her worry he'd disrupt her perfect life. Giving her a little payback might be unworthy and a touch callous, but it was oh-so-tempting.

Her direct and icy stare left him cold. "Quit playing games, Aiden."

He narrowed his eyes. "You lost your right to say who I can or can't see years ago. Butt out."

"Have you told your family?"

"I haven't told anyone … yet."

"Please be careful?" she whispered as she glanced over her shoulder. "Harrison will be looking for me, and the lovely doctor is on her way over." She turned and disappeared into the house.

"Was it something I said?" Emily's smile flickered and faded as the door closed behind Tiffany. "I don't think she likes me much. I'm not sure why, since we've only met."

"She has issues with me."

"Oh?" Emily's perfect brow rose, a knowing look in her eyes. "Something you'd care to share?"

"She's my ex, but it's been over for years." He held his breath.

"That explains a lot." She rested a hand on his arm. "You should have said so before, but I'll let it go. This time."

"I didn't want it to be awkward."

"Not like I didn't know you've dated other women. Don't keep secrets, okay?"

A twinge of guilt hit. Technically, he'd told the truth, but what he hadn't said might haunt him.

He noted people were drifting toward the door. "We've put in our appearance. Would you mind if we called it a night?"

"Not at all. We both work in the morning."

Aiden and Emily said their good nights and were soon on their way home.

"My place?" Aiden slid his arm around her, letting her lean into him.

She nodded. "How did I do?"

"You were wonderful," he said, pulling her closer. "Not that I was worried."

"Aiden." The receptionist smiled as he arrived at the front desk in the law offices of Hamilton Grayson. "Tom's finishing a meeting in the boardroom, but he'll meet you in his office."

"Thanks, Danielle." Aiden waved and headed down the hallway. "Hi, Sadie," he said to Tom's legal assistant.

"Aiden. Can I get you something while you wait? I planned to make fresh coffee for Tom."

"Coffee sounds perfect." He stepped into the office and poured himself a glass of ice water from the carafe on the sideboard before wandering to the large windows.

"Sorry you had to wait." Tom Grayson's warm voice came from behind him as his longtime friend dropped a stack of files onto his massive desk. The man gave Aiden a hug. "It's been too long, brother. We live a few blocks apart and barely see each other."

Aiden returned the embrace. He and Tom had grown up together and the man was his best friend, confident, and business partner. "We'll have to rectify that and get together for dinner soon. You heard the big news?"

"Jenna mentioned something about a lovely lady named Emily tracking you down in the Vineyard. I haven't met this fabulous woman yet." Tom pressed a hand to his chest. "I'm wounded."

"I meant Alex and Joel and the baby news."

"Oh, Alex being preggo. That's big, but we knew it was coming. You introducing a girlfriend is an even bigger deal in my opinion. Most of the ladies last a few dates and they're gone with the wind."

"Ha ha, so funny." Aiden dealt his friend a shoulder punch. "I took Emily to see Gramma Grace, and I'd like you to meet her. She's a doctor in the ER."

Tom stepped back, a grin spreading across his face. "You're actually serious about this one?" he asked. "She must be pretty damn special. You usually don't keep them long enough to subject them to meeting your family."

"Yeah, she's a keeper."

"Ohhh, is our boy finally settling on one girl? Good thing, because you're falling behind. Joel and Alex are out making babies, and Jenna and I will be planning our wedding soon. Which reminds me, mark the third weekend in September. I still expect you to be my best man." Tom motioned to the plush leather couches. "There's legal business you want me to deal with, right? I thought we had your personal affairs sewn up tight."

"Things change." Aiden rose and shut the office door.

"Serious stuff?" Tom furrowed his brow.

Aiden sat across from Tom and took a deep breath. "Anything I say is strictly confidential. I'm not ready to share, not even with Jenn. You have to promise."

A look of concern settled on his friend's face. "Now you have me worried, but I promise. For this discussion, we're client and lawyer. What's up?"

Aiden slid a hand into the inner pocket of his coat, pulled out the envelope and extended it to Tom.

His friend raised a brow as he examined the address on the front. "So who is she?"

"Ahhh, read it."

Tom cleared his throat. *"Aiden James Thomas Franklin Hamilton is not excluded as the biological father of Savannah Jayde Phillips. Conclusive 99.99%."* He stared at the paper. "Holy crap. You have a daughter?"

"Yes."

"What is she angling for?" Tom rubbed his hands over his face. "The mother, I mean. Is she demanding a huge settlement? Child support? How old is the kid?"

"My finances aren't in jeopardy. It's voluntary." He met Tom's gaze. "We gave Savannah up for adoption when she was a baby."

"You signed legal papers allowing the adoption?" Tom's frown deepened. "How long have you known about Savannah? And who's the other half of this we?"

"I've always known." Aiden took a deep breath. "Savannah turns fifteen on January fifth."

"What?" Tom's eyes widened. "The kid's fifteen-damn-years-old? You knew about her, and you never said a word? Bloody hell. I mean ..." A humorless laugh escaped. "When you were fifteen you were dating Tiffany. Did you have a little sidepiece? Or ..." He lunged from his chair and paced, throwing looks at Aiden. "A teenage daughter?"

Aiden almost laughed at the priceless expression on Tom's face, even though the situation wasn't funny. He pulled out his phone and scrolled through before offering it to his friend.

Tom snatched the phone and squinted at the screen. "Damn." He examined the picture. "She's a carbon copy of Tiffany. Beautiful girl." He rubbed the back of his neck. "How?"

Aiden raised his brows. "How?"

Tom waved a hand. "Not *how*, how, but how in the hell did we miss the fact Tiffany was knocked up? We were together for the entire summer. Tiffany stayed with Alexis, and then ..." He snorted, scrubbing his jaw. "She went to Portland. That's where this lab is located. Please tell me one of the adoptive parents gave permission for the testing."

"It was legal, and her dad knows I've been in touch with Savannah."

"Start from the beginning, and don't leave anything out, or I'll beat the daylights out of you." Tom wagged a finger at him. "I should disown you for keeping secrets this big."

Aiden spent the next half-hour talking, filling in as many details as possible, Tom shooting the occasional question at him. The more he talked, the more the weight lifted from his shoulders. Sharing this with his best friend was a relief. "She's visiting me soon."

Tom sighed. "Tiffany simply refuses to be involved? At all?"

"She's adamant. What would Harrison say, or worst of tragedies, what if he loses his edge in the political race?"

"It's a tough situation. I feel for her, but this is her child." Tom perched on the edge of the couch. "You have no legal obligation to leave this girl anything, but you want to anyway? Then again ... you were coerced into signing, and adoption laws have progressed since the time you were fifteen, but ..." A crease appeared in his brow.

"It's a convoluted and tricky situation, legally and morally speaking. I considered searching for her a few years back, but everything was such a mess I thought it best to leave it alone. Our baby girl had been gone for years, and things with Tiffany fell apart. I was in medical school. What was I supposed to do? Spend years fighting the system, track Savannah down, and take her away from the only family she'd ever known? Subject an innocent child to David Baxter and my grandfather?"

Aiden leaned forward in his seat. "Why fight a battle no one could truly win? Now I can provide something for her. If I ever find the right woman and have other children, we'll revise my will, but it could be years before that happens."

"What about Emily?"

"With my track record and the shit my family pulls, it might only last another week. Hell, I have to break the news about Savannah. That alone might make her decide my life's way too fucked up. Not to mention the other thing I'll have to share once this all comes out."

"You haven't told her?" Tom blew out a puff of air. "If she leaves over this stuff, she's not the girl for you. What kind of relationship can you have with someone who can't accept your past?" A grin spread across his face. "I'd love to meet Savannah. I have a niece. That's actually awesome. Freaky that she's fifteen and you're her daddy, but wonderful too."

Aiden couldn't help the smile that appeared at the thought of his daughter. "She's great, but it's weird. I'd pushed her existence to the back of my mind for so long. As far as meeting her, we'll see. I don't want to overwhelm her. She barely knows me so piling on a bunch of aunts and uncles might be too much, at least for now. But soon, I promise she can meet Uncle Tom."

"Not a pile. Just your best friend … remember him?" Tom smirked but it soon faded. "You're planning to tell Emily?"

"If I don't, it's over before it begins. The only reason I can't tell everyone is they know Tiffany, and she'll kill me if I say anything. I'm in a tough spot."

"I don't like your odds of survival." Tom sipped his coffee. "I'll have to plead client confidentiality when my fiancée tries to smother me with her pillow."

"I'm sorry to put you in this position, and I'm truly sorry for not telling you years ago, but it was one of those things."

"I get it, your grandfather wasn't one to be crossed." Tom shook his head. "You should tell everyone. The sooner the better."

"I promised."

His friend rolled his eyes. "Yes, you two have a past, and you caught a lot of flack from Jenna and Alexis, and even Joel about how crazy you were to let

Tiffany walk, but stop sheltering her. Tell everyone the truth about why you split up."

"I don't want our friends taking sides." Aiden stared at his hands.

"Damn it, man. They already have. You're letting them be swayed to Tiffany's viewpoint. You and Joel have drifted apart because of Tiffany's friendship with Alex. You need to straighten this shit out."

"Isn't that how it works? A couple breaks up and one of them keeps the friends?"

"Not in this case. My patience's worn out on this Tiffany situation." He shook a finger at Aiden. "Quit protecting her."

"You didn't live it. I did." Aiden crossed his arms.

On one level, Tom was correct, but it wasn't so simple. If he made the wrong choice, they'd all pay.

Tom tapped his watch. "I have to take this next client. I'll talk to Jenn about Saturday night. Dinner. Our house. We'll invite Alex and Joel, and you can bring the fantastic Emily." Tom accepted the papers Aiden held out to him. "I'll revise your will, but this discussion is far from over."

Chapter 13

Savannah

The December break drew closer, the inevitable time slipping past with a flurry of small parties with Savannah's closest friends. Still, she'd kept her secret from most of them, unsure of where the relationship with Aiden might go. Would he love her? Or would he lose interest in her like she'd seen with her other friends with estranged parents?

"Savannah." The cane Leanne had graduated to after her cast had been removed clunked against the linoleum floor. "Watch out people. Invalid here."

Savannah waited for her friend to maneuver her way through the crowded hallway.

"What happened?" Leanne asked the moment she arrived, slightly out of breath. "Did you book flights to Chicago?"

"Keep your voice down." She ignored the curious stares of the other students milling in the hallway. Everyone was incredibly nosy, and it was almost impossible to keep secrets, especially when her friend loved to broadcast at the top of her voice. "Aiden did," she whispered. "I leave after the last day of classes. I'm staying in his guest room."

"You're staying at his apartment?"

"Yes." She giggled. "My dad's been checking his background. He tried to deny it, but he never erases his search history on the computer. Anyway, he and Aiden agreed it was safer than a hotel room." The smile slid off her face. "I can't believe it's happening."

"You're so lucky to get another trip to Chicago. I never got to see any of it, aside from the hospital and the stupid airport. Our trip was so messed up." Leanne studied her. "You don't seem excited."

"I'm super nervous. Aiden is nice, but what if he doesn't like me? What if he's disappointed?" Savannah nibbled at a finger nail.

"Stop." Leanne yanked her hand away from her face. "I hate it when you chew your nails."

"Way to make me feel better," Savannah mumbled. "Half of the time, I don't even know I'm doing it."

Leanne captured one of Vanna's hands, staring at it in disgust. "You are on edge. We need to fix those before you go. And stop worrying. You're his daughter. That means he'll like you, no matter what."

Savannah rolled her eyes. "That's not true. Rachel doesn't get along with her dad, and she's known him all her life. What if Aiden doesn't like me? Or we don't get along? Or his girlfriend hates me? Why did I ask to meet her? I bet she's all perfect and amazing."

"He has a girlfriend?" Leanne furrowed her brow.

"I'm not surprised. He's thirty and single, not to mention he's a doctor. How about all those nurses drooling over him?"

"When you're right, you're right. He seems like someone who'd have a beautiful girlfriend."

"Her name's Emily and she's a doctor. Did you meet an Emily when you were there? The name's familiar, but I don't know why."

"Nope. None of the nurses mentioned a girlfriend." Her friend tapped a fingertip against her pursed lips.

"They haven't been dating long." Savannah gazed over Leanne's shoulder, catching sight of Justin as he traversed the hall with his best friend, Tony. She offered him a faint smile, which to her joy, earned her a wave and one of his heart-stopping grins.

"Vanna?" Leanne frowned before glancing down the hall. "Oh, I see what, or who," she giggled, "caught your attention."

For a moment, it looked as if the two teenage boys were heading in their direction, but then ... Savannah's heart dropped as Christina appeared, laying a perfectly manicured hand on Justin's arm and tossing her blonde hair. Vanna turned her head, not wanting to see what happened next.

"He likes you," Leanne whispered. "Go pry Christina off of him."

Vanna shook her head. "No way. He said I talk too much, and we played together in his sandbox when we were five." Her face flushed as she remembered all the embarrassing things the boy had witnessed over the years.

"I dunno." Her friend cast a critical eye her way, a slow head-to-toe scan. "You're beautiful, and you don't even know it. And—"

"Don't say it." Savannah held up her hand. "So … did you hear anything about Emily from those nurses?"

"What? Oh … Dr. Hamilton. Nope. They gossiped about some ER nurse who's been begging for his attention. Tanya?" Her nose wrinkled. "Or was it Tammy? Definitely no Emily. That's kind of a perfect name." Leanne waved a hand dismissively. "Never mind, you're going. I bet he doesn't date a high-maintenance princess." She smirked.

"Want to bet? I've seen pictures of him online at these swanky charity functions. The women with him look like supermodels." A frown creased her brow. "I found a picture of him with Jazlyn Leitner."

"No … really?" Leanne's eyes widened. "She's beautiful and she actually is a supermodel. You must be mistaken."

"I don't think so. Her name was under the picture. It was taken at some fashion show in New York." Savannah's hand traveled to her mouth again. "Emily will take one look at me and hate me, and then he'll hate me, and—"

"Savannah. You're driving yourself crazy. He'll love you, and if he doesn't, then he's wrong. You're completely lovable. Not to mention pretty. Lucky, you share his genes."

"You have to say that, you're my best friend." Savannah's smile peeked through, the typical Leanne positivity making her feel better. "He's a guy, so looking like him isn't exactly a good thing."

"No, I suppose not." Leanne giggled. "Lucky you only have his eyes. Maybe you take after your mother. I'm sure she's beautiful."

"I'll never know." Savannah's smile faded.

Leanne gave her a hug. "Hey, I'm coming over after school to help you put together some outfits and pack. He'll like you, don't worry."

⁓

As promised, after school they headed to Vanna's house.

"Hey, Mr. Phillips." Leanne waved before they went to Vanna's room. "How's he taking this Aiden thing?"

"Better than I expected. It's weird. I thought he'd discourage me, but he really likes Aiden." Vanna tugged her suitcase from the back of her closet and set it on her bed. "This one?" She held up the soft pink cardigan for her friend to inspect.

Leanne shook her head but hobbled over to join her at the closet and they began sorting through her clothing.

An hour later, Savannah slumped onto her bed, looking at the scattered mess, feeling defeated. "I have nothing to wear. It's all so old and crappy. I don't have time to go shopping. How am I going to meet the supermodel looking like this?"

Over the past year, she'd barely purchased any new clothing. She'd hesitated to ask her dad. His pension wasn't much, and even with her mom's income, they'd never had much extra money. Anyway, Ross hated shopping and thought people put too much emphasis on appearance. He'd tell her she was being silly.

"Don't worry. He's your dad, and he wants to see you, not your wardrobe. How about these?" Leanne assembled a few outfits, tucking them into the suitcase. "That'll do. You're going to visit and hang around his apartment." Leanne giggled. "Call him and tell him you're coming."

"You're crazy. Anyway, he already knows. He bought the tickets. Remember?"

"I know, but you're not chickening out of this. I won't allow it." Leanne dug in Savannah's bag, pulled out her phone, and scrolled through the contacts. "Hamilton, A." She hit the button as the grin appeared.

"You didn't just do that." Savannah lunged toward her friend, grabbing at the phone.

"Uh-uh." Her friend managed to keep it out of reach, only surrendering it when Aiden's voice mail kicked in.

With a glare in her friend's direction, she left a message. "Hi, it's Savannah. I had a question, and I know it's late in Chicago, but can you call me?"

Leanne wrestled the phone away, typing and hitting send.

"What did you say to him?" Her heart sank. "You asked if he was out with Emily? He'll think I'm a weirdo stalker."

"Don't be ridiculous." Leanne typed again before handing back the phone. "I told him to call, and you'd be up for a while. He gave you his number, and you said you were allowed to call him whenever you wanted. So? Talk to him. It might calm you down."

"Since you're spamming him, he might change his mind and think I'm the crazy daughter he was lucky to get rid of. So stop. It's not funny. I barely know him." Savannah clutched the phone and stared at the screen, but no response came to the string of text messages Leanne had typed in. She sighed and flopped on the bed. "He's not answering."

"He will. Relax. I have to go. My mom will be pissed if I show up late." Leanne gave her friend a cheeky smile. "Say hi for me, and quit worrying. It'll be fine, you'll see." She scooped up her things and waved on her way out the door. "See you tomorrow."

Savannah stared at her phone, her heart sinking at the string of spammy messages. Aiden wouldn't be happy, and he wasn't answering her. What if Leanne ruined it? The half-packed suitcase taunted her.

She hoped Aiden would forgive her for text stalking him.

Chapter 14

Aiden

AIDEN TRAILED HIS FINGERS UP and down Emily's warm bare skin. "I'm exhausted."

"Mmm, sorry, but it was worth it." She cuddled closer.

"Don't be sorry." He kissed the top of her head as she relaxed across his chest. He savored the moment as he held her in his arms, her breath warm and sweet against his skin.

Things continued to heat up between them, and he'd been trying to let go and sink into the relationship. Allowing her into his life opened him up to the danger of getting burned, but it seemed impossible to slow down or hold back.

Their lives had intertwined as her belongings appeared in his apartment, never finding their way home. His closet filled with her clothing, and the inevitable toothbrush and feminine items were stowed in his bathroom. It seemed natural. He'd decided to go with it and let it happen.

"What does this mean?" Emily ran a fingertip along the back of his shoulder, lightly tracing the black ink outline. "Never figured you for the type to have a tattoo. You're full of surprises."

If she only knew. "It's a Celtic Spirit Wolf."

"I love the way the wolf's emerging from the flames. The footprints are so detailed. Does it have special meaning? It's a vicious animal to ink on your body."

"Misunderstood, yes, but vicious? Never. Wolves are pack animals, and they're extremely loyal and protective of their family. They're considered spirit guides. The flames represent transformation, growth, and change."

"Why a Celtic tattoo?"

"My family originated in Ireland and Scotland. There's a long line of Dukes and Earls in Scotland we can trace back through our family tree. The main reason though, it's unique."

"Hmm." She tilted her head. "Why get a tattoo at all?"

"My teenage years were rough." He relaxed as her soft warm fingers brushed over his skin.

"How?" Emily placed a kiss on his shoulder. "What would make you get a tattoo? Teenage rebellion? Being misunderstood like the wolves?"

"Something like that." He slid from the bed and fished his boxers from the floor. "I need a drink. Want something?"

"Just water," she said with a smile. "Don't think I'll forget. I want to know what's going on in your head. Something's bothering you. I can always tell."

"That transparent, am I?" he muttered as he wandered into the kitchen and rummaged in the fridge for a slice of leftover pizza, holding it in his teeth while he poured two glasses of ice-cold water.

He leaned against the counter, debating what to say as he bit into the pizza. *Procrastination.* His forte when it came to matters of the heart. Aiden sucked in a long breath and gulped down his water. This could be the defining moment in their relationship.

As he returned to the bedroom and set her glass of water on the bedside table, Emily narrowed her eyes, the corners of her mouth turning down. "What's the matter?" He reached out to rub her arm.

She pulled back, a wrinkle appearing in her brow as she hugged a pillow across her chest. "Where's area code 503?"

"Oregon?" The anxiety welled up, and a bad feeling about where this conversation was headed crept over him. He froze. His phone was no longer where he left it. "Why?"

"You missed a call and several texts from Savannah." Her stare accused him. "Isn't she the teenager from the derailment?"

Aiden held out his hand and motioned for her to return his phone. "Why are you reading my texts?"

"Why is Savannah visiting you in December?" Emily threw his phone onto the bed between them. "Something to hide? Is that why you're so concerned about me seeing your precious phone?"

"No, but I'd appreciate you not snooping. I don't look through yours." Despite the fact he was being secretive, her looking at his phone annoyed him. A behavior reserved for crazy, insecure women.

She folded her arms across her chest and jutted out her chin. "It rang and the text popped up. I saw it by accident. What do you have to hide? That you lied to me?"

"About what?"

"Your involvement with Savannah? Why is she texting and phoning your personal mobile asking to stay in your apartment? She's a patient, who's fourteen. And no bullshit about mentoring."

"It's not even close to what you're thinking."

"What about her parents? Do they know about this contact? You're not seriously considering letting her stay."

Aiden rubbed his face before reaching for her hands.

Emily pulled away, her dark lashes fluttering over shimmering eyes. "What the hell, Aiden?"

"It's not like that." He bit his lip. The time had come to confess, or he'd ruin another relationship. "I planned to tell you anyway, so now's as good a time as any."

"What could you possibly say?"

Aiden moved closer, taking her by the shoulders. "Look at me, Em." He slid a finger under her chin, forcing her to comply. "She's a blood relative."

"What?" Her eyes widened.

He wrapped his arms around her and tipped his forehead against hers. "I don't know how to tell you."

"Say it, Aiden."

He sucked in a long breath as he fought the nerves and the fear. "Savannah's my daughter."

"How can she be your daughter? You'd have been maybe fifteen …" Her chin rose. "Damn."

"We were young. I never saw Savannah, and I didn't know it was her, until she told me."

"How did she know who you were? And why have you never shared this?"

He took her hands in his. "The adoption was closed and sealed, so I never thought I'd see her. It's been almost fifteen years, and I put it behind me as best I could. She had a picture with my name written on the back that her mother left tucked in her baby blanket."

"She found you with a picture?"

He nodded. "It's crazy, right? She wanted to find her mother, but that's not going to happen …" He glanced at her. "Her dad agreed to a visit."

"Why didn't you tell me? You had to know I'd find out sometime."

"It's not so easy to share. Telling someone you've only dated a few short weeks that you have a teenage daughter who was born when you were fifteen isn't a light topic. I buried the whole experience. It wasn't a fun time and caused untold issues for me and for her mother. I haven't even told my parents or my grandmother."

"Wow, they'll be surprised. How did they feel about it at the time?"

"It was a secret, and by that, I mean it was kept from most of my family. This will be a major deal when it comes out."

"They don't know about your daughter?" Her voice rose, her expression reflecting disbelief. "How could they not know?"

"They weren't around." He swallowed a long gulp of water, hoping loosen the lump in his throat. "My grandfather didn't see the point of involving them. My girlfriend's parents and her aunt knew, along with my grandfather and the lawyer. Nobody else."

"Who is Savannah's mother?"

"She's not in the picture and she won't be."

"What happened to her?"

"Nothing, but she doesn't want to be involved. I don't want to talk about her."

"But you told your daughter about me? Savannah referred to me in her text."

"She wanted to know if I had a girlfriend and hopes to meet you. Would you consider it?" he asked. "It's a lot to ask. I was planning to tell you all of this before her visit, but I didn't know how."

"You were so young."

"Totally irresponsible and stupid, right?"

Emily cupped his cheek in her palm, then patted gently. "Call her back and then we'll talk. She seemed anxious."

"You don't mind?"

She shook her head and stood. "I'll freshen up."

"You don't have to leave."

"I'll only be a minute. Make your call." She shut the bathroom door.

He checked his texts.

Where are you? You didn't answer your phone. Out with Emily?

Then he read the next message.

I can't wait to visit. I'll be up for a while doing my homework. Call me tonight, please?

He read three more before checking the time. The last text was less than half an hour ago. "Savannah."

"You called." She sounded half-hesitant and half-relieved. "I'm sorry about the calls and the texts," she said. "Don't be angry, but Leanne took my phone. I promise I'm not a stalker."

Aiden almost laughed. Now the text-bombing made total sense. "Ahh, so she's the crazy text girl. How is Leanne? Recovered, I hope?"

"She's fine. Her leg's much better, although she has physio and stuff."

He sat on the bed. "I'm looking forward to your visit."

"Me too. Did you tell Emily? Do I get to meet her?"

"Yes."

"She doesn't mind that you have a daughter?"

"Emily is pretty great. Did you get the itinerary? The dates okay?"

"My dad showed it to me when I got home from school. You'll pick me up from the airport?"

"I'll wait by the baggage carousel. You have my number so you can text or call anytime. Maybe keep Leanne away from your phone, though."

This coaxed a soft laugh out of her. "Good idea."

"Get some sleep. It'll be fine, I promise." Aiden sensed the girl was anxious about the trip. "I'm looking forward to seeing you, Savannah, I have a bunch of fun things planned."

"Thanks, Aiden. Goodnight."

"Sleep well."

Emily stood in the doorway of the bathroom. After a moment, she sat beside him on the bed. "This is surreal. I've known you for years, yet I often feel I don't know you at all. Is your daughter the big thing in your life that caused you to get a tattoo?"

"She was part of it." He wished he knew what this incredible woman was thinking.

"Uh-huh." She took his hand. "I wish you'd shared this long ago. You're far too secretive."

"So I'm told." He put his other hand over the top of hers. "I'm sorry. It's a lot to take in. It was for me too. I didn't know how you'd react, or how it would affect us. We have something great."

"We do." She gave a small nod. "Where does she fit into your life? How often are you planning to see her?"

"Long term, I can't say. It's not like she needs a parent. Her adoptive father is a good person. Maybe she won't want more than a few answers, but my hope is we build a permanent relationship." All he had was vague hope and a multitude of his own questions, but no real answers. "It's weird, right?"

"A little." She linked their fingers. "You were worried about us?"

"Of course." He squeezed her hand. "Maybe you won't want to deal with it. If you don't want to or can't, please tell me before you meet Savannah."

"Are you asking if I'm planning to stick around?" Emily raised a brow. "Why do you assume your daughter's a deal breaker?"

Aiden's thoughts went straight to Tiffany. "For some women, it is."

"Just how many women are you dating?" She gave him a saucy half-smile.

"That's not what I meant, and you know it." The attempt to lighten the mood, though appreciated, fell flat given his soul-shattering pain and disappointment in his ex. He faced Emily, taking her hands and squeezing gently. "Imagine telling a teenage girl her mother wants nothing to do with her." He bowed his head. "For some women, my daughter is too much."

"I didn't know." She slid her arms around him and pressed a kiss to his cheek. "I'm sorry. So you went to see this woman? How well do you know her?"

"It wasn't a one-night stand," he said. "I owed it to both her and Savannah to tell her, but she doesn't want her identity revealed, which is problematic." So many promises he'd made that might prove impossible to keep. "There are many things to figure out, like who to tell and when to tell. Sharing it with you is the easy part. The emotional upheaval is just beginning."

"I understand." She relaxed against him. "Maybe this is a silly question, but how sure are you about Savannah being your daughter?"

"About 99.99%."

"What?" Emily's brows rose.

"DNA testing."

"Ahh. Right. Did you always know?"

"It's a mess, but yes." Now any woman he contemplated involvement with would have to accept his daughter. It changed everything.

Emily held his face between her palms. "I'm honored you shared it with me and that you're inviting me to meet her." A smile twitched her lips. "You're the father of a teenager. That's crazy."

"Isn't it? I've been living in some weird dream these past few weeks. I'd banished it from my mind for years, but now …" He squeezed her hand. "You'll keep it to yourself, right?"

"Why hide it? Having a baby isn't a crime."

"No, but I owe it to Savannah's mother to protect her identity, but I want to know my daughter. It's a balancing act. One I don't know how to manage."

"Don't tell anyone who her mother is."

Aiden slumped his shoulders. "It seems obvious, but Tom took one look at Savannah's picture and he knew."

Emily's eyes widened. "Your friends know Savannah's mother?"

"Every single one. One look at Savannah and they'll know."

"You have a picture? I saw her so briefly at the hospital."

Aiden pulled up the picture on his phone, tipping it toward her.

"She's lovely." Emily took his phone and stared at the screen. "Oh," she said. She pushed off the bed, still inspecting the picture. "The ex-girlfriend who was at your grandmother's? She's marrying that guy running for Governor."

Aiden closed his eyes, attempting to quell his nausea. His next revelation was inevitable. "Got it in one." Time to let the secret out, no matter the cost. "She's not my ex-girlfriend ... she's my ex-wife."

"You need something?" Aiden turned into the mall parking lot at Emily's direction, amazed this beautiful woman was still by his side. His revelations, though shocking, had proven something invaluable. Emily was a keeper.

"No, but you do." Emily patted his knee.

"And what's that?" At this moment, he was sure he had everything that mattered.

"Your guest room is lovely, but it needs a feminine touch. Your place is more chic boutique hotel than teenage girl."

"I'm a guy." He gave a low laugh. "I don't do frilly frou-frou stuff." He pictured the room they'd chosen for his daughter's visit. The blue-gray tones and elegant clean lines. Maybe Emily had a point.

"A tiny bit of frilly isn't a bad thing." She raised her brows.

Aiden shrugged, but slid from his seat and rounded the car to open Emily's door. He held out his hand, taking her small soft one in his.

"It won't take much to make the room inviting for Savannah. I'll pick, you pay," she said as she winked, "and carry the bags."

"Swooping in for the rescue, are you? Lead on, then."

First stop was a fancy soap store where Emily selected a variety of products in mere minutes. Aiden handed over his credit card without protest. Next she chose cozy pajamas, slippers, and a luxurious blue bathrobe.

"Drugstore next." She loaded a basket with small items.

"Razors, toothbrush, and tampons?" Aiden raised his eyebrows as he trailed behind, managing the bags.

"Teenage girl? If you stock the necessities, that room will become her sanctuary. It's important to make her feel welcome."

"You're absolutely right." He held up a hand in surrender. By the time they left the mall they were laden with several large bags which he tucked into the back.

"Now we buy groceries." Emily smiled.

Aiden realized how little he knew about his daughter about the time they were a quarter of the way down the first aisle in the market.

"Are you going to stare at those packages forever?"

"What does a teenage girl eat?"

"Don't get so worked up." Emily rubbed his back. "You're a terrific cook. Whip up a few of your gourmet meals. I bet she'll love it."

Aiden relaxed. He knew how to put together great meals and needed to play to his strengths so he added his own selections to the cart, and by the time they reached the till, it was full.

"I coped with medical school and can bring someone back from near-dead, but the thought of feeding a teenager is overwhelming." Aiden sighed as the cashier bagged the groceries. "I feel useless. I can't even imagine how I'd have done this when I was fifteen."

"You'll soon know what she likes and what she doesn't. Don't be so hard on yourself." Emily wrapped an arm around him. "And I bet you would've done fine if your family had supported you. Which they clearly could have." Her voice was tinged with bitterness. "They simply chose not to."

"Isn't that the truth." A wave of sadness ran through him. He couldn't bear to think about how different his life could have been if his family had shown even an ounce of caring. However, it was over and done, and there was no point in dwelling on it. "She'll be fifteen in January, and I've never given her anything."

"Except life, of course," Emily said with a teasing smile.

"Ha, funny."

"Relax. You'll come up with something great," she said. "Hmmm. I've never dated a guy with a teenage daughter."

"Yeah, lucky you. You picked the messed-up guy." He wheeled the cart toward his SUV.

"You're not messed up, although the ex-wife part was a surprise. It sounds like you did your best and your daughter grew up in a good home. Not many adoptive parents would be so open to letting you in, and it seems Savannah wants to know you."

"I wish her mother would—" He waved a hand. "Never mind."

"Finish your thought."

"See what she's missing?" Aiden sighed. "It's not easy, protecting her and Savannah. Maybe for future visits, I'll go to Portland or take Savannah anywhere but Chicago." He loaded the groceries into the SUV.

"Your secrets are safe, though I'm not sure why you're afraid. Or why Tiffany is uptight about it."

"Our families' political ambitions? Her fiancé?" He shrugged. "If it came out and ruined my father's run for DA, he'd have me killed."

"He must care about you more than his career."

"Don't count on it. I haven't had a holiday with them in over ten years, and I see them once every six months, but only if I go to New York. I lived in boarding school or with my grandparents from the time I was thirteen." He hit the button to close the power hatch, wishing he could slam it and release some frustration. "The only reason they remember my name is because it's so similar to his."

"You really think they don't know about their grandchild?"

"If they did, I would've heard about it." Aiden had endured enough lectures from his father, so he was fairly certain he wouldn't have let this go by without comment. "My family is great at lecturing, but lacking in true communication. I'm sure my grandfather didn't tell them so if it ever was discovered, they could plausibly and categorically deny any knowledge of the situation." He held open her door, waiting for her to get settled before he slid into his seat.

Emily's lip curled. "She's a real person, not a situation," she said, her voice laced with disgust.

"To my grandfather, two teenagers having a baby is unsavory and to be handled. Bury it in the past. Pretend it never happened. No escape, though we tried."

"What do you mean?"

Aiden kept his focus on maneuvering the SUV through the heavy traffic, his grip tightening on the wheel. "You sure you want to hear this?"

"Tell me."

"I took some money and we tried to disappear. Unfortunately, my grandfather had top investigators on his payroll. You can run but you cannot hide. Not from Thomas Hamilton and his crackerjack team. And you couldn't lie. The downfall of having criminal lawyers in the family is they have resources along with their built-in bullshit detectors." He peeked from the corner of his eye to gauge her reaction. "Their clients lie all the time."

"Wait. Hold on a second." She held up a hand. "You ran away with her?"

"Yes."

"Wow."

Silence hung over them for several moments.

"But why?"

"We were scared kids. We knew they'd force us to give her up and we didn't want to, so we ran. My grandfather sent his posse of investigators after us. We eluded them for almost a week, which was amazing in retrospect. I received a severe ass kicking. Not to mention the money I borrowed from the safe."

"Borrowed?" She smirked. "Without permission?"

He shrugged.

"Gutsy."

"Stupid." He almost swore she looked impressed. Or was she simply biding her time before locating the nearest exit? "I wish I'd known how to disappear properly because we didn't get another chance. They locked me down. We used to go to the Vineyard, but that summer they sent me away from my friends, and away from her. It broke us, them forcing us apart. Then when I was eighteen we compounded our errors and got back together."

"And ended up married."

"Double the stupidity. We eloped and she moved to Philadelphia. We worked on our degrees. It became an epic fail within two years. From there we endured a painful divorce after ripping each other apart." He motioned to himself. "See? Messed-up guy."

"I'm sorry. It sounds like you loved her."

"I did, but our families did their best to break us. It worked. They took it all," Aiden said as they pulled into the parking garage. "Now you know the story, can we not talk about it?" A dull ache grew in the pit of his stomach. It appeared whenever he thought about what could have been if they'd been allowed to keep their baby girl. All the broken promises were coming back to haunt him.

"We don't have to discuss it, but know that you can talk to me. You've kept this buried a long time. I can't fathom what it must have been like to go through something so life altering with so little support. I'll keep anything you say in confidence."

"I appreciate it." He took her hand. "Let's put these groceries away. We have a dinner tonight. Do you want to come with me tomorrow to pick her up?"

"You should have a night alone so you two can talk. I'll come over the next morning and we can do something fun. Besides, it might set a better example if I'm not sleeping over."

Aiden laughed. "I think the good example thing is shot to hell. She was born when I was fifteen."

"Uh-huh. But still, don't overwhelm her. See how it goes." She squeezed his hand. "You do groceries. I'll fix her room."

"Deal." Aiden helped her carry the bags into the bedroom.

Within two hours, Emily had transformed the bedroom in a teenage girl's paradise.

She'd replaced the bedding and curtains. Now a fluffy white duvet covered the queen sized bed, accented with colorful pillows and a cuddly throw blanket. The new bathrobe and slippers in vibrant blue were draped across the foot of the bed.

A dainty row of products sat along the edge of the bathtub and a basket on the counter overflowed with supplies, and the cupboards were well stocked.

"My lovely miracle worker." Aiden planted a kiss on her lips. "Thank you. This looks amazing."

"My pleasure. You have a gorgeous place, but it needs a feminine touch."

"You have a gift for decorating. Now, time to get dressed. We have dinner at Tom and Jenna's. Tom knows, but nobody else does. Can you keep our discussion between us?"

She nodded. "Let me freshen up and change. The apartment is perfect and ready for tomorrow."

Chapter 15

Savannah

Savannah followed the crowd toward the baggage claim area. She sighed when she spotted him. "Hi, Aiden." She threw her arms around him, happy when he embraced her just as warmly.

"Savannah." Aiden kissed her cheek. "Which bag is yours?" He scooped up the one she indicted before leading her to the familiar SUV. "How's school going?" he asked as they merged into traffic.

"Fine. My teacher said I should look at the University of Maryland, and a couple of other centrally located ones for journalism, but I need a scholarship. My dad's worried about tuition and living expenses, and the cost of flights, and would prefer I stayed closer to home."

"Understandable, that would be less expensive by far, and I'm sure Ross will miss you."

They pulled into the underground garage and he parked beside a black convertible sports car.

Savannah peered in the window while Aiden retrieved her suitcase.

"You like the car?" he asked.

"Which of your neighbors owns it?"

"That's mine." He led her toward the elevators. "If you're here during the summer, we could take it out."

Savannah glanced over her shoulder. It looked expensive with its sleek paint and leather-wrapped steering wheel. "What is it?"

He pressed a black fob against the scanner, the tiny light turning from red to green as the doors slid shut. "A Maserati."

"No kidding," she mumbled, sneaking a look at him as the elevator rose. Maybe Alice felt like this when she went down the rabbit hole. The magical dream intensified as the doors swished open, revealing a gleaming marble foyer. The small but private entrance led to French double doors, inset with fancy frosted glass and an electronic keypad.

"I have the only unit on this floor, but I like the privacy and extra security of the doors." Aiden punched in the code.

Savannah trailed after him, speechless as she took in the surroundings. The front entrance was spectacular, with more shiny marble and a huge closet. Following his example, she removed her shoes and hung her coat in the closet.

After leading her through the myriad of rooms, he ushered her into a large bedroom and set down her bag.

A delighted smile spread across her face. The large windows faced the lake and below, she saw a well-lit park. "This is amazing."

"Glad you like it. Settle in. When you're ready, I'll give you the grand tour."

Once he'd left, she peeked into the bathroom. Everything looked perfect, like a five-star hotel. She practically skipped down the hallway to the main living space.

"Ready to see the rest?" He motioned for her to follow.

The living room had enormous windows, which would allow a gorgeous day-time view over the lake. They continued down a short hallway arriving in the massive master bedroom.

The palatial bathroom had its own fireplace, an expanse of counter with his and hers sinks, and a makeup table with a large mirror and a bench. The glass and tile shower was big enough to dance in with two rain shower heads coming from the ceiling.

She ran a finger over the makeup containers and pot of brushes. "Where's Emily?"

"Home, I think. She'll join us for breakfast tomorrow. She's excited to meet you."

"I can't wait." Savannah's nerves jangled at the thought of meeting his girlfriend. "I love this place. My house would fit in here at least twice." Or maybe even three or four times.

"It's overkill for one person, but I love the location and the unobstructed view of the lake. The Lincoln Park Zoo is there." Aiden pointed out one of the windows. "One day I'll take you."

They talked until midnight. Savannah filled him in on Leanne's recovery and told him more about school and some of her hobbies before Aiden suggested they retire.

"I worked this morning, so I'm ready for bed. If you need anything, don't be afraid to ask."

"Thanks, Aiden."

Savannah awoke cuddled into the softest sheets ever, warm and cozy under the downy duvet. She sighed as she ran her hands along the fine linen, enjoying the floating sensation afforded by the plush mattress. At home, she could stay in bed for several more hours, but she didn't want to waste a single moment of this trip.

She wandered into the attached bathroom, giggling as she adjusted the controls in the tiled shower, choosing a lavender scented shower gel and one of the fluffy white towels from the rack. The place was fully equipped with everything she could ever imagine needing.

After a hot shower, she dressed and wandered down the hallway into the well-appointed kitchen.

Aided sat at the expanse of gleaming counter, sipping an oversized cup of coffee. "Morning. Sleep well?" He smiled as he flipped the screen closed.

She gave him a hesitant smile and a small nod.

"Can I get you something to drink?"

"Tea or juice?"

"If you'd like tea, you can pick one from the cabinet." Aiden pointed. "Juice is in the fridge."

Savannah nodded and opened the cupboard as Aiden filled the kettle and located a cup.

"This is an amazing kitchen." Savannah peered at the large gas cooktop paired with the flat grill on the side.

"It was a bit rough when I bought this place, but after a renovation, it's perfect." Aiden took the canister of tea from her, measuring some into the fancy teacup and pouring in the hot water. He tucked the canister back into the cupboard, setting her cup onto the raised eating bar beside where he'd been sitting. "Are you okay for a few minutes before we eat? I thought we'd make omelets."

"Sounds yummy. Can I help?"

"Absolutely. But you have to help clean up afterward."

"You sound like my dad." Savannah giggled, realizing how funny that sounded. "I mean ..."

"I know what you mean." He glanced at the bright screen of his phone. "Emily is on her way."

Savannah sipped her tea, watching as Aiden moved easily around the kitchen, pulling a variety of items from the fridge. As she came around into the main area, Aiden handed her a cutting board.

"Knives are in the block, pick whichever one you like. I love to listen to music when I'm working in the kitchen. Do you mind?" Aiden turned up the sound system.

"My dad hates having music on, but I love it." Savannah hummed along with the tunes as they worked, swaying to the eclectic range of music flowing through the room. "Interesting playlist."

"Do you like it?" Aiden looked up from where he sliced mushrooms. "Or would you prefer something else?"

"Don't change it. I'm surprised you like the same stuff I do. My dad listens to yucky country, like the old style, not the newer stuff. You know, super twangy? Gross."

"Maybe you got your musical taste from me." He grinned. "I don't listen to country, but I love most everything else."

It made her think. Her dad was much older, retired, and into his senior years, where Aiden was like a cool big brother. She related to him on an entirely different level, and she relaxed even further as the conversation flowed from topic to topic.

"Aiden?" A woman's voice rang through the apartment.

"In the kitchen, Em." Aiden clicked on the gas burner and selected a pan from the rack hanging over the island, adding the onions and mushrooms to sauté.

A slim well-dressed woman rounded the corner. "It smells amazing. I'm starving."

Savannah's immediate reaction was she wasn't wrong about Aiden dating gorgeous women. Though slightly shorter than Savannah, the woman had dark hair, flawless olive skin, and perfect white teeth. Long thick lashes framed vibrant green eyes. Even with her scant makeup, she looked like a supermodel, and her dark-washed jeans hugged her curves in a way that made Savannah envious.

"Savannah, this is Dr. Emily Anderson."

A warm smile appeared on Emily's face and she hugged the girl. "It's lovely to meet you, Savannah. Aiden has told me all about you."

"I wasn't sure Aiden would even introduce us." Savannah's eyes widened, but a smile crept over her face. This was not the greeting she expected from this elegant woman.

Emily released Savannah, taking a small step back. "He and I agreed it was an excellent idea for us to get to know each other."

"Absolutely." Aiden wrapped an arm around Emily, giving her a squeeze. "Coffee?"

"I'd love some, but I'll get it. You look busy." She opened one of the cabinets and selected a cup.

"I've seen you before." Savannah studied the woman. "Wait. You asked Aiden for help with a patient. He was giving me stitches." *The flirty doctor.*

"That's right." Emily added a touch of cream to her cup before she tasted it. "Mmm, perfect. What are the plans for today? It's chilly outside." She took another sip of her steaming coffee.

"Could we go shopping, or visit the Art Institute? Do you like art, Emily?"

"I do, though I haven't been to the Institute in forever. What kind of shopping?"

"Christmas shopping. My dad's notoriously hard to buy for, and there are some great stores here."

"Drag the poor guy to the mall?" Emily laughed as Aiden plated breakfast. "The Art Institute too. You're testing him."

"I've been known to shop, and I love art. In fact, I'm an amateur photographer."

"You are?" Emily asked.

"It's a hobby of mine." Aiden set the plates onto the table along with a carafe of fresh squeezed orange juice. "Let's eat while it's hot."

"Rather than the mall, can we go to the shopping street downtown?" Savannah took a bite of her breakfast, savoring the combination of ham, cheese, and mushrooms. "This is so good."

"You mean the Magnificent Mile? The expensive part of town," Aiden said in a light, teasing tone.

"Do you mind?"

"Wherever you'd like is fine. It's not far from here. If you don't find what you want, we can go to Wicker Park or Bucktown another day."

After breakfast, she brushed her teeth and fussed over her outfit, finally selecting a pair of worn jeans and her favorite pink sweater. She eyed the mess on the bed, wrinkling her nose. Nothing in that pile compared to Emily's clothing.

By the time she arrived at the front door, Aiden had donned a cashmere scarf, wool overcoat, and a pair of casual leather boots.

Emily slid on a elegant wool coat and slung her small purse across her shoulder.

"I love that." Savannah said.

"Cute, isn't it? Perfect for a day of shopping as it leaves my hands free for the bags." Emily smiled.

Savannah flushed, hiding her cheap purse and accepting her thin jacket from Aiden before they rode the elevator to the lobby. Maybe visiting a fancy shopping street wasn't the best idea, but how could she back out after begging to be taken there?

The cold raw air cut through her coat as they stepped into the street and she shivered, rubbing her hands together as the crisp breeze swept through her hair.

"You look frozen already." Aiden wrapped his scarf around her neck and tucked it inside her collar before offering his leather gloves.

"Won't you be cold?" She slid on the large gloves, grateful for the cozy lining.

"I'm used to it, and I have a proper coat. I should've warned you to bring something warmer. Chicago winters are different from Portland." He dug in a pocket and produced a black beanie which he placed on her head. "Better?"

Savannah nodded. "It's always so windy." She patted the hat that was similar to the one he'd given her at the derailment.

Aiden's gaze traveled to her thin and worn sneakers with the hole in the toe. "We need to make a stop." He slung an arm around Savannah, which protected her somewhat, but she was still trembling as the wind nipped at her.

Emily frowned. "I think you're right."

They didn't walk far before Aiden ushered them inside a department store. "Let's see if we can't find you something better for Chicago weather."

Emily led them into the ladies wear section where they spent the next hour trying on boots and mid-thigh length wool overcoats.

Savannah selected a heather gray coat along with a scarf, hat, and gloves in a lovely shade of pink and a pair of low-heeled boots.

Aiden nodded in approval. "Perfect. Can you take all the tags off please?" he asked the cashier as he offered a shiny black credit card.

Savannah shoved her worn sneakers and old coat into the shopping bag, conscious of the disdainful look the sales clerk gave her. "Thank you, but you shouldn't have bought these."

"We can't have you catching pneumonia."

"Thanks, Aiden." She hugged him, and he dropped his arm over her shoulders as they continued.

She peered from under her fringe of hair, as she tried to figure him out. He was nothing like she'd imagined, nor was Emily.

People bustled down the crowded sidewalks past the multitude of shops with brightly lit windows, seeming oblivious to the abundant decorations and cheerful holiday music floating through the air.

"Let us know which stores you want to visit," Aiden said as she gazed around the busy street.

She pointed at the closest one, and Aiden held the door for her and Emily to enter. The sales person greeted them immediately as they walked inside the perfectly ordered boutique. Savannah wandered through but saw nothing that interested her, and they moved to the next store, then the next, and the next.

Neither Aiden nor Emily commented on the endless stream of boutiques. So very different from Ross who detested the mall, and who only shrugged when asked for his opinion and cringed when Savannah mentioned buying clothes.

"True Religion. I never go in there." Savannah stared at the window display, noting the red sign announcing their holiday sale.

"Here's your chance." Aiden ushered her inside.

She perused the racks, wishing she could afford to buy something, but even on sale, her meager supply of cash wouldn't cover much.

"What are you trying on?" Emily flipped through the stack of denim. "I bet these would look incredible. What size?"

Savannah scooped up a pair. "These should fit. And these, and maybe these?"

Emily nodded, adding a soft blue sweater to Savannah's selections.

Aiden sat while they tried on the clothing, either nodding or shaking his head at each pair.

By the end, Savannah had fallen in love with a pair of crisp white jeans that hugged her curves and had a touch of stretch that made them comfortable. The sweater paired with them perfectly, and looked fabulous with the pair of soft medium washed mid-rise jeans. She sorted through her wallet, hoping to find a couple bills tucked away out of sight.

"Nothing?" Aiden raised an eyebrow as she emerged from her fitting room empty handed.

Savannah shook her head, looking at the floor. "It's fun to try stuff on, but I never spend that much on clothes."

"They looked good on you. Go get them. At least three pairs." He steered her toward her change room. "Don't forget the sweater."

"No." She looked up, trying to read his expression. "Really?"

"No arguments."

She gathered them up and followed Aiden to the register. "I wish I could wear them." She ran her fingers over the white jeans.

Emily came up beside them, holding her shopping bag. "Save those for when it's warmer. White's never a great choice for Chicago in December, but the dark washed ones would be perfect."

"Take off the tags, please," Aiden said to the young man behind the counter. "And the sweater. Go change, Savannah. I'll finish here."

Vanna bounced on her toes as she examined herself in the mirror wearing her new clothes. After folding her old clothes, she carried them to the register. "What should I do with these?"

Aiden tucked then into the shopping bag. "We'll put them here for now."

"There's a clothing donation bin around the corner," the young man behind the counter said, without looking up.

Aiden frowned at the clerk, but Emily tugged him toward the door, shaking her head.

Savannah's cheeks burned as they exited onto the street. "Can I donate them? I mean," she said, bowing her head, "I won't wear them again now I have my new ones."

"Great idea," Emily said, giving her a one-armed hug. "Let's find that bin."

They found the big blue canister, and Savannah added her old clothes, including the jacket she no longer needed. "Thank you." She threw her arms around Aiden, hugging him and planting a kiss on his cheek.

"You're welcome." He slung his arm around her as they continued down the street.

Now she relaxed and the day seemed brighter. She'd never been on a shopping trip like this, ever. Aiden added several more tops and sweaters to Savannah's collection, and Emily purchased a to-die-for pair of black high heels.

"On sale." Emily sighed as they wandered down the street. "I've been coveting them from afar."

"Time for food." Aiden tapped at his watch. "I'm starving."

Savannah agreed. Her feet were sore from all the walking. They chose a small bistro, finding a table close the window.

"Put your bags away, and we'll make dinner." Aiden handed Savannah the parcels he'd carried for her, setting Emily's purchases on the floor in the marble tiled foyer.

Savannah hung her new items in the large closet. The day had been fun from start to finish, with Aiden being generous and accommodating, even buying her a new pair of sneakers.

After admiring her new outfit in the mirror, she emerged from her room. Soft music floated through the air along with the murmur of low voices from the kitchen. She paused as she entered the room, smiling at the way Aiden curled his arms around Emily's waist. The woman laughed as he whispered something in her ear before she turned her head to accept a long kiss.

Savannah cleared her throat.

"Hey, you decided to join us." Aiden stepped away from his girlfriend. "Grab a knife, and we'll put you to work on the salad."

"Okay." She washed and tore the lettuce as chicken hit the hot pan, and the aroma of garlic and butter filled her nostrils. "How long have you known each other?"

"Years." Emily uncorked a bottle of wine.

"You met at work?"

"We were both fourth-year students and we worked together during my first emergency rotation," Aiden said. "I accepted a surgical internship, and Emily decided on emergency medicine."

"Are you a resident now, Emily?"

"No, I'm an attending physician and have been for a couple years."

"If you were in the same year, why is Aiden chief resident while you're an attending?"

"Aiden decided to moonlight as a surgical intern, then he realized emergency is where the real action is." Emily prodded him in the ribs. "He could be an attending, but he accepted the chief position. It's a smart move as people fight tooth and nail for the job. You manage the scheduling and supervise the medical students and residents, plus there's a ton of teaching involved."

"Dad thought it was a big deal." Savannah nodded. Her dad had been visibly impressed when he learned Aiden was chief resident.

"He's right." The older woman nodded. "Especially chief resident of a Level 1 trauma center in a major city like Chicago. We deal with the critical cases and triage on-scene during major incidents."

"You've done actual surgery?" Savannah hadn't thought much about the reality of Aiden's work as a doctor, which seemed odd considering how they'd met. She avoided thinking about that day. The entire terrifying experience remained a blurry, unfocused memory that she'd prefer to forget.

"It was interesting, but I like emergency medicine better. Surgeons get the glory, but we make a real difference to people's lives in the ER. In July, I'll become an attending."

After dinner, they watched a movie, and at ten, Emily stretched. "I should head home. I have an appointment in the morning."

"You don't have to leave on my account."

"I have to be up early, but I'll see you later in the day. Today was fun."

Savannah hugged the woman before allowing the couple privacy to say goodnight. It had been a good day, and all her fears had been unfounded.

"I know, Dana, but—" Aiden sighed. "A half-shift, that's it." He set his phone on the counter and rubbed a hand through his hair.

"What's up?"

"I'm sorry, I've been called if for a six-hour shift."

"I can manage on my own." She forced a smile.

"Emily's on her way. You two could go."

"That would be fun, if she doesn't mind."

"I'm happy you two get along, though I figured you would. I should change but that'll only take a minute."

Savannah flopped onto the couch, playing with her phone until Emily appeared.

"Hi, Emily. Aiden is changing."

"I thought he'd be ready. He texted ten minutes ago wondering where I was."

"Sorry." Aiden reappeared. "Dana caught me. I have to work, but you ladies could go without me."

Emily smiled. "Having a girls' day sounds like fun. What do you think, Savannah?"

"I'm in."

"Perfect. Sorry for the change in plans, but I'll make it up to you tomorrow." Aiden handed Emily his credit card, murmuring something indistinguishable in her ear. "Enjoy."

"Ready?" Emily tucked the card into her wallet and tucked her keys inside her purse.

Savannah donned her new coat and boots, trailing her into the elevator. "He gave you his credit card." Did he do this with all his girlfriends? Emily had gone home last night, but she understood that was for her benefit. "You usually stay with him, don't you?" She observed the woman.

Emily simply smiled at her.

"Sorry, that's personal, right? He's my father, and you're dating him, but ..." She sighed. "You left stuff in his bathroom."

"If you have questions, ask Aiden," Emily said in a gentle voice.

"You don't have to pretend and go home on my account."

"Noted," she said. "What shall we do?"

"Can you help me buy some new bras? My dad's so uncomfortable and he can't help me figure out what fits."

Emily laughed. "Men are hopeless at that kind of thing."

They chose Bloomingdale's lingerie department and spent the next hour choosing bras, along with some cute lacy panties Savannah loved.

"Thanks, Emily. I never knew shopping for underwear could be fun." She grinned as she located her wallet and extracted her remaining cash.

"Put it away." Emily waved a hand and presented Aiden's credit card.

The clerk examined it. "I'm sorry. I can't accept this unless you have ID confirming your name is Aiden Hamilton." The woman regarded them with narrowed eyes.

"I have the PIN. Or you can contact Aiden. I have his permission to use it." Emily smiled, looking hopeful.

"No, sorry. I'm supposed to cut up the card."

"Emily?"

Savannah turned toward the voice, looking into the crystal blue eyes of a stunning blonde woman.

"Tiffany. Nice to see you," Emily said.

"Are you having an issue with Aiden's card?" Tiffany's gaze flitted to Savannah, and her eyes widened as she stepped back.

"He got called to work. I'll use my card, and he can pay me back."

Tiffany shook her head. "Jill, could you run it, please? I'm sure Aiden authorized Dr. Anderson's use of his card." She cleared her throat, her gaze darting to Savannah's face before she angled her body, the staccato beat of her tapping foot echoing against the tile.

Savannah shifted and ran a hand through her hair, smoothing it as she fought the urge to check in the mirror. *Do I have something on my face?*

"Of course, Ms. Baxter." The girl smiled and swiped the card and motioned to the terminal on the counter. "You can input the PIN."

"Nice to see you. I have to run." Tiffany spun, the red soles of her shoes flashing as she hurried toward the escalator.

The clerk handed Aiden's credit card to Emily. "Sorry for the inconvenience, we have to be careful with all the credit card fraud. But as Ms. Baxter vouches for you ..."

"I understand. Thank you." Emily handed the bag to Savannah, a thoughtful look on her face as she tucked away the card.

"That was weird," Savannah whispered as they headed for the exit. "That Tiffany woman knows Aiden?" The woman was beautiful, even if a bit odd.

"She does. They went ... I met her at a dinner party." Emily's smile seemed forced as they stepped onto the street.

Savannah frowned, certain Emily had been about to say something else.

"That was fun," Emily said.

"Do you think Aiden will mind we spent so much?"

"Aiden gave me his card for a reason, sweetie." Emily squeezed her hand.

Savannah held on to the woman as she returned Emily's bright smile. "It feels unreal, though. He's fun, like a cool big brother."

Emily gave a slight nod.

"Did he tell you what happened in Portland?" Savannah's smile faded. "I wasn't even sure I wanted to see him again, but I'm glad I did. Not because of the shopping thing, though, it's ..." She tipped her chin down, not sure how to express the swirl of confusing emotions and thoughts.

"You don't need to explain. This has to be difficult for both of you," Emily said. "Anytime you're in Chicago, I'd love to see you."

"Maybe if Aiden visits Portland, you could come and meet my dad? And Leanne. You know he visited Leanne when she was stuck in the hospital?"

"No, I didn't. I'll talk to Aiden about visiting." Emily held open the door. "Do you mind going to a later movie? I need to stop at my hair salon."

"Nope, I don't mind."

They trudged through the heavy snow until they arrived at a salon, and Emily motioned for her to enter.

"Emily." A young man waved. "What can I do for you, love? Our appointment is next week, right?"

"Josh, this is Savannah. Josh is a miracle worker with hair."

"Hi, Josh." She waved.

"My, look at this beauty." Josh lifted a chunk of Savannah's hair. "I'd love to work some of my magic. When was the last time someone cut this?" He inspected the tips. "Far too long, honey." He clicked his tongue. "I have time."

"I couldn't." Savannah shook her head. "We're supposed to go to a movie."

"Don't worry about the movie. It's a super idea." Emily looked at Josh. "You can keep the length?"

Josh tilted his head and then nodded. "Give me an hour."

"You sure?" Savannah glanced at Emily, noting that the woman's lips twitched as if she were trying not to smile.

"It would be my pleasure. Let's wash these marvelous locks of yours." He ushered her toward the back. "Love, why don't you let Magda do your nails while you wait for your beautiful young friend?"

Savannah flushed and tucked her hands under her legs as he seated her in his chair before the large mirror, willing Josh not to spot her messy nails. They were nothing like Emily's elegant hands.

A wicked smile playing across his face. "Honey," he said as he raised a brow, "perhaps you need more pampering. Magda," he glanced over his shoulder, "can you save a spot for our lovely Savannah?"

Vanna opened her mouth to protest but then shrugged. What was the point in arguing when she wouldn't win? "Can she do French tips?"

⁓

Three hours later, Savannah felt like she'd gone to heaven.

"Come again, sweet Savannah. I'd be pleased to see you." Josh handed over the bag of hair products he'd recommended for her.

Savannah hoped Aiden didn't get upset about the enormous amount they'd charged to his credit card, but she loved her hair. Josh had styled it so it fell in soft smooth waves. Her nails were tidy and polished and they'd fit in a pedicure and shaped her eyebrows. She felt like a new person. "We missed the movie." She giggled.

"We can go another time. Why don't we pop into this little bistro and have dinner? Aiden and I come here often." Emily held open the door as Savannah maneuvered inside with her bags.

"Josh is amazing. I loved him," Savannah said as they slid into a cozy booth. "Aiden sure won't be happy when he gets his credit card bill." She inhaled deeply, her mouth watering at the tang of tomato sauce and fragrance of fresh bread.

"Aiden won't be upset, trust me. The next time you visit, we'll book an appointment to touch up your hair. It's been a while since you cut it, right?"

"It's been over a year."

"Well, it looks gorgeous." Emily set her menu aside. "They make this insane Veal Piccata with roasted baby potatoes and vegetables. I love their garden salad. What would you like?"

"The same?" Savannah had never eaten veal, but Emily had impeccable taste in everything.

Emily seemed like a big sister or a favorite aunt, and they chatted like they'd known each other forever. She was incredibly sweet and absolutely gorgeous, and Savannah wished she could look as downright sexy. Maybe then Justin would notice.

"Late movie, or sack out on Aiden's couch, order pay-per-view, and pig out on popcorn?" Emily dropped her credit card on the table once they'd eaten.

"Let's do that. He might be home."

Emily checked her phone. "Nope. He won't be back until later, but he sends his apologies. There was a major accident, so it's just us girls tonight."

"Doesn't it bother you that he stuck you with me all day?"

"I've enjoyed the girls' time and getting to know you. I'm sure you'd have preferred to spend the day with Aiden as he's the reason you came to Chicago, but the reality of being chief resident in a major trauma center is you get called into work at the most inconvenient times. It's part of the job."

"It was a good day. You're pretty understanding about his work, though."

"Two years ago, I was chief resident." Emily laughed. "Don't forget, I'm a doctor in the same department of the same hospital, and I know how hard he works. When I'm on call and have to go in or get held up at work due to an incoming trauma, he understands. He never freaks out because we missed the movie or had to change dinner reservations. It's not the easiest job or lifestyle, but we make it work."

The moment they reached the apartment Emily said, "I'm putting on something more comfortable." She disappeared into Aiden's bedroom.

Savannah changed in to her pajamas, and after she'd put away her purchases, she joined Emily in the kitchen.

Emily looked cozy in flannel sleep pants paired with an oversized men's shirt. The popcorn maker spun the kernels while she melted butter in a small pan. "If you check that cupboard"—she pointed—"you'll find Aiden's stash of chocolate."

She peeked inside and giggled. "Oh. M&M's."

"Perfect." Emily dumped the popcorn into a bowl and drizzled on the melted butter before adding a sprinkle of salt and dumping in a handful of the little chocolate candies.

Savannah poured two glasses of ice-water and followed the woman into the media room.

"Cozy. We just need fluffy throws." Savannah plopped onto the couch while Emily turned on the big-screen TV mounted to the wall. She loved this room. The heavy blinds shut out the cold snowy weather and the gas fireplace cast a heavenly warmth into the room.

"In the chest." Emily pointed as she turned on the sound system. "Grab me one, please."

Savannah pulled out two blankets then joined Emily on the couch. "You must spend a lot of time here."

"My apartment's nice, but ..." Emily shrugged. "We tend to hang out here. It's bigger and closer to work."

"When you marry Aiden, you'll move in?"

"Don't rush it. We've only been dating a few weeks." Emily laughed. "It's too soon to be discussing marriage."

"He trusts you with his keys and his credit card."

"We've known each other several years."

"You like him."

"I do." Emily gave her a meaningful look. "It's too early to plan the wedding."

Savannah got her point, but she persisted. "Tell me what you like about him."

"That's easy. He's compassionate, kind, sweet, and generous, extremely intelligent, driven career-wise, and he's at the top of his game professionally. He'll never be one to sit around. He's fun, but serious when it's called for."

Savannah nodded. "What else do you like about him?"

"Hmmm, he's a fantastic cook, he cleans up after himself, and he's house trained." Emily grinned. "He's an excellent doctor, and well-liked by the patients and the staff, probably because he works hard."

"And the not so perfect side?"

"I'll let you discover that on your own. Shall we watch our movie?"

Savannah snuggled under her blanket as the movie started. The cute romantic comedy had them both giggling. By the end of the movie, Aiden still wasn't home.

"Can you stay?" Even knowing the apartment was secure, Savannah didn't want to be alone.

"Sure."

Savannah helped clear the dishes and fold the throws before hugging Emily. "Thanks again for today. Say goodnight to Aiden?"

"Why don't you text him?" The woman rubbed Vanna's arm. "Goodnight, sweetie. I had fun today."

Savannah crawled into the bed, totally exhausted. It had been a busy day, but she'd learned a lot about Aiden and Emily. After a goodnight text to Aiden, she drifted to sleep with a contented smile on her face.

Chapter 16

Aiden

Aiden had known it would be a bad day the moment he stepped into the icy, snow-packed street. Not only was there an influx of patients involved in vehicular collisions, but a barrage of other injuries.

Then he'd been sent to the scene of a major incident on the Kennedy, involving a rough flight on the helicopter, followed by hours triaging in frigid conditions. The final reward had been the gash in his arm gained by crawling into a crushed car to apply pressure to a young boy's wounds as the firefighters cut apart the vehicle.

Finally, his shift ended. He rubbed his aching arm as he settled in the lounge, intent on checking his charts and patient updates before heading home. "Damn." He scrubbed the back of his neck.

"What's the problem, Dr. Hamilton?" Dana appeared behind him.

"The heart attack patient from this morning died in the cath lab." Aiden ran a hand over his face. "He had young kids."

"You did what you could. Go home. You've put in enough hours today."

"Good idea. One quick stop first. I should check on the toddler from the car." Aiden craved good news. He dialed the surgical floor, lucky to catch the surgeon before he left for the evening. "How's the boy?"

"The one you brought in from the accident?" The surgeon's voice was low and level. "I'm sorry, he didn't make it. You did a great patch job, but he had massive internal injuries. There was nothing we could do."

Aiden slumped forward, massaging his temples with his fingertips. The kid hadn't made his third birthday. The reality of life as a doctor was you couldn't save everyone.

"Rough shift?" Tara dropped onto the couch. "You should join me for a drink."

"Thanks, but I'm done in and need to take my pain meds and antibiotics." He rolled his shoulder.

"I heard about the boy you brought in." Tara rose and moved behind him. Her hands descended to his shoulders, her fingertips digging into his muscles. "Better?"

"I'll be fine." He stood, shaking her off. "All I want is a hot shower and my pillow."

"Sitting at home alone isn't a good idea after a day like today. One drink." She nibbled at her lip. "You could come to my place."

"Bad idea." He scoffed at the woman's assumption he'd be alone. "It's been a crappy shift, so … goodnight."

"Maybe another time," she said. "Night, Aiden."

Without a backward glance, he exited the ER into the lightly falling snow. It looked magical and deceptively calm and peaceful, but behind the doors of the ER, the battle between life and death continued to rage.

Aiden let himself into the dimly lit, silent apartment. The supposed six-hour shift had turned into over twelve and it was well past midnight.

He threw back two of the pain pills he'd been prescribed, chasing them with a glass of water. Soon they'd kick in and he could hardly wait. The over-the-counter meds he'd taken earlier had barely made a dent in the throbbing ache. He hadn't eaten much and he felt grimy and chilled to the bone.

In the guest room, Savannah was buried under the fluffy down duvet, her breathing deep and even.

He tiptoed to his room, quietly shutting the door behind him.

Emily seemed to be sleeping too, curled up in his bed, breathing softly. He tiptoed through, peeling off his clothing as the shower warmed up. The steamy water cast off the chill that had sunk into his bones.

"I'm happy you're home," Emily murmured as he slid into bed. She nestled against him, running her fingers through his damp hair. "You went on the chopper in that nasty weather. I worried."

"The pilots are great, no need for concern." Despite his protest, it felt amazing to have someone worry about him for a change. "I'm beat."

"Bad one?" Her fingers touched the fresh dressing he'd applied after his shower. "What happened?"

"A few stitches. I crawled into a car after a kid. The entire scene was horrible." He curled an arm around her. "Let's not talk about it."

"I hate those days." She held him close, her fingers trickling up and down his back. "I'm glad you're safe." Her voice soothed him, her hands soft and warm as she pressed gentle kisses against his flesh. "You smell yummy. I could eat you up."

"Mmm, careful, it's been a few days."

"I can be quiet if you can." She nibbled on his earlobe as she slid her hands under his shirt, working it over his head. "Much better." Her soft caresses raised goose bumps on his flesh. "Let's get rid of the rest."

"Stealing my clothes again?" He peeled off the oversized shirt, leaving her in tiny satin thong panties.

"They're comfy."

"You look sexy in my shirts, but … even sexier out of my shirts." He slid down the covers, the cool air washing over their bodies. "You're beautiful." He breathed against her skin.

"So are you." Emily wrapped him in her arms.

Emily rested her head on his chest, her fingers grazing his side.

"You'll get me into trouble with my daughter." He kept his voice low and dropped a kiss onto her hair. "Or maybe she got what she wanted. She's said it's okay for you to sleep over while she's here."

"She commented to me, as well. I didn't hide my makeup and she noticed."

"They grow up so fast."

"She told me I should marry you. How about that for matchmaking? Savannah's known me for less than forty-eight hours, and she's ready to marry us off."

"She didn't say that." Aiden laughed. "Did she?"

"I bet she was a precocious young child. Anyway, she's almost fifteen, not six. She clearly understands adult relationships."

"Still, it's a little weird for my teenage daughter to invite my girlfriend to stay over."

"Maybe but …" Emily sighed. "Perhaps it's her way of opening a conversation. I doubt Ross discusses teenage girl issues, and she wouldn't be comfortable if he did. The man's pushing sixty. That disconnect is hard for any teenage girl, especially one who lost her mother. You've come into her life at the perfect time."

"Do you think so?" Ross seemed to be a caring and loving father, but Emily could be right. Nothing about Savannah's recent life had been easy.

"She was excited about shopping and begged me to help her buy the necessities. Savannah seems to think buying bras, panties, and those kinds of things makes Ross uncomfortable. She's not even fifteen and experienced overwhelming losses. I sense the emotional struggle."

"Did she say anything that concerns you?"

"No, but she needs extra support, along with some exposure to the real world. Keep an eye on her, and offer to be a resource," Emily said. "I orchestrated a little run-in with Josh because I noticed she needed some pampering. I spent a lot of money on her today. Sorry."

"No, Em. Thank you. This is the first chance I've had to help my daughter. I can afford to buy her some appropriate clothing and pay for a haircut."

"Mmmm, but she still felt bad about charging your card." She tipped her head. "There's a huge hole in her life. Having time alone with a woman to talk to seemed like a major event."

Some of the girl's comments and actions fell into place in his mind. "That makes sense, and we know how grief works. We see it often enough. I'd bet Jayde took care of all these details. Maybe it's too much for Ross." Aiden sighed. "I wonder if she'd be receptive to asking me the sensitive questions. Boys, sex, health concerns?"

"Talk to her before she goes home. Don't push, but at least offer. I'd happily give her advice if she'd feel more comfortable talking to a woman. I remember how hard it was as a teenage girl."

"Thank you. I can relate as I never had any sort of conversation with my parents, ever. They weren't around, and my grandparents were unapproachable. My friends weren't the best source of information and I got myself in a world of trouble."

"Ah, the total wild child, were you?"

"You could say that. We sneaked out, partied, and had a lot of sex. All when we were way too young to handle the consequences. We had money, so nothing was off limits."

"I wasn't the poster child of innocence either. My mom is wonderful, but her Spanish heritage shows. She's strict, and her talks were more of the "just don't do it" variety. Who knows what Jayde discussed with Savannah."

He shook his head. "I'm glad you two had a good day."

"We did." She rolled toward him. "We saw Tiffany at the store."

"What?" Aiden bolted upright, his heart pounding.

"She recognized me and when Vanna turned around, Tiffany practically ran the other direction. Savannah found it weird, but I don't think she clued in."

Aiden put his arm around her, pulling her closer. "So that's it? Tiffany didn't say anything?"

"She saved your credit card from being hacked to bits by the overzealous sales clerk and left as soon as humanly possible."

He rubbed the back of his neck. "How could she ignore the daughter standing right in front of her? Seriously, the woman needs a reality check, but what do you want to bet she calls tomorrow and takes a strip off me?"

"For seeing your child?"

"For bringing said child to Chicago where she might be recognized."

"The resemblance is unmistakable." Her intense gaze burned into him. "You two acted like you barely knew each other that night at your grandmother's house, but you were married. It's weird that you're divorced, and no one at work knows."

"We lived in Philadelphia at the time, and divorced before I started residency."

"How long were you married?"

"Two extremely volatile years."

"And how long together in total, including when you dated as teenagers?"

"Six, if you count the number of times we broke up and then got back together."

"What's the longest you've been with one woman since Tiffany?"

"Four, maybe five months? What's your longest relationship?"

"I was with Jason almost two years."

"Didn't know he lasted that long. He's an idiot."

"Yes, I think so. But why do you think so?"

"He cheated on you. That makes him an idiot."

"You should talk, mister four to five months." Emily poked his ribs.

Aiden frowned. "Just because my relationships don't last long doesn't mean I'm a total asshole. I don't cheat." He hadn't expected this judgmental attitude from Emily. "I have been cheated on, so I get how it feels."

Emily brushed her hand over his hair. "That was a stupid thing for me to say."

"You of all people should know how hard it is to find the right person. You date, and I don't assume things about you."

"You're right." She cupped his face. "I'm sorry. Forgive me?"

Aiden contemplated her, noting her unwavering gaze and pursed lips. "Yes, you're forgiven." He leaned in for another kiss. "Promise you won't tell anyone about me being married. I hope Savannah's getting past the fact her mother doesn't want to see her, and Tiffany doesn't want her to know."

"I won't tell. I haven't said anything about her to anyone, and I won't. You can trust me." She kissed him again. "I like your daughter a lot."

"She's quite the kid, isn't she?"

"She is. Get some sleep. I have to work tomorrow."

Aiden pulled her close. "Night, sweetheart." He closed his eyes, drifting off to sleep

Chapter 17

Savannah

Savannah squinted at the clock. It was early, but she heard movement in the hallway. She slid out of bed and wandered down the hall to the kitchen, brushing her unruly hair back from her eyes.

"Good morning." Emily smiled as she poured hot coffee into a travel mug. She wore navy dress pants with a crisp button-down blouse and looked sleek and professional. "Sorry I woke you. It's not even six-thirty."

"Where are you going?" Savannah rubbed her eyes.

"I work at seven. Sorry, I can't chat, but it was fun. You go home tonight?"

"My dad wants me back before Christmas. He's overprotective."

"Dads are like that." Emily hugged her, rocking on her feet. "Let Aiden sleep a while longer. He arrived home after one."

"I'll watch TV or write."

"It was great meeting you, Savannah. I enjoyed our girls' day."

"Me too. Thank you." Vanna blinked hard. The time with Emily had been fun, and she hoped one day they'd do it again.

The doctor slid on low-heeled boots and her long wool coat and tucked a knit hat on her head before wrapping up in a scarf and gloves. She collected her small bag and coffee mug, waving as she disappeared out the door.

Savannah took her time in the shower and dressed in a pair of her new jeans and her soft, cozy sweater. After brewing some hot tea, she lit the fireplace and curled up on the overstuffed couch with her notebook. Snowflakes fluttered past the large windows, but she bent her head, becoming fully absorbed in her writing.

"You're up early."

Savannah jumped, placing a hand over her racing heart. She stared at him wide-eyed.

Aiden leaned in the doorway holding a steaming cup of coffee, dressed in a thick sweater and jeans. "I didn't mean to scare you."

"It's okay." She snapped her journal closed, passing her hand over the cover. "Emily went to work."

Aiden nodded. "You had fun with her?"

"She's great. Amazing, actually. Emily helped me buy a few things but we used your credit card."

"She told me, and it's not a problem. You got your hair done? It suits you."

Savannah ran her hand over her smooth, thick hair. "Emily took me to see some guy called Josh. He was cute."

"Ahh, Josh. Em loves him." Aiden sat facing her on the opposite end of the couch, his legs tucked up casually.

"We went for dinner, and came home and pigged out on popcorn."

"Sorry I got held up at work, but it sounds like you had a good time." He sipped his coffee and motioned to her notebook. "What are you working on?"

"I keep a journal, but I never show it to anyone. It's more like a diary." She rested her hand on top. To her relief, Aiden didn't ask to see it.

"I write sometimes, but not a personal journal. I stick to medical articles."

"Really? What happens to them?"

"I've published several in medical journals. Sometimes we run across interesting cases at work. It's a way of sharing our findings with other doctors. Emily writes too."

"Wow, she's smart and beautiful. You get along really well." Savannah smiled. "You should marry her."

"Whoa, whoa." He held up a hand, the corners of his mouth twitching. "Let's hold off on the whole marriage thing." His face settled into a serious expression. "You can't rush relationships. Emily's great, but we need time to make sure we're right for each other."

"So don't get too attached, is that what you're saying? I should expect a new girlfriend the next time I visit?"

"That's not it. Not even close. I hope things work, but it's early in our relationship. Seriously, she's amazing but don't expect to be a bridesmaid anytime soon. Okay?"

"Yes." Savannah knew she shouldn't push her luck, as she didn't know Aiden well, or for long, although she already felt comfortable talking to him.

"Art Institute after breakfast?" he asked.

"I hoped we could go today."

"Let's eat and get ready. It's best to go before it gets crowded."

An hour later they were on the train speeding toward their destination. Savannah watched the city flash by.

"This is us." Aiden pulled her off the car through the incoming crush.

"This is a huge city. So many people."

"Almost three million." Aiden kept a tight grip until they escaped the crowded platform.

Savannah enjoyed every minute, and she learned Aiden had a deep interest in art. Maybe she'd gotten her artistic talent from him, but it was impossible to know. She would have liked to ask questions about her mother. To find out even the barest bit of information would have been amazing, but she wasn't sure Aiden would be receptive or answer.

"Wow, that was great." They'd decided it was time for a late lunch and were now sitting in a small restaurant not far from Millennium Park. "Aiden? Have you told your family about me?"

"Do you want to do this again? You coming out to see me, or having me come out to Portland? Or we can go somewhere? I know you haven't had much opportunity to travel."

"It might be fun to visit other places, though I love it here." She frowned. He'd answered her question with his own. "You told Emily about me, and she's only your girlfriend. What about your family?"

"Emily's supportive. My family isn't, so I thought I'd wait to see if you wanted to meet them before I approach the subject."

"If you visit Portland, Emily should come with you."

"You'd like to continue seeing me?"

She nodded. "You'll tell your family? And I can meet them?"

"I'll talk to them." Aiden folded his menu and reached across the table to take her hand. "Whether you'll meet them or not will depend on how they react. I won't put you into an uncomfortable situation."

"You're not sure?"

"No. If it goes well then we'll go to New York for a visit, or out to my grandmother's. If it goes badly, I won't put you through it." He hesitated the squeezed her hand. "Sorry, my family's dysfunctional, but I'm sure you've already picked up on that fact."

"Why wouldn't they want to meet me?" Her eyes filled with tears at the thought of more people who didn't care, just like her mother.

Aiden shook his head. "I'm sorry. It's them, not you. I don't see my family often."

"It's okay." Savannah buried her nose in the menu, brushing the dampness from her cheeks. "I'll have the ravioli in tomato sauce," she said to the server who'd appeared at the table.

"It's not okay, Savannah," he said after the server left with their orders. "It never will be, but it's the unfortunate reality." He stared out the window as heavy flakes blanketed the ground in a sheet of white. "How do you feel about staying another day or so?"

"Like my dad would allow it."

"I'd bet flights will be canceled for the next twenty-four to forty-eight hours. They're forecasting a major dump of snow." He motioned at the virtual blizzard outside. "This is nothing compared to what's coming."

"I get to stay?"

"Until the airport reopens at least. Unless you'd rather sit on a train for a couple of days."

Her heart soared at the news, and she grinned. "Can Emily come over tonight? What will we do?"

"I'm sure we can find something to keep us busy. Why don't I call her—" His phone rang, but after a cursory glance, he silenced it and placed it face down on the table.

"You're not going to answer?"

"I'll get back to them later. Let me text Emily and see if she's free. Might be a night in with this snowfall. Transit could come to a standstill."

"We could make her dinner. I bet she'd love it. We could play some games or watch a movie or something." Savannah's excitement level rose at the thought of spending more time with the couple.

"Good idea. We'll pick up ingredients on our way home. What did you have in mind?"

They ate and chatted about dinner plans, and Aiden texted Emily, inviting her for the evening.

"Aiden."

Savannah looked up, taking in the well-dressed man standing beside their table.

"Tom. What brings you here?" Aiden smiled, glancing at Savannah.

"I was in the area to meet a client and decided to stop for a coffee."

Savannah eyed the handsome man, admiring his piercing blue eyes, dark hair, and expensive suit. He resembled a briefcase carrying GQ model.

"Join us if you like. Savannah, this is Tom Grayson."

"Do you mind, Savannah? I don't want to interrupt your lunch."

"No, it's fine."

Tom slipped off his coat and seated himself in the booth beside her. He waved down the waiter for a cup of coffee and a slice of apple pie with ice cream. "Either of you interested? The pie is amazing, Savannah. They bake it on site."

She nodded, and Tom ordered slices for both her and Aiden. The next hour flew by, and she found herself liking the man immensely. He drew her into the conversation and asked questions. She wondered if this man knew she was Aiden's daughter. He didn't seem surprised by her presence or inquire as to why his friend was having lunch with a teenage girl.

Tom glanced at his watch. "I have one more client before I head home. You enjoy the rest of your visit, Savannah."

"Thanks, Tom. Nice to meet you." Savannah watched him go as Aiden paid the bill, and then they walked back to the apartment.

Savannah called her dad as soon as they arrived home, and had a brief conversation, filling him in on her day. Once she was done, she decided to find Aiden. She started down the hall, freezing at the tone of his voice.

"No…. I won't do that…. Stop it…. It's your problem, not mine…. We're not having this discussion…. I'm hanging up now."

Vanna backed away, one slow step at a time, listening intently, but only greeted by deep silence. She crept toward his room. "Aiden?"

"Come in." A shirtless Aiden opened his dresser drawer, extracting a fresh shirt.

She pointed to the red mark on his well-toned bicep. "What happened?"

"I cut it when I crawled into a car at the accident scene." His voice was level and calm.

"Does it hurt?"

"It's fine. I'm just changing the dressing."

Savannah caught a glimpse of an intricate design inked on his shoulder. "Holy crap. You have a tattoo? That's so cool. Can I see it?"

"Sure." He turned, allowing her a better view.

"Wolves are my favorite animals. When did you get this?"

"I was eighteen."

"My dad would freak if I got a tattoo, but maybe when I'm eighteen. Will you get another?" Savannah inspected it closely, examining the incredible and beautiful artistry. She ran her fingertip over the design. The wolf even had tiny, detailed paw prints.

"You never know. I need to grab a fresh bandage. I'll be right back."

Savannah sat on the massive bed as he reappeared, ripping the wrapping from the sterile dressing. "Need help?"

"Thanks. It's easier if someone else does it."

Savannah carefully lined up the dressing so it wouldn't stick to the sutures and pressed it on with her fingertip. The tattoo fascinated her, drawing her gaze, and more of the details grabbed her attention. "I." She traced the letter, following the delicate lines to others intricately woven into the design. "N. I. O. N. Weird. What do the letters mean?"

"You see them?" Aiden's eyes widened.

"Did I miss some letters? This isn't a real word."

He picked up the shirt from the bed and slid it on, starting on the buttons. "It's real," he said.

"Does your tattoo mean something?" Savannah's curiosity rose as she studied it. "I've never seen one like it. It's abstract and so beautifully designed. Maybe I'll get one like this someday."

"They're Celtic, both the word and the design." Aiden turned to look at her. "No one has ever noticed it before. Fitting you would, though."

"Why?"

"I'll tell you, but it's between us." He took her hand. "It's pronounced *ih nee in*. It means daughter."

Savannah stared as he sat beside her on the edge of the bed. "Daughter?"

"The footprints are Celtic knots symbolizing father and daughter."

"It's about us."

He nodded. "Wolves are fierce protectors of family. Flames represent transformation. My wolf holds the secret."

"It's my tattoo?" Her eyes burned as a tear escaped and trickled down her cheek.

"Hey, don't cry," he whispered, catching the tear and brushing it away.

"You never forgot." Her voice cracked.

"No." He slid an arm around her shoulders, letting her lean into him. "You were lost to me, for so long, and us meeting was a miracle. I often wondered if you were okay, if the family who adopted you were good people, and if you were happy."

Another tear escaped. Even if she knew nothing about giving up a child, she understood loss far too well.

"It hurt to give me away." She placed her palm over his heart. "Like it hurt when my mom died." Savannah's thoughts traveled to his comment about the loss of someone he loved and now she wondered if that person was her.

He rested his hand on hers, gripping it lightly. "Never seeing you, holding you, or even having a single moment to say goodbye ... that's an unbearable agony. My consolation is your parents were good to you, and that you have your dad. He loves you."

"I love him. I complain, and he's overprotective, but he's a good dad. My mom was amazing too."

"Most teenagers complain about their parents. It doesn't mean you don't love them. I bet he'd do anything for you."

"He would, but I can't always talk to him. There were some things I told my mom about. I miss her all the time. My dad doesn't understand. It's like he wants to keep me his little girl forever, but I need to grow up." It felt good to give voice to her thoughts. Aiden's nod made her think he understood her dilemma.

"You miss having a woman around. Some things might not be comfortable topics to discuss with your dad."

Savannah nodded.

"Is that why you want me to marry Emily?"

It seemed like Aiden saw right through her, and she felt guilty for being transparent about her motives. "Silly, right?"

"Not at all," he said. "Emily and I don't need to be married for you to confide in her. And you can talk to me. My views are vastly different from your dad's as we're different generations. They adopted you when they were older, right?"

"My mom was almost forty, and my dad over forty. He's close to sixty now. How old is your dad?"

"He's fifty-five, and my mom's fifty-two. I know how hard it can be to make parents understand. My father and I rarely get along, and we don't have much of a bond. You're lucky because you're close to your dad."

"I am, but it's weird bringing up certain subjects."

"You could talk to me."

"It might be even stranger." Savannah peeked at him, noting he didn't seem the least bit uncomfortable with the conversation. "Would you tell my dad?"

Aiden let out a long breath. "Most things you say could be kept between us. I'd only get Ross involved if it was serious."

"Serious how?"

"Life or death serious. Otherwise, I'll keep it to myself. Remember what I do for a living. Being a doctor is like being a counselor most days."

Savannah considered him. "What about boys? Or dating? All that kind of stuff?"

"I'm here, Savannah. I won't judge, or lecture, and I'm not the morals police. You can be open with me, perhaps in a way you can't with your dad."

"You won't tell my secrets?"

"I won't. Being a teenager is tough." He smiled and lifted a shoulder. "I'm a doctor. If you tell me it's confidential, I can keep it to myself. We have more in common than you think."

"We do?" The comment perplexed Savannah. What parallels could she have with a privileged guy who'd attended elite boarding schools?

"I never confided in my father. I sure the hell didn't go running to him for help when your mother got pregnant. My mother left me when I was young. I understand how it feels to not have any adults to turn to with my troubles."

"Oh." Sadness enveloped her. She'd lost her mom, but he'd lost both parents, even if they weren't dead.

"Don't look so concerned. My life hasn't been so bad. I spent a lot of time with my grandparents during the holidays, though my grandfather wasn't exactly the warm type. I've traveled and had the benefit of the best education even if they hate that I'm a doctor instead of a lawyer. And I have great friends, who became my family."

"I thought everyone wanted their kids to be doctors?"

"Not mine. They wanted me to be a lawyer. Anyway, I know we're just getting to know each other, but I'm here if you need me. For anything."

Savannah evaluated his statement. "I can call anytime?"

"Yes. Whenever you want."

On impulse, she leaned in for a hug. "I'm glad I decided to see you again. I almost didn't, you know?"

"I do. I'm grateful for this chance to get to know you." Aiden hugged her back and dropped a kiss on her hair.

She felt safe and warm and somehow she knew, no matter what happened, he'd be there. The thought was comforting. "Does Tom know who I am?"

"Yes. I've known him all my life. I trust him."

"He knows my mother. Right?"

"He does. Why?"

"Just curious." Savannah shrugged. "I like him. He treated me like a person, not an annoying teenager. Some adults act as if teenagers are too much trouble to bother with." It felt truly wonderful knowing Aiden had shared her existence with the people closest to him. "I'm glad you told him about me."

"I'm sure you'll see more of him." He kept his arm around her shoulders. "Should we make dinner? Emily will be here soon."

"Sounds good." She let him pull her from the bed and followed him into the kitchen. Funny how things turned out. Taking the opportunity to visit Chicago and spend this time with her father might be one of the best decisions she'd ever made.

Chapter 18

Aiden

*I*T WAS ALMOST TWO IN the morning, and his phone buzzed on the bedside table.

"Shut off your damn phone." Emily grumbled, half asleep.

"It's Savannah." He propped himself up on one elbow, smiling at her text.

I'm home safe. Had a lot of fun. Say hi to Emily, and I hope we can see each other again soon.

Thanks, Vanna, enjoyed your visit, and I'd love to see you. Sleep well.

"Savannah's home. She says hi." He slid an arm around Emily and kissed the back of her neck, inhaling the sweet vanilla scent of her body lotion. It soothed him, and he relaxed with Emily wrapped in his arms.

"Now sleep. We have to be up by six."

He closed his eyes as her fingers entwined with his. The world seemed right for a change.

The alarm rang all too soon, both of them dragging themselves out of bed and into a hot shower.

"Hurry, or we'll be late for our shift." Aiden handed Emily a travel cup of coffee.

"Thank you, *mi amor*." Emily planted a kiss on his lips before they dashed out the door.

Aiden watched the city flash by, and soon they were at their stop.

"I'll go in first today." Emily squeezed his hand before disappearing down the stairs.

Aiden followed five minutes later. From the moment he walked through the door, he was immersed in work, with barely a chance to take a break. The moment the ER quieted down, he headed for the lounge.

"What's up with you? You've been off in your own little world." Tara cornered him. "We haven't hung out in forever."

"I've been busy. Pre-Christmas stuff, and I have a trip to New York planned. Man, who made this stuff?" He dumped his cup, renewing his vow to avoid the coffee.

"New York, huh?" Tara wound a strand of her hair around her finger, batting her eyes at him. "I've never been there."

"You should go sometime." Aiden popped open his locker, digging for his wallet. "Want a coffee from across the street? I'll bring you one."

"Maybe I could keep you company."

"Oh, get your coat."

"No. I mean ..." She sighed. "Maybe I could come to New York. It would be fun. Don't you get tired of traveling by yourself?"

He gave Tara a sideways glance. "Who said I'm going alone?"

"Oh, I assumed, since—" Her head popped up. "Wait. Are you seeing someone?"

"My girlfriend wouldn't be happy about you joining us."

"Since when do you have a girlfriend?"

"Since a while ago."

"You never told me. You're taking her to New York to meet your parents?"

"I wasn't aware I had to report my relationship status to my colleagues." He shoved his arms into his jacket.

Emily stepped into the lounge. "How's the coffee?"

"Nasty." Aiden grimaced, even as he sent a silent thanks to Emily for interrupting the interrogation. "I'm going across the street. I'll get you one."

"I'll come. I need the fresh air." Emily grabbed her coat.

"You hear the news?" Tara crossed her arms.

"What news?" Emily pulled on leather gloves.

"Aiden's new girlfriend. He's been quiet about this development. So who is she? Some socialite?" Tara raised a brow at Emily. "Did you know he had a girlfriend?"

"Mmmhmm." Emily focused on buttoning her coat. "You ready, Aiden?"

"You told her," Tara said, narrowing her eyes, "but not me?"

Aiden held open the lounge door for Emily. "Shall we?" He didn't look back as they crossed to the sliding glass doors, both shivering as the frigid air struck them. "I hate winter." Aiden adjusted his scarf to cut the wind. "I booked plane tickets for New York. You sure you're up for this?"

"I've managed to deal with meeting your grandmother, and you've met my mom. Time to meet your parents. It'll be fine."

"So you say now. Just wait, and you won't be so confident in that assessment. Anyway, we have reservations at the Park Hyatt, which is close to their place."

"We aren't staying with them?"

"Are you kidding?" He reached for her hand. "You'd be talking me down from the top of a tall building if we stayed with them. This way we can escape when they get too overbearing. You'll thank me later." He held open the café door. "Can I buy you lunch?"

"Tempting. Maybe a chicken wrap as we need to—" She sighed at the distinctive blare of an ambulance horn and the staccato bleat of a siren. "Aaaaand now we have to go back."

"I'll deal with the incoming. You take five and eat." He slid his wallet into her hand. "Order me a chicken wrap and an extra-large coffee. You know how I like it." He winked and dashed out the door, arriving in time to meet the paramedics. He snagged a stethoscope from one of the nurse's necks.

"Tara." He wheeled the gurney toward Trauma 1, a second-year resident appearing alongside it. "Stabilize the airway."

Phil called out for the correct sized tube as Aiden assessed the patient. The monitors started to beep.

"He's losing pressure. What should we do?" He looked at the young doctor across the table.

"Check for bleeding. Hang some blood." The young man issued orders to the nurse and began a search for injuries. "There." He placed a clamp, adding sutures under Aiden's watchful eye.

"Good. That'll hold until the surgeon can do a proper fix," Aiden said.

"Surgery will be down ASAP." Tara placed the receiver back in the cradle before snapping up the side of the gurney.

"Perfect. Monitor the patient until he's transferred," Aiden said to the resident as he snapped off his gloves.

"Who's this wonderful mystery woman?" Tara trailed after him as he left the trauma room.

"Umm, not sharing that quite yet." He yanked off his gown and tossed it all into the waste. "I'm taking five. Emily promised to bring me lunch."

A scowl appeared on Tara's face at the sight of Emily disappearing into the lounge. "You shared with her," she muttered.

Aiden pretended not to notice and grabbed the coat he'd tossed across the admissions desk. The nurse wouldn't be pleased when she clued in, but so far no one at work had picked up on the relationship. He considered it a major miracle.

"Thanks, Em." He gave her a kiss and sat across from her at the small break table. "I'm starving. You eat something?"

"I didn't leave the café until I had my wrap, or I'd never have eaten. I'll get the next trauma, but I'll sit with you for a minute." She sipped her coffee. "Tara seemed pretty interested in your new girlfriend. I thought we were keeping the whole thing quiet."

"She tried to invite herself to New York. What was I supposed to say? I told her my girlfriend wouldn't like it." He took a bite of his savory chicken wrap.

"She did?" Emily frowned. "Pretty forward of her. I can't say I love her putting the moves on you." She fiddled with her cup. "It's been weeks. I'm meeting your parents, and you've met my mom. Maybe we should open up about our relationship. We're doing pretty well as a couple. And it would keep Tara off you. What do you think?"

"You're jealous."

"Is that a no?" Emily raised her brows at him.

"You're right. We're doing great, so whenever you're ready, we can let people know."

Emily moved around the table, taking the cup from his hands and straddling his knees. Tipping her head down, she captured his lips and played with the hair at the nape of his neck. She smirked as they broke apart and she wiped her thumb across his lips, catching the faint bit of gloss she'd left there. "When we're back from New York. For now, I'll get out there and keep the wolves and pesky brunette nurses at bay. I'll see you in five."

She threw a smile over her shoulder as she left the lounge.

Aiden shook his head. That woman spelled deep, deep, trouble.

"I'm flying first class from now on. Crazy how fast we got out of that terminal." Emily crossed the room and gazed out over Central Park. "This is gorgeous."

"I did well, then." He moved behind her, wrapping his arms around her waist. "We should get ready. If we're late, I'll never hear the end of it."

Emily turned, stretching for a kiss. "They'll blame me for being a bad influence on their son."

"Everyone knows you're far too late to corrupt me." He swatted her on the bottom as she moved away and opened her suitcase.

"Can you help me with this?" Emily handed him a gold chain and swept aside her hair, which she'd left down tonight.

"You look amazing." Aiden moved close behind her, fastening it before nuzzling against the nape of her neck. He slid his arms around her waist.

"Thank you. You look pretty good too."

Their eyes met in the reflection from the mirror, a soft smile lingering on her lips.

"No time for that." She pushed him away and added simple earrings. "James and Caroline, right? I don't know why I'm so nervous."

"You'll do great, and you look beautiful. Relax, and don't let them intimidate you." He wrapped his arms around her and squeezed before helping her with her coat. "They'll try to scare you, but hold your ground."

"It feels like I'm going to the inquisition."

"Almost." Aiden linked his arm with hers for the short walk from the hotel to the restaurant.

"Handy. It's so close." She grinned as they approached the front doors. "After I'm grilled, we can get totaled and stumble back to the hotel."

"Or we can get totaled in the hotel bar. Less distance to stumble."

"Even better." Emily scanned the crowded establishment and the groups of diners that were waiting to be seated. "No waiting?"

"Are you kidding? ADA Hamilton never waits." He snickered after they were seated at a prime table. "And here we go."

Emily took in the distinguished couple proceeding toward them, casting a nervous glance at Aiden. He squeezed her hand as he rose to greet his parents.

"Aiden." Caroline Hamilton offered a cheek and accepted a kiss from her son. "You must be Emily."

"Aiden." His dad gave him a formal handshake, forgoing anything further. "Dr. Anderson."

As they all sat, a waiter descended to offer drinks and fill their water glasses.

"I hear you work with Aiden at the hospital." James sipped his Macallan.

Aiden was grateful for her presence. With Emily taking center stage, he didn't have to endure the criticism typical of these get-togethers. He wasn't sure why he even bothered, except for the fact they were his parents and he felt duty-bound to visit them. Enduring the meal always became an exercise in control.

"You should come to the apartment for a drink," James said at the end of dinner.

Aiden had expected the invitation and warned Emily beforehand he'd accept it. The main reason they'd even made the trip was to tell his parents about Savannah. However, a busy restaurant wasn't a suitable venue for the conversation.

Emily nodded and smiled on cue. "Sounds lovely."

Caroline looked pleased with her response. "The car's out front, you can ride with us."

In a few minutes they were on their way up to his parents' apartment overlooking Central Park. The magnificent home encompassed an entire floor with a 360-degree view of the city and large windows in the living room.

If it had been warmer, Aiden would have shown Emily the rooftop garden designated for the exclusive use of the Penthouse apartments.

"This is beautiful," Emily said as Caroline handed her a glass of wine.

"Thank you, we love it here. We bought it when we moved to New York, and the location is perfect. We'd always wanted Aiden with us, but with boarding school and his grandparents taking him to the Vineyard or sending him on trips over the summer, it never materialized."

Aiden hid the eye roll at the ridiculous notion that they'd ever intended for him to live in New York. It was typical for Caroline to make herself appear the perfect concerned mother when she rarely remembered his birthday. It seemed enough he could be paraded at the occasional event while his parents played happy family before shuttling him back to Chicago.

He stared over the park, the festive twinkle of lights reminding him of the approaching holidays. His parents would board a plane to the Caribbean or some place equally tropical as they had ever since he could remember, though he'd never been invited to join them.

"Aiden?" His father appeared beside him. "Join me in the office for a chat. Will you excuse us, ladies?" James led him into the room, where cheery flames flickered in the stone fireplace, casting a deceptive warmth over the room. He gestured to one of the plush chairs and poured cognac into crystal tumblers. "Emily's a beautiful woman. Are you planning on keeping her around for more than a couple months?" James asked. "Is there an announcement coming? You rarely introduce ladies to us."

"It's too early to be proposing."

"It's about time you settled down, though."

"Ah. So that's what this is about? You think I should marry her?" Aiden sighed and downed his drink.

"Couldn't hurt." His father shrugged. "She can hold her own. She's beautiful, stunning really, and intelligent. She'd be a suitable wife." James tipped back his glass before refilling both of their drinks.

"We've been dating less than two months, so let's hold off on booking the Plaza." Aiden took another swig of the liquor. "If it's okay with you, of course."

"Sarcasm. Shame. You were so well behaved at dinner."

"As were you," Aiden said. "Where's the Christmas trip to this year?"

"St. Bart's." A smug smile appeared. "You?"

"I'll make an appearance at Grandmother's house. Emily invited me to her mom's for Christmas dinner."

"Right." His father swirled the golden liquid in his glass. "Dave called. Seems you're keeping some interesting company."

Aiden's mind whirled at this oh-so-casual comment. "David Baxter?"

"His daughter's upset. Are you trying to ruin Harrison's chances for Governor?" His father's gaze settled on him.

"How would I do that?" His heart pounded, a sinking feeling settling on him. This conversation was headed in an ominous direction.

James stared into his glass, avoiding Aiden's gaze. "You've been seeing a particular young lady from Portland."

Aiden narrowed his eyes, his anger rising. "David called you?" He ran a hand through his hair. "You already know."

"Your grandfather informed me the minute you cleaned out the safe and headed to Canada with Dave's daughter." His father glowered. "Here's what's going to happen. You'll cut off all communication with that girl and go on with your life. Find a lovely wife and produce legitimate grandchildren. Your beautiful doctor will do quite nicely, don't you think?"

Aiden slammed his glass on the table, James wincing at the harsh clunk of crystal against antique wood. "Seriously?" He crossed his arms. "You expect me to marry a woman I've been dating for less than two months to make you happy? And by the way, *that* girl is your granddaughter."

"It doesn't matter." His father gave a dismissive wave. "There's no point in dredging up what happened when you were a kid. You'll damage Tiffany's reputation and sink the political career of a promising young man. Not to mention this could affect my career. I'm on track to become a judge."

"Unbelievable." Aiden shook his head. "Why would I give a shit about any of that?" He rose from his chair and strode halfway to the door before his father could get any further words out.

"Aiden, be reasonable—"

He spun and glared at his father. "You're unreasonable."

"If you won't do it for her, do it for me. You know they'll dig into my life, into all of our lives, and this could affect my chances."

"What have you ever done that would be worth me giving up my daughter? Nothing. That's what," he said as he turned toward the door.

"Aiden." His dad's stern voice echoed behind him before the slamming door muffled it.

Aiden stalked into the living room and scooped the wine glass from Emily's fingers. He snatched her handbag from the side table as he escorted her toward the door and they donned their coats.

"What's going on?" Caroline trailed behind them. "Aiden?"

"Merry Christmas, Mother. Have fun in St. Bart's. You know where I live if you ever wish to see me." He hit the elevator button firmly, not letting go of Emily, who kept throwing concerned looks his way. A slight shake of his head warned her not to ask.

"What did he say?" Caroline asked as they stepped into the elevator.

"Why don't you ask him what secrets he's keeping?" Aiden turned to look at her. "He always put his career before his own family. I'm not his damn puppet, and I refuse to let him control my life."

"What happened?" Emily brushed his cheek with her fingertips as the doors glided shut. "Aiden?"

"I'll tell you everything, but later."

"Okay." She gripped his hand as they exited onto the main street.

Aiden turned, holding tight to Emily as he strode down the sidewalk.

"Hey, slow down." She clutched his arm. "Aiden."

He came to an abrupt halt. "Sorry, sweetie." Leaning back against the stonework on the building, he stared up at the sky, blinking hard, fighting back the wave of anger and discouragement threatening to engulf him. A few soft flakes of snow settled on his cheeks. "It's a couple of blocks to the hotel. Are you okay to walk?"

"As long as we're not jogging." Emily moved in closer, resting her palms against his cheeks. "It'll be okay." She embraced him. "Let's get to the hotel, and we can talk."

Aiden nodded as her warm hand slipped into his. "Good idea." He peered at her high-heeled shoes. "I'll get a cab. Those aren't designed for icy New York streets."

"No. The fresh air will do us good, but we're not running a marathon."

His phone buzzed several times as they walked, but he hit decline.

"Who's that?"

"My father. I'm sure he wants to vent his displeasure."

"What happened? You were gone for less than ten minutes."

"He already knew. And he said nothing."

"About Savannah?"

"Yup. And get this. He's never told my mother, and he doesn't want her to know. And David Baxter called him."

"Tiffany's father?"

"She's been whining to Daddy. I've been ordered—not asked—to stop seeing Savannah. Don't want to ruin Tiffany's happiness or ruin Harrison's precious political career. And my father thinks he might run for the Supreme Court. If I don't do it for her, I owe it to him," he said. "As usual, it's about everyone else."

"They don't want to meet their granddaughter?"

"That discussion never came up. He doesn't care and never has. They spout crap all the time. A perfect example was my mother's asinine comment about me living with them. They've never said anything like that, ever."

Aiden held open the lobby door and ushered her inside, the warmth enveloping them. "I need a drink. They have a lounge upstairs." He pulled her into the elevator.

"Where does your happiness figure into this grand scheme?" Emily asked as they claimed a table and ordered drinks.

"My needs are trumped by the wishes of the politicians."

"What will you do?"

"Refuse to have anything to do with him? He puts himself first, every time. He's distanced himself from me."

Emily slid closer and curled her arm around his waist. "I'm sorry."

"No, I'm sorry, but I couldn't stand another minute of their lies. I'm clearly a huge expendable disappointment to my parents."

"And your mother?"

"She made her choice long ago. I was delusional to hope they'd want their granddaughter. They're more worried about moving the next step up the ladder."

The server set another round in front of them as Aiden tipped back the last of his first drink. "You know what's even worse? Tiffany's turned into one of them. She used to be amazing and now she's ... a cold, conniving bitch. Or a coward. Either way, she's trying to control me through her damn father. Un-fucking-believable. You think you know someone." He downed his drink, signaling for another.

Emily grasped his face between her hands. "Slow down. You're already half cut. There's no way I can carry you to bed."

"Mmm, I can carry you."

"Uh-huh, sure you can. Last call." She waved over the top of his glass as the server placed another drink on the table. "He's cut off." Emily signed the bill before sliding out of the booth and beckoning. "Let's go."

He downed his drink in one gulp. "Do we have to?"

"Yes, before it truly hits. Come on, mi amor, I'll tuck you into bed."

"Only if you're coming with me."

"Sure, let's go." Emily grasped his hand.

"Promisesssss." The word sounded funny to his ears, and things were growing fuzzy. Alcohol sang through his veins clouding his thoughts, but he didn't much care. It numbed the constant pain.

Emily kept her arm around him as he stumbled into the elevator and leaned against the side. He rested his head against the wall, too tired to hold it up.

"Aiden." Emily shook his arm. "Come on."

He forced his eyes open. Had he fallen asleep in the time it had taken to go from the lounge to their floor? Without protest, he allowed her to lead him to the room. He wobbled across the carpet and collapsed onto the bed.

"You'll be feeling it tomorrow. I'm surprised you made it back." She pulled off his shoes and propped him up to peel off his jacket and tie before she worked at the buttons of his shirt.

"Love it when a beautiful, sssexy lady undresses me." He flopped back as she unfastened his belt.

"Alright, Casanova, lift." Emily slid his pants off and held up the covers. "In."

The room spun and his eyelids grew heavy as she tucked the fluffy duvet around him. "Think I'm drunk."

"No thinking about it." She brushed her lips across his forehead. "Sleep it off, mi vida, and we'll talk in the morning."

Aiden rolled over and buried his head in the pillow. Seconds later, darkness descended.

Chapter 19

Savannah

Leanne's eyes widened at the sight of Savannah. "You look incredible." Leanne grabbed her arms and hopped up and down.

"Thanks." Savannah gave a little twirl. "Just a few things I got in Chicago."

It felt amazing. Her dad had been taken aback, but even the minor changes made her feel good in a way she hadn't in a long time. Her hair fell into waves and it looked soft, shiny, and sleek like Emily's. She had opted to wear her new boots, along with a pair of the curve-hugging jeans and the soft blue sweater Aiden had purchased for her. Every stitch she had on today came from her Chicago trip, right down to the lacy panties. Emily had even given her some makeup tips.

"Your hair. I love it. When did you do all this?"

"I have so much to tell you. It was incredible. The trip was so much fun." She pulled her friend down beside her on a bench in the middle of the bustling mall, which was crowded with last minute Christmas shoppers.

"So? What's he like?" Leanne asked. "I missed you so much, you were gone so long. Texting isn't the same."

"I missed you too, but you know, the snowstorm delayed flights. I liked staying with Aiden for the extra days. He lives in this cool Penthouse only a few blocks from downtown. You can see the lake and a huge park, and it has massive windows. I swear it was better than staying in a hotel. He gave me my own room, and Emily helped him decorate it. Anytime I visit, I get to stay there. The pictures I sent don't even come close to doing it justice."

"I'm jealous. Your father's a rich Chicago doctor. How lucky are you."

"He's amazing. Thanks for talking me into seeing him, and for encouraging the visit. I learned a ton about him, and Emily was awesome too. I was so nervous and worried, but it turned out great. They took me out because I wanted to buy a couple of Christmas gifts, which became this great shopping trip, and we went into all these crazy expensive stores."

"What was Emily like?"

"She's so beautiful. I swear she could be a model. But she's sweet, not all stuck up or bitchy. When she first walked in I worried. She looked so perfect, but she wasn't anything like I expected. She was super nice to me. Not in that phony, 'I'm the girlfriend, and I'll pretend to like you to impress the guy' way either."

"Oh, like how Marley's always complaining about her dad's girlfriends? She's terrified she's going to end up with a horrible step-monster."

Savannah giggled. "Not funny, I know. Poor Marley, her dad brings home the absolute worst women. I wish Aiden would marry Emily. That's how much I liked her. Aiden got called into work, and we spent the whole day together. It was so much fun. Seriously, I could deal with her as a stepmother. Not that it'll happen. They've only been dating a few weeks."

"What's he like? In real life, I mean? He visited me in the hospital, but outside of work he must be different."

"Yes and no. He really is as caring as he seems at work and being a doctor suits him. We got along great. He's amazing. It's hard to believe he's my dad, but I plan to see him again. I saw a ton of Chicago, and we were busy all the time. And we talked about all sorts of stuff."

"Did he tell you about your mother?"

"No. It's weird. He says he has to respect her decision and it's complicated. Whatever that means. I wish I knew who she was, but at least I have some answers. I know he wanted me. And I met his friend, Tom, so that was good."

"Maybe one day your mother will want to see you too. It's only been a few weeks."

"I've vowed to put it out of my mind." She lifted her shoulder. "Aiden is visiting his parents in New York. He might take to meet them."

"New York City? Your grandparents live there?"

"Uh-huh. His dad is some big-time lawyer and works for the District Attorney's office."

"I wish I could come with you. One trip, do you think Aiden would let me stay in Chicago with you? He has room, right?"

"Tons. Maybe once I know him better. I'd feel funny asking him now. He plans to phone my dad and see if he could join us to celebrate my birthday. He might bring Emily with him. Then you could see him again and meet her. You can tell me what you think."

"Then you'll see him again soon."

"I'll see what my dad says, but it shouldn't be a big deal because Aiden stays in a hotel when he visits."

Leanne nodded but seemed focused on something across the mall. "Look who it is. He's staring at you." Her friend turned toward her. "You've always been pretty, but now you look amazing. He's noticing."

Justin was with a group of his friends who seemed to be milling aimlessly and playing around, but the boy was definitely looking their way.

"He's coming over." Savannah giggled and ducked her head, not daring to look until a pair of sneakers came into view.

"Hey, Vanna."

She lifted her head, brushing a strand of hair back from her face as she gazed into beautiful blue eyes surrounded by thick dark lashes. "Hi, Justin."

"Haven't seen you around for a while."

"I went to Chicago for a few days."

"Cool. Umm ... Tony and I were heading to a movie. Did you and Leanne want to come with?"

Savannah shot a glance at Leanne, whose eyes widened. Her friend kicked Savannah's boot, a well-aimed but subtle jolt that brought her back to the present.

"We'd love to." Leanne batted her eyes.

"Okay, let's go."

"Yeah, let's." Leanne dragged Savannah to her feet, and they headed toward the theaters.

Tony chatted with Leanne as their two friends fell into step behind them.

Justin shuffled his feet along the tile floor. "What do you want to see?"

Once they'd chosen a movie and purchased snacks, they took seats at the back of the theater.

Savannah sat with Justin on her right, and Leanne on her left, with Tony seated on the far side of Leanne. Her heart thumped as she glanced at Justin, feeling like she'd died and gone to heaven. Their fingers touched as they shared popcorn, causing a tingle to her hand.

Part way through the movie, Justin set the empty popcorn bag on the floor, his gaze turning toward her briefly, a smile crossing his face.

She peeked out of the corner of her eye; Leanne motioned with her head, her eyes on Justin's hand, which was curled around his drink cup. Savannah wiped her damp palm on her pants, summoning enough nerve to rest her hand on the arm of the chair and leave it there.

The movie droned on, and she could barely keep her attention on the screen, almost jumping when his fingers enclosed hers and pulled her hand down to rest on his knee as Leanne's elbow dug into her side.

"Ooh."

"You okay?" Justin shot her a concerned look.

"Fine." She elbowed Leanne once Justin had turned his attention to the movie. She leaned toward him, rewarded as his arm slid around her shoulders. It wasn't terribly comfortable with the armrest digging into her side, but she wouldn't complain. This is what she'd dreamed about, and she leaned closer, the earthy scent of him tickling her nose.

"Wanna go for pizza?" Justin asked after the movie.

"Sure." Savannah smiled, studying the boy as he held out his hand. She took it, not so nervous now.

Tony and Leanne trailed behind them. She knew her friend wasn't wild about Tony, but she was being civil. Or quite friendly, now Savannah thought about it. She almost giggled when Tony held Leanne's hand and her friend batted her eyes at the boy.

It seemed Leanne liked him, though she'd never admitted it. Savannah figured she'd have fun later teasing her best friend about flirting with Tony.

The next two hours she spent laughing, playing arcade games, and eating pizza. Vanna couldn't remember the last time she'd had so much fun with school friends. Admittedly, she had withdrawn somewhat after her mom died. It had seemed wrong to have fun when her mom was resting in a box in the cold hard ground and her dad was crying himself to sleep.

"You're really pretty." Justin stared at her so intently she blushed, her attention coming back to the adorable boy in front of her.

"Thanks." Savannah looked at her feet, her face flushing at his attentions.

"Would you like to go out again?" Justin shuffled his feet. "Can I call you? Is that weird?"

"Yes. I mean, yes call me. It's not weird." She lifted her chin, immersing herself in his dreamy blue eyes.

"Give me your phone."

She passed him her mobile, smiling and batting her lashes flirtatiously like Leanne had with Tony.

His lovely lips curved upward, white teeth flashing as he tapped his number into the dinosaur electronic device. "There. Maybe Friday? We still have over a week off before we have to go back to school."

"Sure, sounds good."

To her surprise, he leaned in and kissed her on the cheek. "This was fun. I'm glad we ran into you and Leanne." He tilted his head. "We used to hang out all the time. What happened?"

Savannah shrugged. "You're always with Christina and her group. I thought you liked her."

"Oh. She's okay, but I'd rather be with you." He regarded her. "I'm not dating Christina. You know that, right?"

"I didn't. She's so perfect and pretty and everything."

"You're prettier, and nicer too. Will you go out with me again? Will it be okay with your dad?" He scuffed at the tile with one shoe. "I got the feeling your parents didn't want you dating, so I never asked. I like your dad, but he seems kind of ..." He shrugged and shoved his hands into his pockets.

"Overprotective?" She wrinkled her nose. "I'd like to go out again. My birthday's coming up. Maybe my dad will let me date. It's not fair if I have to wait another year."

"I had a good time, Vanna." He leaned in and kissed her cheek again. "I'll call you." After waving, he strode off with Tony at his side.

She and Leanne made their way onto the bus toward their houses.

"He asked me out again." Savannah giggled and bounced on her toes. "Justin asked me out."

"He barely took his eyes off of you the whole time. When are you seeing him again?"

"You should talk. What was that with Tony? I thought you didn't like him."

"He's not so bad. He's gotten cuter now he's matured, he was fun to hang with, and he took my phone number. Maybe we can double date."

They gave each other excited hugs before parting ways.

"See you Christmas Day for dinner." Leanne called over her shoulder.

Savannah waved, heading into the house, a wide smile on her face. Maybe, after all of this time, life was getting better. At least she hoped so.

Chapter 20

Aiden

AIDEN OPENED HIS EYES TO darkness, his mouth dry and pasty. He rolled, his stomach churning and rebelling against the exorbitant amount of alcohol he'd poured into it.

That wasn't how he'd pictured last night. Not even close. He'd wanted their first trip together to be romantic, not him getting drunk off his ass and her tucking him into bed like he was a child.

His head pounded and he stayed frozen, terrified to move. Vomiting on your girlfriend wasn't the way to get sympathy or win points. He spotted a glass of water on the bedside table and guzzled half of it before settling against the pillow.

"You okay?" Emily's soft hand brushed over his hair.

He tried to calm the rolling sea inside with several deep breaths. "Dunno, feel sick," he mumbled before bolting for the bathroom, barely making it to the toilet before he emptied his stomach contents. As he sank onto the cold tile floor, he held his pounding head in his hands, willing the waves of nausea to stop.

Emily crouched beside him and rubbed his back. "You're freezing. Come to bed."

"Not yet." He sank into the warm arms encircling him, relaxing as her lips touched his hair in a light caress.

"Let me get you a blanket."

"Don't go." He held her tighter, his breath hitching as his stomach cramped and twisted. "You might want to—" His entire body rebelled, and he hung over the porcelain again.

Emily didn't leave but stroked his back and offered him water to rinse his mouth. The upside of dating another doctor. The woman wasn't faint-hearted or squeamish.

"Back to bed." She helped him to his feet and tucked him in before joining him.

"Sorry, so not romantic."

"Don't worry about it. We both know it wasn't a great visit with your parents. Sleep. You can make it up to me tomorrow."

Aiden woke much later to the buzzing of his phone, the bright orange numbers on the bedside clock announcing it was 11:07. Other than his insistent phone, the room was silent and empty. He scrambled for the jacket draped over the chair, patting it down for his phone. By the time he fumbled it out of the pocket, it had lapsed into silence.

The display showed a Chicago area code, so not his father, but it wasn't Emily either. Maybe the woman was running for the hills. Why would she stick around after last night? She'd tucked him into bed. Twice. Like an errant child. Or an unruly teenage boy. *Stupid, stupid, stupid.*

The screen lit up, the same number appearing. "Hello?"

"Aiden?"

The familiar voice made his lip curl. She'd betrayed him. Yet again. "To what do I owe the honor?" *Conniving little rat.*

"What the hell were you thinking?"

"I could ask you the same question. Running to Daddy? Mature, really mature. What are you, five?"

"You talked to James."

"Ha. I stopped trying to talk to him long ago." He paced back and forth in front of the couch, sweeping his fingers through his hair. "I'm to pretend she doesn't exist? Did you know that James knew about her?"

Aiden suspected she possessed more of the facts than he did. She'd obviously whined to her father to have James coming down like a sledgehammer.

"Yes." Her guilt-filled voice carried down the line. "He talked to my father when they brought us home from Canada."

"Why didn't you tell me? All those years and never a word. Unbelievable." Had he been blinded by his love for Tiffany, or had she always been this person? Or maybe she'd changed under the constant pressure from David and Harrison. Whatever. He didn't like this insipid shell of a woman.

"I was ordered not to tell. You know how it was, Aiden."

"I trusted you. I'm such an idiot for ever thinking we were in it together. What else don't I know?" *A bad nightmare.* Wasn't that her take on their entire relationship? Had she ever loved him or just used him? He didn't know.

"We couldn't have taken care of her, Aiden. Giving her up was for the best."

"Yeah? Well, I'm not giving her up again."

"Please? For me?"

"Why would I do anything for you? What do I get out of this whole deal?"

"Aiden …"

"Right. I get nothing. Don't expect me to play along. I won't."

"At least quit parading her around Chicago. She was at Bloomingdale's with your little girlfriend."

"Stop being so damn condescending. Emily's a far better person than you'll ever be. Quit being a selfish …" *Bitch,* he finished, unable to say it out loud, even if she deserved the title. From the moment he'd walked into that gallery, it had been all about her. Her life. Her precious fiancé. He sucked for air. Maybe that's who she'd always been.

"Does she know? Who she is to you? That I'm her mother?"

"Emily?"

"No, the Queen of England."

"Yeah, so?" Aiden fought to keep his anger under control. Not only was she demanding things she had no right to demand, she was getting up in his personal business about his girlfriend. *Hell no.*

"You're serious about this one? This Emily woman?"

"Check your tone. It's hardly any of your business and pretty rich coming from Miss-I'm-So-Important-Because-I'm-Engaged-To-A-Senator. But don't you worry, princess, all your dirty little secrets are safe."

"I'd hoped you'd see reason. It'll affect your reputation too."

Aiden hated whiny, fake sounding women, and this pale, narcissistic version of Tiffany was not the woman he'd loved. "I don't give a shit what anybody thinks. We're not in high school. She's my daughter, she's amazing, and you're missing out. Anyway, like half the men in Chicago don't have bigger and far more interesting secrets."

"Harrison won't like it. He'll leave me if he finds out. I need to marry him, not ruin his career. Please, please stop seeing her."

"Quit being a doormat. If the guy loves you, he'll accept it. If not, then consider it a lucky escape. Who'd want to marry someone like that? Enough of this bullshit. We've nothing further to say to each other. Don't call, don't write, and do me a favor and decline any further invitations to my grandmother's house so I don't have to look at you."

"Daddy won't like it."

"Isn't that too fucking bad for Daddy. Quit being such a conniving, two-faced, self-centered, whiny little bitch." It felt good to let it out. It wasn't his usual style, but she'd been begging for it. "Stay away from me, from Savannah, and from Emily. We've managed to avoid each other for the past eight years, so another fifty should be easy."

The sniffle carried down the phone line, but he vowed not to cave to her crocodile tears or be tempted to feel sorry for her.

"How can you say that after all we meant to each other?"

"Meant. Past tense. You make me sick and angry as hell. How can you turn your back on your own daughter? After everything, I can't imagine what's going through your head." His hand curled tightly around his phone, and he wished he had something to punch. "Remember all those times you wished you knew?"

"It's different now. I have a fiancé, my own life, and including her would be too hard."

"What a weak, spineless ... You know what? I've wasted enough breath on you. Crawl back into your hole, whatever rock it's under."

Aiden disconnected and tossed his phone onto the bed, pacing and clutching his hair as he tried to breathe. Unbelievable. She tried to manipulate him by bringing up what they used to have? Like he'd bend to her demands when she was the one who'd destroyed everything?

The buzzing of his phone caught his attention. He dared a glance at the screen.

Text me when you revive. Love you.

The thought of Emily made him smile and drew him out of his anger. She never said she loved him and he wasn't sure how to take it. Did she? Even after last night, after meeting his parents and seeing the dark side of the Hamilton family?

I'm sort of alive. Where are you? Miss you.

After a moment of contemplation, he typed those words he'd vowed never to say to a woman, ever again.

I love you too.

No matter how inconvenient, it was the truth.

Bet you say that to all the girls.

A smile twitched at his lips, his heart lightening despite the ache thudding through his temples.

I definitely don't. Ever.

He stared at his last text, wishing he could take it back when the screen faded to black. For sure Emily would run now. He sucked in breath when the phone lit up, the small dots dancing in their tiny row.

Café Lorenzo on 5th. 1 pm.

It's a date.

Aiden hunched his shoulders against the chill wind whistling down the street as he hurried toward the restaurant, both looking forward to seeing Emily but also nervous about the brief text exchange. At least the short journey to the café gave him a chance to calm down after the conversation with Tiffany, who never failed to rile him.

He claimed a table, watching the people bustling by as he sipped a hot coffee.

"Hi, honey." Emily planted a kiss on his lips when she arrived loaded down with shopping bags. "You're looking better."

"Hard not to. Sorry, that was really stupid." He met her gaze, fighting the embarrassment flooding him. "I let my family get to me."

"No worries. It's not like you do it often." She winked. "You don't, right?"

"No." Aiden laughed. "Only around my father. He drives me insane. The trigger will be gone as our relationship is done. I refuse to let him bully me into neglecting Savannah. Bad enough he knew all these years and never said a word."

"And your mother?"

"Not like she wins the mother of the year award." He shrugged. "I don't understand my family."

"Neither do I." A faint smile crossed her face. "Damn, I like New York. Does that mean we won't visit again?"

"Sure. We just won't visit them." He reached across the table, appreciating her effort at lightening the mood. "Thank you for last night, and for being so understanding. Maybe James is finally right about something."

"What would that be?"

"You don't want to hear it."

"Oh, come on. You can't say something like that and not tell me."

"He's convinced I should marry you."

"Whoa, cowboy. Don't get ahead of yourself. It's only been a few weeks so perhaps we should give it another month or two."

"I told him to hold off booking the Country Club." He looked at the menu, desperate to change the subject. "What do you want for lunch?"

They both ordered and then sipped coffee while snowflakes danced against the café window.

"I bought Savannah's birthday present. You know how she admired my purse? I got her a similar one. I hope she likes it." She patted one of the bags on the seat beside her.

"She'll love it, but you didn't have to do that. You're spoiling my daughter."

"There's a difference between have to and want to. I enjoyed her visit. She's a great kid." Emily reached across the table to entwine her fingers with his. "Did you send her gift?"

He couldn't contain his smile. This woman was incredible. He'd dropped several major revelations onto her, and she'd accepted everything and welcomed his child into her life. He was in massive danger of falling hopelessly in love. "I'll need your help in choosing. It's the first birthday we've shared, so it needs to be special." He contemplated the wonderful woman across the table for a moment. "I'm worried."

"Why? She'll love anything you get her."

"I worry about upstaging Ross. He was great about the phone for Christmas, probably because I'll be paying for all the long distance calls, but I don't want to overdo it. The clothes, the phone, the hair, and we took her to that concert. I'm spoiling her."

"I see your point." Emily leaned back as the server delivered their food, then stole one of his fries. "What ideas did you have?"

"A new laptop? Or jewelry? I'm not sure what she wears, but perhaps a watch or earrings or a ring? Or an education fund?"

"You want to adopt me?" Emily laughed. "I have major student loans if you're interested."

Nope. I won't adopt you, but the marriage idea certainly had merits. As much as they'd joked about the idea, he was ready to commit to a woman, and Emily might just be the one.

"Ha ha, funny. You've spent time with her. What's appropriate?"

"They're all good ideas, but I'd go for jewelry. We can look this afternoon. The education fund would be a great graduation gift. How much were you thinking?"

"Enough to get her a degree and cover tuition and living expenses for a top university. Ross is worried how he'll pay for post-secondary."

Emily's eyes widened. "That's a ton of money." She flagged down the waitress and motioned to her coffee. "A refill, please."

"She's my daughter, not a waif off the street."

"True enough." She eyed him over the rim of her cup. "Did you ever doubt Vanna was yours? Like when Tiffany told you she was pregnant?"

"Not for a second. We were almost inseparable, and we were careful most of the time, but ..." He shrugged. "We were young and stupid, and it happened. I'm glad I did the DNA testing though, considering how crazy everyone's acting."

"There's no doubt she's Tiffany's daughter?" Emily waved a hand. "Never mind. The resemblance is uncanny." A soft smile appeared. "So no other children will appear in the future?"

"Not that I'm aware of." He winked. "No other ex-wives either."

Emily scrunched her nose, the corners of her mouth twitching. "Funny."

"Speaking of ex-wives, Tiffany called a couple of hours ago. She knows that you know, and it scares the crap out of her."

"I won't tell."

"I trust you." Aiden played with his spoon. "What made you stay?"

"What do you mean?"

"Last night. The pressure will get worse. I have a crazy controlling family, a psychotic ex-wife, a bonus surprise daughter, and I got stupid drunk over it all."

"Nobody's perfect." She linked their hands, brushing her thumb across his fingers. "I'm here because I care about you and Savannah. The rest is white noise, which I can handle. It shows great strength to resist the will of your family." She lifted one shoulder. "The drunk part doesn't concern me."

Aiden let out a long slow breath. "I'm glad you're here."

"Me too."

They'd just finished lunch when Aiden's phone rang. He answered with a deep sigh. "Mother."

"Where are you?"

"What does it matter?"

"Are you still in New York? You're not registered at the Plaza."

"What do you want?"

"Your father refuses to tell me what you two fought about. I wish you'd come to dinner tonight and talk it through."

"Absolutely not."

"Why don't you tell me? Please, Aiden, you're my son. Don't cut me out of your life."

"You can meet me for coffee, but don't bring him."

Two hours later, Aiden let his mother into the hotel suite, accepting a brief hug and a kiss on the cheek.

"Coffee?" At her nod, Aiden poured her a cup and motioned to the couch.

"Where's Emily?"

"It's best if we had a few minutes to talk privately."

"You shouldn't keep secrets from her."

"That's rich coming from you."

His mother sighed. "Tell me what's going on. Your father's been moody."

"Is he throwing a tantrum because he's not getting his way? So like him. He dumped me in boarding school and has ignored me for most of my life, yet he assumes he can order me around."

"You know how he is."

"Yup, I do. That's why I decline to visit. I don't even know why you two decided having a kid was a good idea."

Caroline frowned. "You make it sound like you were abandoned. You were safe at school or with your grandparents."

"Sure. The best babysitting money could buy." Aiden set his cup down. "You won't like what I have to tell you, but it's time you knew. You can yell at James later. You have a fifteen-year-old granddaughter. Her name is Savannah, and she lives in Portland."

"What?" Caroline's cup thumped against the table, hot coffee sloshing over the sides. "Where has she been all these years?"

"Grandfather arranged for her to be adopted, but she found me recently. James is worried about his career and ordered me to stop visiting her. That's what we're fighting about."

His mother stared at him. "Does this have anything to do with Tiffany Baxter? David's been calling."

He nodded. "James and David are concerned about Harrison's run for Governor. What I want doesn't matter. It's only about what's good for them. Let James disown me. I don't care. It's not like I ever see him."

"What about Tiffany? Doesn't it matter what she wants?"

"How do you know what she wants?" He scoffed. "Why should I care anyway? We've been divorced for years."

"Isn't it for the best—"

"No." A frisson of anger appeared. "Pick your side. See me or don't. It's up to you."

"Can I see a picture?" Caroline wiped a tear from her eye, and he almost swore it was real emotion. "Please?"

Aiden pulled an envelope from his bag. "You can have this."

Caroline pulled out the photo and took a long look. "She's gorgeous. My, she looks like Tiffany. What's she like?"

"She's sweet, and kind, and truly amazing. I had her visit me in Chicago. I don't know what else to say."

"I wish I could say I was surprised he kept this from me, but James and Thomas were both so secretive. I'm sorry, Aiden, but it was probably for the best." Caroline ran her fingertip across the photo, nodding as a deep frown marred her usually calm complexion. "I wish I could meet her."

"I could bring her to New York."

"Your father wouldn't like it. If he doesn't want you seeing her, he's not going to like me visiting."

"You're going to let him order you around?"

"He's my husband, and he's all I have."

Aiden felt a stab of pain. "You should go." He stood as she held the picture out to him.

When he didn't take it, she set it on the coffee table. It was disheartening to see her outright rejection of her granddaughter. This cold, unfeeling woman disgusted him. This virtual stranger he'd called his mother all these years had let him down for the last time.

"Don't be like this, Aiden."

"You make your choices, I make mine. It's to be expected that you'd let him keep you from your grandchild. You never wanted me either. Go back to your life, Caroline. I'll be fine. I've survived this long without you."

"That's all you have to say?" She rose to her feet.

"I won't ignore my child or choose anyone over her." Aiden held out her coat. "Please leave." Why bother getting angry? It wouldn't make any difference.

When she stretched to kiss his cheek, he stepped back and folded his arms across his chest. "Don't." He opened the door. "We're done."

Her eyes widened, but when he didn't move she stepped into the hallway, marching stiffly toward the elevators without looking back.

Aiden shut the door firmly behind her.

⁓≼

Aiden glanced at the imposing wooden front doors as he passed, circling around to the garage at the back of the mansion. It was time for the hard part. Or was it the rest of the hard part?

He clenched his hands around the steering wheel, dreading the conversation to come. This might be his last visit here.

"Just get it over with," he said under his breath before he headed in through the side door.

"Aiden. So nice of you to drop by for dinner." His grandmother's lilt carried down the hallway. "I didn't expect you until Christmas."

Aiden greeted his grandmother with his traditional peck on the cheek. "Gramma. How are you?"

"Fine. You look serious." Her hand brushed across his cheek, and she patted gently. "What's wrong?"

"Can we talk?"

"Always." She beckoned him into the library. "Pour me a martini?"

Aiden mixed her drink, setting it in front of her before pouring himself a double shot of Macallan.

"You went to New York, correct? How are your parents? " Grace took a delicate sip of her drink. "Mmm, perfect as usual."

Aiden shrugged and stared into his glass of amber liquid, swirling it before taking a long swallow.

"What's troubling my favorite grandson?"

Aiden lifted his eyes, seeing the concern reflected back at him. He'd usually make some crack such as 'I'm your only grandson' but today his spirit felt beaten. His heart ached with the knowledge his parents didn't give a damn about him or Savannah either. "I have something to say, but maybe you already know. Father hasn't called?"

Grace shook her head. "James called before your visit, but not since. What's going on?"

"You really don't know?"

She shook her head again.

"So much I need to tell you." Aiden let out a long slow breath. "I'm not sure where to start."

"At the beginning. I'm listening."

"Remember when I was fifteen and Grandfather and I had that big argument?"

"I worried about you. Thomas seemed to think you were mixed up in something bad, so we sent you to that summer program. You'd missed quite a few classes and skipped school. We didn't want you getting yourself in trouble."

Aiden almost snorted. It was a little too late to keep him out of trouble at that point.

Grace stared at him.

"You don't know what it was about?"

"No, aside from Thomas being angry and the fact there were numerous calls between to your father and to Tiffany's father. It seemed like she got herself into the same pot of hot water."

"You could say that. Tiffany was pregnant."

"What?" His grandmother sat ramrod straight. "Did you just say ...? Oh, my." She gaped at him.

"Your great-granddaughter is almost fifteen."

"How's this possible? I worried you'd gotten mixed up with a bad crowd and maybe into drugs. I didn't have the heart to know. But a baby?"

"They sent Tiffany to Portland. I was skipping and sneaking there to see her." He fiddled with his glass. "I took some money, and we tried to run away. We made it as far as Canada."

"Why is this coming up now?"

Aiden spent the next half hour telling her about meeting his daughter, the visits, the trip to New York, and the reception from his parents. He held nothing back.

"Oh, my boy." Grace wiped a tear from her cheek before squeezing his knee. "I wish I'd known. I'm disappointed."

Aiden's gut twisted at hearing those words from her lips. He always managed to disappoint his family and expecting support from any of them was clearly out of the question. He set his glass on the table and rose, unable to handle any further rejection. "I understand if you don't want anything to do with me, or her, or any of this."

"Please don't leave." She gripped his arm. "I'm not disappointed in you. It's what's been done to you, to Tiffany, and to that poor child. You were young, only a boy, and you made mistakes. Instead of supporting you, they fed you to the wolves. Even now. Not wanting to know their grandchild. Unimaginable."

She rubbed his cheeks with her thumbs like she had when he was young and he'd skinned his knees falling from his bike. It comforted him, making him feel less alone.

"I'm proud of you for not backing down. I should've been there for you, but I wasn't. I knew you were having a hard time, but I let Thomas discourage me from being involved." Grace smiled. "Next time she's in Chicago, you must bring her to see me."

"You want to meet her?"

"She's my great-granddaughter." She squeezed his hand. "You've always been the light of my life. I loved my husband, but he had his faults. Thomas was pigheaded and stubborn and your father took after him in many ways. Getting ahead, wanting to succeed, those were always the goals. When they moved to New York, I insisted they leave you in Illinois."

"What?" Confusion swept through him. "Why would you do that?"

"The boarding school in New York would have been so far away. Forgive me, but Caroline has always been a weak and selfish woman and too easily led by James. I wanted you close so you'd come for holidays. Aiden Grayson suggested you attend the same school as Tom and Thomas agreed."

"You wanted me here?"

"Your parents were busy with their dinner parties and political maneuvering, never bothering to come for holidays. They didn't put up enough of a fight. You may not remember, but even when they lived in Chicago, you often stayed with me."

"I remember." Aiden nodded. "I always wondered why they left me here. It was because of you?"

"I insisted. I'm sorry if it's upsetting, but I did it for you."

"I'm not upset. It makes sense. I often wonder why they bothered having me in the first place. They certainly have no interest in being my parents, and they have no interest in their granddaughter. You probably saved me from endless holidays stuck at school. They haven't made any sort of effort and I'm done trying."

Grace gave him a long searching look. "You aren't talking to them anymore?"

He shook his head. "Does that bother you?"

"It certainly does." She patted his hand. "But I understand why. I did my best. I wish you'd come to me." She studied him. "Why didn't you?"

"Fear. I have my regrets too, I wish I'd stood up to grandfather, but I didn't and they took her away. I won't let them scare me this time. I'm not fifteen anymore."

A twinge of resentment flowed through him. If he'd gone to his grandmother, they wouldn't have taken his baby girl away. He wouldn't have missed her birth and holding his precious daughter. The dull ache deep in his soul reminded him of all he'd lost the day he'd signed those damn papers.

Grace let out a long slow sigh. "I don't blame you for being scared. Thomas knew how to put on the pressure. He was a good man, but his priorities were off."

Aiden bit his lip. He'd never seen the softer side of Thomas Hamilton. His grandfather had never been affectionate or paid him much attention. After the events of that fall, Aiden avoided spending time with the man.

Grace leveled her gaze at him. "I suppose you have every right to be angry. They took a child away, but you were a child yourself. You weren't ready for that kind of responsibility. It's likely she would've been given up for adoption in any case."

"Maybe, but it should've been our choice, not the old boys club. With help, we could have taken care of her. Not like we didn't have the money. They never let me see her. I didn't get to say goodbye. No one cared. They sent me away, separated me from my friends, and destroyed everything I had with Tiffany. We can't even be in the same room."

"Chances are you wouldn't have stayed together. It's clear you've never forgiven any of them."

Aiden smothered a snort, holding back the contempt he felt for the lot of them. "Forgive them? Why should I? It's not like they care."

"They love you in their own way."

"They have a funny way of showing it." Aiden ran his fingers through his hair. "Do you really want to meet her?"

"Nothing could make me happier."

"She'd like that." He returned the squeeze his grandmother gave his hand, hoping Grace Hamilton would show some warmth and compassion to his daughter. He had so little family, and he needed to give her the opportunity to make it right.

Chapter 21

Savannah

On Christmas morning Savannah rose early and plugged in the tree lights before starting breakfast. She decided to make the traditional cinnamon buns. Her mom had made them every Christmas morning for years.

Her dad looked tired as he ambled into the kitchen two hours later. Savannah knew he'd had a restless night, and had been up several times. This was the second Christmas without her mother and it wasn't getting any easier. Despite his close friends, she knew he was lonely and missed her as much as Savannah did.

"Merry Christmas." Savannah poured him a coffee.

"Merry Christmas." Her dad smiled and gave her a hug and a kiss on her cheek before sitting at the table with his cup cradled in his hands. "Cinnamon buns? What time did you get up this morning?"

Savannah popped the newly risen buns into the hot oven. "A couple hours ago. I was craving them." She slumped into the seat across from him, a hot cup of cocoa in front of her. "I miss her, Daddy."

"Christmas isn't the same without her."

Savannah shook her head. "No, it's never going to be the same without Mom." She smiled through her tears. "Remember when I was little? I'd come in and wake you at three in the morning, wanting to open my presents. I couldn't wait, but she used to pull me into the bed and rub my back until I fell asleep again. You know I came in early just so I could cuddle in the middle of your bed?"

"We thought you were overexcited, which isn't unusual for kids. We loved every minute, and we missed it when you decided you were too old for that. You're growing up too fast. I wish I could keep you my little girl forever. One day you'll spread your wings and fly away."

"I'll always come back. You know that, don't you?"

"I hope so. I'll miss you when you leave for college."

"Maybe I should apply here."

"Don't choose to be near me. Pick the school that will provide a great education. They invented airplanes for a reason. I'm retired. We'll get together during the holidays. It'll be fine."

"What about the money? I won't get any scholarships with my grades." She wrapped her hand around her mug, pushing the mini marshmallows around with her fingertip. "It's been difficult without Mom." After that devastating night, things had fallen apart. Months had passed in a haze, and her schoolwork had suffered.

"I don't think it'll be an issue."

"Why the sudden change?" Savannah lifted her gaze to meet her dad's.

Ross heaved a sigh and stared into his coffee cup. "Improve your grades and when the time comes, we'll figure out finances. Your mom would want you get the best possible education. No sacrifices, Vanna."

A thick silence descended.

He sipped his coffee. "I talked to Aiden."

Savannah straightened and shifted forward in her chair. "About what?"

"I like him, that's no secret. He and I talked while you were in Chicago." A faint smile appeared. "You don't believe I'd send my daughter across the country without getting to know the man she's spending time with, do you? I'm a dad, I worry."

"Aiden's great."

"Mmmhmm. He's a responsible and accomplished young man. I respect his determination. Anyway, the visit went well, right?"

"I'm glad I took the chance."

"He answered your questions?"

"He still won't talk about my mom." She forced a smile. "At least I wasn't totally unwanted."

"Never, Savannah. I'll always be grateful for receiving the gift of a child, and I have Aiden to thank." Her dad brushed at his eyes. "Your mom was thrilled to have a daughter, and she loved watching you grow. She'd be proud of you."

Savannah circled the table and wrapped her arms around his shoulders.

"Aiden wants to come for your birthday, and he'd like to bring Emily. What do you think?"

"He asked you?" On one level she knew her dad needed to agree for Aiden to be at her party, but she assumed she'd be doing the asking.

"He respects there are boundaries, and he's worried about stepping over the line. I have to admit when you came home with the new clothes and the hair it concerned me. Like he was trying to change you. But you don't act different except for being happier."

"It's surface stuff. He bought me a coat because I was freezing, and I haven't been for a haircut in over a year. It was due."

Ross held up a hand. "I haven't been paying enough attention. Your mom took care of so much. I'm not upset Aiden took care of you as he did. I understand. He missed you growing up."

Savannah nodded. "He would've liked to be there. I couldn't imagine being responsible for a baby at fifteen. How do people do it?"

"Sometimes they don't have a choice. I suspect he'd have done okay and been good to you, even though he was only a kid himself." Ross cleared his throat. "So, your birthday. Would you like them to come?"

"Are you kidding? Yes."

"You can phone him later today and tell him, and I'd love to meet Emily. Sounds like she'll be around for a while."

"What?" Savannah brightened. "Are they getting married?"

"I've no idea. I didn't ask, but he wants me to meet her. Don't read anything into it."

"Oh." Savannah's shoulders sagged.

"Don't sound so disappointed." Her dad smiled for the first time this morning. "You like her that much?"

"Yes. I want him to marry her."

Ross laughed. "I hope you didn't tell him that."

She avoided his gaze.

Her dad's eyes widened. "You did not get into that conversation. Savannah?"

"I might have mentioned it. He wasn't mad, but he told me not to rush it."

"The man has patience but you didn't inherit that trait, did you?" Her dad shook his head. "How about we open presents?"

Savannah opened the new journal her dad had bought her for Christmas and tapped her pencil on the page. She ran a fingertips over the Kate Spade handbag she placed close by.

The brand new phone from Aiden buzzed and a text notification appeared. The attached image of Emily in her elegant cocktail dress and Aiden in his dark, expensive looking suit brought a smile to the surface. They looked perfect together. She scrolled through her contacts and found Aiden's number.

"Savannah, hi."

"How's the party?" It sounded lively judging by the noise in the background. "You still at your grandmother's house?"

"We're at Emily's mother's house now, and her sisters and her niece are here. How was your dinner?"

"Good." She picked at a nail. "Christmas isn't the same without Mom."

"I'm sorry, sweetie. Want to talk about it?"

The voices and music faded as a door clicked closed.

"I'll get used to it. Thanks again for all the gift cards. I can't wait to see you on my birthday."

"I'm looking forward to it. Emily says hi and Merry Christmas."

"I feel bad, she gave me such amazing presents, and I can't do the same for her."

"Don't. She understands and worked hard for her money when she was a teenager. That's how she is."

She bit her tongue, not wanting to reiterate her wish he'd marry Emily. "Did you tell your family about me?" The silence made her heart sink.

"I have, actually," he said, "but I wanted to talk to you in person."

"Oh." A solitary tear dribbled down her cheek.

"I'm sorry." He sighed. "If it makes you feel any better, my parents barely want to see me. I have some good news, though. Your great-grandmother wants to meet you."

"She does?" Her mood brightened.

"She insists I bring you to her house, which is where I spent a lot of time as a kid." He snickered. "We had to explain selfies to Gramma Grace. Did Em send you photos?"

"She sent a bunch."

"Good. Gramma Grace is excited about having a great-granddaughter. Do you think your dad would let you visit during exam break in January?"

"Maybe. I'd like to come out. I'm sad your parents don't want to meet me, though I'm happy about meeting Gramma Grace."

"Please don't take my parents' decision personally."

"It feels personal."

"Believe me, it's not. It's about them, as usual." His voice softened. "You're great, Savannah. Don't let anyone tell you otherwise. I'm thankful you had the chance to grow up in a normal family, not my messed up excuse for one."

Savannah frowned. Aiden seemed to have everything, but appearances were deceiving. His childhood had been far from normal. Maybe he was right about his parents.

"You still there?"

"Yes." Savannah glanced at her closed door. "Can I tell you something? But you can't tell my dad."

"Of course."

She twisted her hair around a fingertip. "This boy I like asked me out. I said yes."

"What's his name?"

"Justin. I've known him for years. He's not my boyfriend or anything, it's just a date."

"You excited? Or nervous?"

"Both. I can't tell my dad because he doesn't want me to date until I'm sixteen. It's embarrassing. I want to hang out with Justin over the school break. Is it wrong to keep it a secret?"

"I'm not sure I'm the best person to ask about keeping secrets." Aiden gave a low laugh. "Hmm. Ross is bound to notice if you dress up and Justin arrives at the house. And don't even think about crawling out the window."

Savannah giggled. "That would've been a good idea, but I promise I won't. It'll be a double date with Leanne and Tony. I'll tell him I'm hanging out with friends."

"That seems true enough. Is Justin from your school? He's the same age as you, right?"

"He's fifteen. Why?"

"This may sound overprotective but stay away from the older guys. Especially since you haven't dated before. It's a recipe for trouble."

"Sounds like you speak from experience."

"Well, a couple of girls I know got into those kinds of relationships and they didn't end well."

"Like an older guy would even be interested in me." Savannah rolled her eyes. "They wouldn't give me a second glance."

"Uh, wrong. Remember the day you came to see me at the hospital? How you felt so uncomfortable around those residents?"

She closed her eyes and shivered. "Yes."

"Those guys are all mid-twenties. I recognized the looks, and I could tell what they were thinking. Don't kid yourself, Savannah. You're a beautiful girl. Men will try to sweet talk you if they get the chance. Don't fall for it, listen to your instincts, and if it doesn't feel right, then it's not."

"You think those guys were …?"

"Don't underestimate yourself. Any guy would be lucky to have you."

She had mixed feelings about what he'd said, but it made her feel better. "I thought Justin was interested in this other girl, Christina. But he said he knew my dad wouldn't let me date, so he waited. I've known him since elementary school."

"I'm sure you'll have fun. Try to talk to your dad about dating. The longer you wait, the harder it will be to come clean."

"My mother was about the same age as you, right?"

"I'm only a few months older than her." Aiden sighed. "Don't make the same choices, Vanna. Promise you'll be careful, and don't rush into a relationship. You only get to be young once."

"I promise." Savannah smiled to herself. "I should let you get back to Emily. Good night."

"Night, honey. Sleep well."

Savannah rolled onto her back and stared at the ceiling, her phone resting on her belly. She'd created a rosy picture in her mind of how it would be with the welcoming arms of her long lost family. Now it was all fading away. No matter, she supposed. She had Aiden and he'd brought Emily into her life. For now, that would be enough. She'd be grateful for what she'd received.

Savannah fastened the strap of the new suit she'd purchased with one of her gift cards. Excitement flowed through her. Both Aiden and Emily had made the trip to Portland to attend the party her dad arranged at the indoor sports complex.

"Justin will flip out when he sees you in that." Her friend Rachel giggled and pointed at the candy pink bathing suit. "Let's go already."

Savannah shot a nervous look toward Emily. Surely the woman knew she was dating Justin? "See you out there?"

"You girls go." Emily motioned to the door as she stowed her bag in her locker. "I'll be out in a minute."

Savannah joined her group and they headed onto the pool deck.

Justin and Tony were already there, along with two other classmates who hadn't been invited to the party.

"Guys. Ten o'clock," the one boy whispered. They all turned as if one unit and gawked at the dark-haired beauty as she strolled across the deck. "Wow."

Savannah bowed her head, a hot flush creeping into her cheeks. "That's Emily," she muttered to Justin.

"Subtle." Rachel rolled her eyes and turned her back on the teenage boys.

"Crap." Tony dipped his head. "She looks different with her hair up." He looked at Aiden.

It appeared Emily hadn't taken any notice of the stir her appearance had created. She draped her towel over the back of a chair and looped an arm around her boyfriend's neck, stretching to plant a kiss on his lips.

Aiden's brow rose and a grin twitched at the corner of his lips as he returned Emily's kiss and slipped an arm around his girlfriend's waist before turning to speak to Ross.

Savannah laughed at the boys' expressions. "Caught in the act."

"So immature." Leanne tossed her hair over her shoulder. "It's like they've never seen a woman in a bikini."

Tony leaned in. "She's hot. Don't deny it."

Leanne huffed and stalked toward the pool as the boys returned to play fighting and horsing around.

Justin held his hand out to Savannah. "Ready to go down the big slide?" He smiled. "You look pretty."

"You don't look so bad yourself." Savannah blushed as she took his hand and graced him with her sweetest smile. It had taken countless hours in the swim shop to pick the adorable bikini and she was thrilled Justin had noticed. "Let's go."

Everyone dispersed, and soon they were all racing down the various slides and playing in the many pools.

Some of the tension drained from her body. Aside from Leanne, she hadn't told any of her friends the full story. Her friends understood she'd been adopted, but she'd avoided revealing that she'd found her father. The emotions were overwhelming, and she wasn't entirely sure her friends would grasp the significance of her discovery.

"Go again?" Justin grabbed her hand as they crawled out of the pool for the millionth time.

"Let's take a breather. My legs ache from climbing all those stairs." She linked their fingers and pulled him toward one of the quieter pools.

They located a quiet place to sit on the edge of one of the pools, watching the young kids play on the toddler slide.

Savannah glanced at their table. Aiden and Ross appeared to be deep in conversation, which piqued her interest. As if they knew she was staring, they looked over at her and Justin, although the attention seemed to be directed at Justin.

She smiled and waved before turning her attention back to her boyfriend.

"Who is Aiden? You don't have a brother, and he looks far too young to be your uncle." Justin grinned. "He just gave me the *I'm watching you and I know where you live* look."

She giggled. "What?"

"Like when you pick up a girl for a date, and their dad does the Jedi-mind trick and sends mental warnings? That *you'd better be good around my daughter* look."

"That only happens in the movies." Savannah squeezed his hand even as she directed her gaze toward Aiden.

"Nope, it's real." Justin poked her side.

As if sensing their gazes, Aiden looked their way and smiled.

"So?"

"He's my father." Savannah peeked at Justin.

"He's what?" His eyes widened, and he turned to look at Aiden. "Like for real?"

"You know I'm adopted, right?"

"Yeah, but I never really think about it. It's never been a deal to me."

"I wish everyone felt that way." Savannah twirled a lock of hair around her fingertip. Her Mom and Dad were considered old compared to the other kids' parents and she'd be teased about it during the early grades. One boy made her cry when he'd said they weren't her real parents. "Remember the day in first grade and that boy …? What was his name?"

"Randall." Justin flushed.

"I'll never forget your heroic rescue." She grinned and reached for his hand. "He teased me and pulled my pigtails but you saved me. Whatever happened to him, anyway?"

"Juvie. He robbed a liquor store."

"No way. I guess I shouldn't be surprised. Randall was horrible and nasty all through elementary. He used to spit at the girls on the bus."

"Gross." Justin shuddered. "Why didn't you tell me you found your father? How did it happen?"

She swished her feet through the water. "I found him on our trip to Chicago."

"I knew there was something going on. You and Leanne are on about the trip every minute. I thought you two had some sort of weird crush on your doctor."

"Ha ha, no. Not even close." She peered at him. "I wasn't ready to talk about it. I didn't even think that I'd continue to see him."

"It's a big deal, so I get it."

"Aiden lives on the other side of the country, so it's a long flight. I don't know how often I can go to Chicago, but my dad's okay with me seeing him."

"How about your mother?" Justin rubbed her hand. "Did you find her?"

"She doesn't want to see me," Savannah turned her head away to hide her misty eyes. "She decided not to be involved, so it's just Aiden."

"I'm sorry. I know you've wondered about her."

"You did?" Even though Savannah had known Justin for a long time, she didn't think he'd paid that much attention.

"Yeah, I remembered." A flush of red crept into his cheeks. "He's really your father? Crazy."

"It is, right?" Savannah's gaze wandered to Aiden and Ross. The two men laughed occasionally, but for the most part, they seemed serious. Were they discussing her? "Ready for another trip down the slide?"

Justin rose and caught her hand, pulling her to her feet. "Yup. Let's go."

By dinner, the entire group was starving. They piled into her dad's car and Aiden's rental and descended on her favorite pizza place. Before she knew it, everyone was saying goodbye and heading home.

"Walk me out?" Justin checked his phone. "My dad's here."

"Sure." She linked their hands. "Thanks for coming. I had fun."

"Me too." He flashed her one of his adorable grins before he pulled out a wrapped box. "I have something for you."

"You already gave me a present."

"This one I wanted to give you when we were alone. It's a little scary, having both your dad and Aiden watching me. Especially Aiden. He looks like he works out. A lot."

Savannah laughed. "You don't need to be scared of him."

"Oh, I have the feeling if I did anything he didn't like, I might need to be more than a little afraid. He seems protective."

"He's my father, but I doubt he would hurt you." She poked him in the ribs. "Unless you deserved it, of course."

He rolled his eyes. "Ha ha, so funny." He nodded toward the box in her hands. "Open it."

Savannah ripped off the paper and opened the box. "The earrings." She threw her arms around Justin, rewarding him with a warm hug before tipping her head and pressing her lips to his. A tingling sensation ran right down to her toes and she sank against him. Her cheeks flushed as they finally broke apart. Savannah buried her face against his chest, inhaling deeply as he hugged her.

"Happy Birthday, Vanna." Justin planted another kiss on her. "My dad's here so I have to go, but I'll see you at school on Monday."

"Night, Justin." A soft smile emerged as he bounded out the door, turning to give her a small wave. Savannah savored the moment, running a fingertip over her lips before she went inside.

Aiden wrapped her in a warm embrace. "Did you have fun?"

"Yes." Savannah kissed his cheek.

"Tomorrow we're taking you for lunch. You get to pick the place." He grinned and whispered, "You should invite Justin."

Her eyes widened. "No."

"Your choice." He winked and looped an arm around her waist. "We have something for you." Aiden motioned for her to sit in the chair beside Emily before pulling a beautifully wrapped box decorated with a delicate bow from his bag.

The short message in the enclosed card was heartfelt and made her feel even more special. She tugged at the ribbon and peeled away the paper, recognizing the signature blue box. Nestled inside was a shiny heart glittering with tiny diamonds. Her heart thumped and the tears rushed to her eyes as she dangled the delicate pendant by its chain.

"I love it." She sprang out of her chair, wrapping her arms around his neck. "I've never had anything like this. It's so beautiful."

"Let's put it on," he said.

She handed him the pendant and held up her hair, allowing him to secure it around her neck. "How does it look?"

Emily smiled. "It suits you."

"Is it real?"

"Diamonds set in platinum," Aiden said.

"It's gorgeous." One hand rose to touch the necklace as she blinked back the tears.

"One more thing." Aiden handed her another envelope.

Savannah stared at it for a moment before breaking the seal. Her breath caught in her chest as she read the card.

My Dearest Savannah,

I look forward to meeting you on your next visit to Chicago. I couldn't be there for your birthday, but I have a special gift for you.

Education is very important, and I wish to support you in every endeavor.

Happy Birthday, my dear.

Love, Gramma Grace.

Tears slipped down her face, the joy in her heart overflowing as she held the small card to her chest. Even though Aiden had shared the news that her great-grandmother wanted to meet her, she'd barely dared hope it was true. Now she had irrefutable proof.

She unfolded the fancy paper included inside, her eyes widening. "Are you kidding?" Savannah bounced on her toes. "Seriously, Aiden?" Her gaze cut towards her dad and then she read it again. "My great-grandmother wants to pay for college?"

"Gramma Grace didn't have the opportunity to continue her education after high school." Aiden looped an arm around her. "She wants to ensure the future generations have the chance. You'll have to work hard in all your classes, but you can go to any university you choose once you graduate high school."

"Wow. Daddy, you knew about this?"

"Aiden and I discussed it." Ross nodded. "It's a great gift, Savannah. You can do anything you want."

"I should thank Gramma Grace."

Aiden pulled out his phone and dialed. "Hi … yes, she's here now." He held the phone toward her.

Savannah hesitated only for a moment before accepting it. "Hello?"

"Savannah, how are you, my dear?"

She pressed a hand to her chest, tongue-tied as she gasped for air.

"Happy birthday."

Savannah bowed her head, clutching the phone in her trembling fingers. "I don't know what to say, except thank you for the education fund. It means so much."

"Next time you're in Chicago, Aiden will bring you for a visit."

"I can't wait."

"If you ever need anything, please call. Aiden will give you my number."

"I will … Gramma." The word slipped out naturally and felt amazing. She'd never had a grandparent.

"Happy Birthday, sweetie."

Savannah accepted a tissue from Aiden as she returned his phone. This had turned out to be one of the best birthdays ever. She clung to Aiden for a long time before pulling away with a tearful smile. No further words were needed. Surely, he read exactly how she felt. He understood how important meeting his family was, and the acceptance from even one of them was huge.

She hugged her dad. "Thank you, Daddy. I love you so much."

Ross pressed a kiss to the top of her head. "I love you, my sweet girl."

This day had exceeded her expectations and felt like a turning point. She would forever be grateful that her dad had not only allowed, but encouraged Aiden to be present in her life.

Chapter 22

Aiden

Aiden helped Ross load the gifts into the car before hugging Savannah one final time. "Happy Birthday. I love you."

"I love you too." Savannah seemed about to burst into tears, so he planted a kiss on her cheek and opened the car door so she could settle into the front seat.

"Good night, Ross." The two men shook hands, and then the man pulled him into a long hug.

"Thanks for making this such a great day for Vanna," Ross said, patting Aiden's back. "It means the world to her."

"I appreciated the invitation." He blinked hard.

Perhaps the adoption had been for the best. As much as he wished he'd raised Savannah, Aiden questioned the negative influence of James and his grandfather. Even worse was how David Baxter would have treated this sweet and lovely girl.

"I'm ready for sleep." Emily sighed and sank into the passenger seat of the rental car before resting her hand on his knee.

"Thanks for being here." He kissed her fingers before returning them to his thigh. "How great was that? I celebrated my daughter's birthday."

She squeezed lightly. "She's a special girl, Aiden. Thank you for including me."

Once they'd arrived at their hotel, he propped himself against the pillows on the bed and stared at the television, finding it impossible to engage. The day had been emotionally draining.

The sight of Emily as she wandered out of the bathroom drew his attention. Aiden eyed the slim legs peeking from under the hem of the shirt she'd borrowed from his bag. It fell just above mid-thigh, and she looked so damn sexy, he could scarcely keep his eyes off of her.

A coquettish smile crossed her face. "Like what you see?" She exaggerated the sway of her hips as she organized her clothes.

"Always."

She scanned him from head to toe. "Me too."

A shiver of anticipation ran through him. The flirty smile caused a flicker of desire. "You almost done?"

"I need to rinse and hang my swimsuit." She dangled the tiny bikini, waving it gently.

That little suit had sent the teenage boys in a hormonal uproar. For some reason, possessiveness gripped him, although it was unlike him to be jealous when it came to girlfriends. That incredibly sexy scrap of deep blue fabric looked amazing against her honey-dipped skin.

"Aiden?" Emily stared at him, her brow rising.

"Hmmm?" Aiden met her gaze. "Sorry, drifted off there for a second."

"I noticed." She smirked as she propped a leg on the chair, rubbing in her lotion. "The call to Grace was a great ending to the day."

"I thought so. Vanna has been anxious about meeting my family, and Gramma wanted to wish her Happy Birthday."

Emily nodded as she joined him on the bed.

"I thought my grandmother would lose it when I first told her about Savannah, but she's been supportive. I didn't realize how much Savannah wanted it, and having at least one of my family members accept her is a big deal."

"Most families would be loving and accepting. I can't fathom your parents turning away their only grandchild. How could they reject that sweet girl without even bothering to meet her?"

"Why do you think I've cut them out of my life? They're toxic." Aiden tucked a strand of her long dark hair behind her ear.

This amazing woman always managed to get him talking. Emily had found a way to skirt around his outer guard and had begun chipping away at his protective wall. Everything screamed caution and to protect his heart, but this woman captivated him.

"What did Ross say about the gift from Gramma Grace?"

"Ross seems grateful. Paying for college worried him."

"Savannah's reaction said it all. It's amazing your grandmother offered to pay for her education."

"She's thrilled to have a great-granddaughter. I'm sure she figured it would never happen at the rate I'm going. I planned to provide the tuition, but Gramma insisted. It makes her happy, so why argue the point?"

"Why would you?"

Why indeed? His grandmother had stepped up in an unanticipated way. Grace had supported him over the years, but she'd never let on how much she'd endured in the process. During his teenage years, he'd felt alone much of the time, assuming she pitied him.

He felt closer to his grandmother now than ever before. To find out the deep love she had for him was overwhelming as she tended to hide her emotions. With his grandfather gone, they'd reconnected, and he'd learned much about her. Her unwavering support meant everything.

"What else did Ross say?" Emily brushed her fingers over his hands, a small intimate touch that made his heart leap. "You two were in a deep discussion."

Aiden sighed. "James is causing trouble." His family was intent on making everything difficult.

"What?" Emily's eyes widened. "Why?"

"I didn't do what he wanted, so he's attempting to intimidate Ross."

"How?"

His phone lit up and vibrated across the nightstand. "Speak of the devil." He steeled himself for the exchange before answering. "That was quick. Your little watchdogs have a tail on me?"

"Watchdogs?" Emily mouthed.

He shook his head and stepped into the bathroom, leaving the door slightly ajar. He trusted Emily, but some things she probably didn't want to know.

"What are you talking about?"

The overly calm tone of his father's voice told Aiden he was on point. "Don't pretend you don't know. Call them off, or I go public."

"You wouldn't do that to your own father." The man's voice carried a phoney hurt tone. "Besides, you don't have anything on me or David. You're bluffing."

"You want to call me on that?" Aiden ignored the blatant attempt at manipulation. "Two can play, so back the fuck off. It's easy to feed anonymous information to the press. I'll sink your boy's ship so fast he won't have time for his life jacket."

"Like what?"

"Playing dumb doesn't suit you. There are plenty of skeletons in Harrison's closet. He wouldn't want all those potential voters to learn his dirty little secrets. Leave us alone. That means all of you, or I'll hang you out to dry and your so-called friends with you."

"Hmmm, you missed your calling. I'd have loved to see you argue a case in a courtroom. Ruthless. Exactly what a true Hamilton should be." His father sounded strangely proud. "Have your precious little princess but be discreet. Nobody is to know about her mother."

"My daughter's better off without that woman in her life."

"I never knew you were into bullying women and making them cry."

"She got what she deserved." What fairy tale Tiffany had told David about their exchange on the phone? "Do we understand each other?"

"Never knew you had this in you," he said. "Why'd you tell Caroline?"

"Perhaps because she has a grandchild she knew nothing about? It's sickening how you keep your wife in the dark about everything. Even worse, she allows it. Whatever. I don't need her or you. Are we done?"

"I suspect we are." James sighed. "It didn't have to be like this."

"Oh? If I'd done what you said like a good little boy, would it be okay? Are you suggesting a cozy group hug?" This release was cathartic after holding in his resentment for so long. "You expect my loyalty? For me to do the same thing to my own child?"

"Don't be melodramatic."

"I'm not a fifteen-year-old boy you can bully. Oh, wait. You didn't bully me. You had your daddy do it for you. You're a fucking coward."

The ugly truth. His father was a bully, coward, philanderer, and borderline criminal. A low life who left his only son to endure the darkest and most painful moments of his life alone.

Aiden hit disconnect and sank onto the side of the tub. James might retaliate, but the calculated risk was worth it. This time he wouldn't allow anyone to interfere. His daughter was too precious.

The way Emily looked at him when he emerged from the bathroom made him shiver.

"How much did you hear?" This woman was someone he wanted in his life, so she might as well see the good, bad, and ugly right now. If he were to lose her, it would be easier on his heart if she left now. "Emily?"

She patted the bed beside her. "Who in the hell are you? Are you blackmailing your own father?"

Aiden sat beside her and rested his hands on her thighs, rubbing gently. "Does it bother you?"

"It depends." She tilted her head. "Are we getting serious? It feels serious."

Aiden gazed into her eyes. "We are, but …" He dragged in a halting breath, afraid of what they had breaking into pieces. Maybe seeing this side of him scared her.

She leaned toward him, cupping his face between her palms. "Let me in, Aiden."

He swayed, her warm touch drawing him in. This fleeting moment of shared intimacy should be savored. It had been forever since he allowed himself to grow this close to a woman and he craved more. He brushed her lips with his, longing to disappear into this moment and hold onto her forever. "I don't want to lose you."

"You won't."

"What if …" He wrapped his arms around her. "This could get messy. What if you don't like this side of me?"

"Why are you doing it? Maybe I can help." She rubbed his bare back.

Should he take the chance? The final breakup with Tiffany had taken its toll. Allowing Emily in required a fortitude he struggled to maintain. The fear she'd rip open his hidden scars always lingered.

"James tried to cut me out of my daughter's life by threatening Ross. Ross told him to go to hell, but he has little power against James. I know things that would damage a lot of high-profile people."

"And?" Emily drew him closer.

"We made a deal. He stays out of my life and away from everyone in it, or I leak something to the press."

"You're protecting Ross and Savannah?"

He shrugged. "I can't let him get away with this low life behavior."

"So this is the dark side?" Her voice carried an inflection he couldn't identify. "How do you know this damaging stuff?"

"I spent a lot of time at my grandparents' house. Harrison was only two years ahead of me at university. I can't tell you exactly what I know, because—"

She pressed a fingertip against his lips. "Keep your part of the bargain."

"You're okay with this?"

"If this is how you have to deal with James, then who am I to argue? You're a papa bear protecting your cub. I respect that."

Aiden inhaled, the tension draining from his tense muscles. "I wouldn't survive losing her again."

"It's sexy," she whispered in his ear. "A man who has a backbone and isn't afraid to stand up and do what he needs to do to protect his daughter. Don't stop." The way she said those words and looked at him set him on fire.

"You're amazing." He claimed her lips, the kisses burning hot and fierce as desire flooded his body.

The rush rose from his toes. Maybe he'd found someone he could trust, open up to, and she wouldn't judge. Maybe she'd even accept his imperfections. Finally, he found his perfect woman.

~

A few weeks later, Aiden sat in a coffee shop, waiting for Alex to appear. He spun his coffee cup, trying to calm the nerves. Tom was right. The time had come to allow those closest to him in on the secret.

Alex finally ambled in the door, looking worn out and rubbing her large belly. "Oh, honey, I'm sorry. Getting out the door is a challenge these days." Her words came out between puffs of air.

"You okay?" Aiden pulled out a chair and motioned for her to sit. "You sound like you ran the quarter-mile." He grinned

A rueful smile appeared as Alex leaned back. "Nope. This little guy is crammed in so tight I have no room to even breathe. I pee every five minutes, I can't see my feet or tie my shoes due to my humongous belly, and I can't sleep. Joel doesn't either, because I take up the whole damn bed. Whoever said pregnancy was joyful must have been delusional or a man. This doesn't feel joyous." She wheezed in air and closed her eyes. "I'm ranting. That's another thing. I swing from weepy to being so grouchy, I can't even stand myself."

Aiden's grin widened. "You only have a few more weeks, and you look beautiful."

"Liar." She snorted. "I look like a beached whale and barely squeezed through the door. Good thing you didn't get a booth. I'd never have fit."

He took in her sparkling blue eyes, lush dark hair, and glowing skin. "You look amazing. Admit it. You're thrilled."

A smile erupted, the glow of true happiness spreading across her features. "It's exciting and miraculous. We tried for so long, and then boom, it happened. I can't wait to meet our son."

"It's what you've always wanted; the husband, the house, and the babies."

Her smile faded. "You'll have it someday. The right woman is out there and waiting for you. Maybe you've already met her. Emily's great but …"

He groaned. Here came the 'give her another chance' speech.

"I don't understand why you let Tiffany go. Kick Harrison's ass to the curb and take her back."

He rolled his eyes. "Has it ever occurred to you I don't want her back?"

"Stubborn man." She shook her head. "I'll never understand the divorce. Anyway, there's something else I needed to talk to you about."

"What's that?"

"Joel and I have discussed guardians for our baby. We're close to you, but also to Tiffany. It's an impossible decision." She stared into her teacup. "This is hard."

"Just say it."

Her gaze lifted to his. "We're naming Tiffany. She's engaged and can provide a good home. I'm not sure you'd want to take it on."

"Oh." Disappointment flooded him, along with a measure of concern. "I would you know. I'd be fine with a child, but it's your decision."

"I sense a but in here."

He shook his head. "Whatever you think. It would be unusual to leave a baby to a single guy when you can pick the woman."

She sighed. "It's not like that."

"Isn't it? Neither of you even like Harrison, but you'd leave your son in the care of the woman who's marrying him? Why don't you ask Tom and Jenna? They'd be great parents."

"They will be someday." She picked at the paper napkin on the table. "I'd always hoped it would be you and Tiffany, but you can't be in the same room. So now I'll pick one of you and make the best of it."

"Okay."

Alex squeezed his hand. "I'm sorry. You have a busy career. Your lifestyle isn't suited to taking on a child."

He pasted on a blank expression and bit back the reply. Having one of his closest friends express doubt about his worthiness to be a parent and his life in general, burned. It reminded him of the snap judgment from Emily after their first night together. If the people who knew him best shared the same opinion, taking his daughter away averted certain disaster.

"You said there was something you wanted to talk about?" Alex's voice shook him from his thoughts.

"It can wait." He couldn't bear to open the conversation. Facing it meant turning everything upside down for everyone in his life and he didn't want to force Alex to take sides. So he sipped his coffee and changed the subject, hiding his true feelings. He'd become good at that.

Chapter 23

Savannah

The frigid temperatures of mid-January in Chicago were a shock compared to the mildness of a winter in Portland. Savannah wrapped her arms around herself and rubbed her arms, shivering despite the blast of hot air coming from the vents.

Aiden flicked a switch and moments later warmth surrounded her. "Seat heaters are a definite must in Chicago." He flashed her a smile as she sighed, the warmth relaxing her.

The typical big city scenery flashed by, and gradually houses packed together with apartment complexes changed to homes set on larger lots and surrounded by trees. The space between houses grew bigger the farther they drove from downtown, and the closer they drew to Lake Forest.

Her eyes widened at the sight of enormous mansions behind iron gates, some practically hidden from view on their large well-treed lots. This was beyond her wildest dreams.

Savannah reached for Aiden's hand. "You grew up here?"

"Sort of." He squeezed her fingers, still concentrating on the icy roads. "It's a little much."

Silently, she agreed. The prospect of meeting Gramma Grace was overwhelming. Even wearing her dark-washed jeans paired with a sweater, she felt under dressed, but Aiden had chosen a similar casual style, so she forced herself to relax.

One hand sneaked upwards, a fingertip finding its way into her mouth, and she nibbled at her nail.

Aiden reached out and pulled her hand down. "She doesn't bite. Often." The smile crinkled the corners of his eyes. "Don't worry. She'll love you."

"Sorry." She tucked her hands under her thighs and willed herself to stop bouncing.

"She isn't much different in person than she is on the phone. Just be yourself."

His calm assurance helped, but her life had changed so much in the past few months, it deluged her some days.

A tiny squeak escaped as they turned into a driveway flanked by wrought iron gates and rounded a circular drive before parking near the house. The sight of the massive gray stone structure made her mouth go dry.

Most of the grounds were buried under a layer of snow, but she could tell come summertime it would be magnificent. Vines crawled up the side and an ornate fountain dominated the center of the circular driveway. It seemed surreal that this imposing mansion was her great-grandmother's home.

Savannah froze, rooted to her seat until Aiden skirted around to open her door.

"You'll do great." He flashed her one of his perfect smiles, peeling her out of the front seat before wrapping an arm around her.

She sucked in several deep breaths, glancing upwards as they approached the double front doors of the towering structure. Hopefully, her grandmother was less intimidating than her home.

The door opened as they arrived on the doorstep. Savannah stepped inside, staring in wonder at the high ceilings and tiled foyer. The grand split double staircase caught her eye. It reminded her of watching princess movies as a child, all dark wood and elegance, combined with gleaming marble and a sparkling chandelier.

"Good afternoon, Dr. Hamilton."

"Good afternoon, Bernard." Aiden assisted Savannah with her coat and handed it to the butler before removing his own. "This is my daughter, Savannah."

"Welcome, Miss Savannah." The man inclined his head and disappeared with their coats.

Savannah giggled before slapping a hand over her mouth. "A butler?"

A grin appeared as Aiden wiggled his brows, making her giggle again. "I used to slide down the banister, and these tiles are really fun. If you get up enough speed you can just …" He made a little gesture with his hands.

Savannah pictured him as a young boy, slipping and sliding around the fancy foyer.

"Don't be teaching her any of your bad habits." An elderly, gray-haired woman appeared in the doorway, her smile and teasing tone putting Savannah at ease. "Oh, my dear. I'm so happy you're here." Grace enveloped Savannah in her arms. There was no formal handshake, only this deep, warm embrace.

Savannah sank into it, wrapping her arms around the petite woman in return. She savored the long-awaited moment. "Gramma," she whispered, blinking rapidly.

Grace stepped back, placing her hands on Savannah's shoulders. Her eyes shimmered. "My, you're a lovely girl. It's such a pleasure to meet you at last. Come, we can talk in the library."

Her grandmother led her through French double doors into a cozy book-lined room. There were hundreds of leather-bound volumes neatly arranged on the shelves. The stone fireplace cast off a warm glow as it crackled merrily, and the furniture was elegant but comfortable.

Savannah inhaled, enjoying the combined scents of wood, leather, and the light floral scent of her grandmother's perfume mingling in the high-ceilinged room.

Grace pulled her hand, encouraging her to settle on the couch beside her. "I want to hear all about you."

―――

Savannah lay across her bed, staring out the large window and contemplating the day. Her notebook in front of her, she idly tapped her pencil against the pages she'd written in the hour they'd been home. It seemed she'd written a ton, using her journal as an outlet for the thoughts crowding her mind.

She knew her dad loved her, but he'd been buried in his own pain, having lost his wife after thirty-five years of marriage. He did his best every day, she knew that, but he was all Savannah had. At least until Aiden had come into her life, bringing Emily and Grace. Now, she had so much more. Her nerves had been for nothing. Grace Hamilton was sweet and kind, with an obvious affection for her grandson.

Aiden knocked on the door frame, pulling her from her thoughts. "Can I come in?"

"Sure." She sat, leaning against one of her bright blue pillows, bringing her knees to her chest and wrapping her arms around them. "What's up?"

"You were quiet on the way home. I wanted to make sure you're okay. Kind of a big day."

"I'm just tired. I was nervous, but Gramma Grace was great."

"I could tell, but it went well."

Savannah smiled at the understatement. He'd stopped her from chewing her fingers off multiple times over the course of the day. "You noticed."

"Just a little bit." Aiden held up two fingers, creating a little space in between. "How's Justin?"

"Good." She grinned. The moment they'd gotten home, she'd called Justin. "Are you going to do the dad thing? Tell me to be careful and all that? Again?"

"Is it wrong for me to show an interest in my daughter's boyfriend? You don't have to hide it. Ross knows."

"Does he? He hasn't said a word."

"I'm not sure he knows how to bring it up. He noticed you spent most of your time with Justin at your party. I know you two talk, but are you uncomfortable discussing boys?"

"Well, yeah." She raised her brows. "I love Dad, but he's not my mom. It's weird talking to a man about some of this stuff, especially my dad."

"I'm here if you want to talk and so is Emily."

"She'll tell you, won't she?" Savannah longed to engage in girl chats with Emily, but she worried. Some things she preferred to keep private.

"I meant what I said, sweetie. You can talk to her without fear of judgment, or punishment, or whatever else goes through a teenagers' mind."

"Like feeling painfully embarrassed or stupid?"

"Exactly. I didn't have anyone to talk to at your age, aside from my friends. I wish I'd felt more comfortable going to Gramma, but I didn't. Being scared and having no one to trust is a feeling I understand. I don't want you to be in that position. If it's Emily or Gramma, that's fine. Just promise you'll talk to someone."

Savannah shifted. "I will." Though Ross sometimes asked her if things were okay, he never pursued the matter. She supposed Aiden was more in touch with teenagers' issues, as he dealt with them in the ER, and he'd been through difficult circumstances himself. It seemed he and her mother had managed alone.

"Enough said." He patted her knee and rose. "You probably want to get some sleep."

"You want to hear something funny?"

"Sure." He stopped in the doorway.

"Justin said you gave him the look."

"The look?"

"The dad look. Like he'd better be good or he'd be in trouble."

Aiden laughed. "I know that look. I got it a few times myself. I guess he and I understand each other."

"You can't go around scaring my boyfriends."

"I didn't do it on purpose." He raised his hands. "I didn't even realize I was doing it, but hey, he'd better treat you right. You deserve it. Is he good to you?"

"He's a sweetheart." Savannah blushed, but it was true.

"Keep him in line. Teenage boys are trouble."

"You were a teenage boy." She smirked.

"And I was trouble." A cheeky grin appeared, but then he grew serious. "Don't accept any bad behavior, okay?"

"I won't. Hey, can we watch a movie and eat popcorn? You know, with those little chocolate candies?"

"Sure." He held out a hand. "Let's go."

Chapter 24

Aiden

On Valentine's Day, the ER was a hive of activity. Aiden positioned himself close to the admissions desk when the promised text arrived.

"Delivery for you, Dr. Anderson." The desk clerk flagged Emily down as she arrived at the front.

Emily's eyes widened at the sight of the bouquet and the accompanying ribbon-wrapped box of expensive chocolates. "These are amazing." She peeled back the elegant wrapping to reveal two dozen long-stemmed red roses. Her lips twitched into a smile as she shoved her nose into the flowers and inhaled.

"That's a spectacular bouquet. Who's it from?" Rosa tried to snatch the card out of Emily's hands.

Emily tucked it against her chest, her eyes sparkling. "Not a chance."

"That's an embarrassing floral display." Tara sidled up beside Emily. "I'd love to meet this guy."

Emily raised an eyebrow. "You already have." A secretive smile appeared as she looked his way.

He twitched his brow in return.

"Holy crap." The smirk slid from Tara's face, replaced by a frown. "Your mystery man is Aiden?" Her voice rose to a shrill pitch as she spun and stared at him, along with the rest of the staff. "How did I not know?"

"Maybe because you can't keep a secret?" He rolled his eyes as he strolled toward the exam room, reading the patient chart on his way.

Rosa appeared to assist with the patient. "Emily, huh?" She squeezed his arm. "No wonder you look so happy." With a wink, she took the tablet from his hands and recorded while he performed his exam.

"The orderly will take you upstairs for x-rays," Aiden said to the patient before he stepped from the room. "Whoa." He stopped short.

Tara narrowed her eyes and folded her arms across her chest. "Are you out of your mind? Anderson? How the hell did that happen?"

"Lower your voice." Aiden pulled her aside. "Who I date is none of your business."

"We've gone out, you and I, and …" She looked down, blinking rapidly. "I thought we had something."

"Pizza and beer or a movie with a work colleague is not a date." He scoffed. "We wouldn't have met at a pub with a group of coworkers to play pool and eat burgers."

"You've been busy screwing … *her*." Tara's lower lip jutted out. "In a couple months, it'll be over, just like every other one of your so-called relationships. Don't think I'll be waiting." She flounced down the hall.

He'd feared this exact scenario. Their coworkers on the sidelines, examining every move and placing bets on how long it would take for their relationship to implode. Being a couple was hard enough without outside interference.

"Dr. Hamilton?" Dana beckoned from an exam room, her stern voice shaking him from his reverie. "Come in and shut the door."

Aiden leaned against the gurney, anticipating her next words.

"It's come to my attention you're involved with Dr. Anderson." Her lips set in a grim line. "She's an attending."

"Is that a problem?" He sighed, wishing he hadn't sent the flowers to the ER.

"She supervises you."

"She's my colleague, not my boss and you do the evaluations. I checked, and there's no rule against it. Besides, we've been professional. Nobody noticed until now."

"How long have you two been dating?"

"Three months, give or take."

"If you felt there was nothing wrong, why did you hide it?"

"We haven't hidden it. We're discreet. It's inappropriate and unprofessional to hang on each other at work. Is that all?"

"For now, but be careful, doctor. We discourage favoritism in the workplace. This case is borderline. You're a resident and she's an attending," she said. "Make sure it doesn't impede your work."

"It hasn't yet. Can I get back to my patients?"

At Dana's impatient wave, Aiden exited. He'd only taken a few steps down the hall when a warm hand reached out and yanked him into an exam room.

Emily slid her arms around his neck. "Thank you for the flowers." Her lithe body pressed against his as she drew him into a long kiss.

When they finally broke apart, he rested his forehead against hers. "I take it you like them?"

"They're gorgeous. Now everyone knows about us."

"Dana lectured me about keeping it professional, and Tara threw a fit."

"Oops. My bad." She giggled as she tipped her chin to kiss him again. "Get back to work before Dragon Lady fires us."

"Ha. I'm so scared." Aiden kissed her again. "Ahhh, but I do have a ton of patients waiting."

"Go." She swatted him on the butt as he turned to leave.

"Sexual harassment. Be careful, Dr. Anderson." He winked as he left the room.

The rest of the shift sped by, accompanied by many comments about his involvement with Emily. Their secret was out, but being in the open was a relief.

Emily relinquished her bouquet for the short walk to the train. "It was a long one and so busy." She yawned, leaning against him as they rode home.

Once they were at his apartment, they changed into comfortable casual clothes. He opened a bottle of wine and retrieved the ingredients for dinner from the fridge.

Emily wrapped her arms around his waist from behind, leaning against his back. "What are you making?"

"Chicken and pesto linguine, herb garlic bread, and Caesar salad."

"Yum. I think I'll keep you around." She kissed his cheek then wandered to the sound system. Soon strains of soft jazz floated through the apartment. "Who knew you had so many ... talents."

"Are you flirting with me?" He grinned.

"Maybe a little." Emily reached into the cabinet, procuring two wine glasses.

"I'm sorry we couldn't do something fancier." He shrugged. "If I'd made reservations, we'd have gotten stuck at work."

She poured the wine and handed him a glass. "I'd rather be here having a quiet night with good food and company than in some overpriced stuffy restaurant, jammed among the hordes out for Valentine's."

Aiden loved how appreciative she was of the simple arrangements, especially after a long day of work. "I promise we'll go another night when we can take our time." He dropped the pasta into the water as a pan heated to sauté the chicken. With the bread in the oven, and the salad ready to dress, he relaxed.

Emily perched on a stool at the counter, a soft smile gracing her lips. "If you like, but this is perfect."

Within a few minutes, they were seated at the table.

"Happy Valentine's." He tapped his glass against hers, both drinking before tucking into the meal.

"This is delicious." She took another bite, sighing happily. "Thank you for cooking."

"You're welcome. Julissa, my grandmother's cook, used to make this, and it was one of my favorite meals. We often visited Florence and there was a market with this little Italian mama. She made pesto and fresh pasta and this reminds me of our time there."

"You've traveled a lot."

"When I was young, my grandmother took me on holiday. When I was a teenager, I'd go with my grandparents or my friends. I wasn't even sixteen when they sent me on a sailing trip in Europe, which happened to be my punishment for running away."

"Your punishment for running away was a trip to Europe?" Emily smirked. "Sounds rough."

"It wasn't a luxury cruise. We were the crew. My family cut me off from everyone and banned me from communication. I'm surprised they didn't disown me, but I made the best of it." Aiden gazed at her. "By the time I returned to the States, I'd obtained my undergrad degree and been accepted into medical school. I paid for my mistakes. Just not in a way most people would understand."

"How much did you take?"

"Twenty-five thousand."

She straightened. "You stole twenty-five thousand from your grandparents? They kept that much in the house?"

"They did, in the safe. We planned for it to last, so we were careful what we spent. When they caught up to us, we still had most of it. Stupid, perhaps, but I did what I needed to do at the time."

"I never figured you for a hardened criminal." Her gentle smile softened the words. "Still, you're lucky your education was paid. I managed a partial scholarship to the University of Chicago, but I ended up with huge loans which I might be paying for the rest of my life. At least I love my job, most of the time. Speaking of which, I'm thinking about applying for a supervisory position."

"Where?"

"Dana applied for another position, and they'll be posting her job. It's a long shot, but what the heck."

"I didn't know you had aspirations to be the replacement Dragon Lady, but good for you. I'll keep my fingers crossed."

After they'd eaten and tidied the kitchen, Aiden pulled her into his arms, spinning them toward the living room.

"Mmm, you dance?" she murmured, her eyes sparkling.

"I was forced to take lessons when I was younger." Aiden nuzzled against her neck, inhaling the soft lavender scent of her body lotion. "I have something for you."

"More? I'm getting spoiled."

"You deserve it." He tugged her onto the sofa beside him, pulling out the small packages and setting them in front of her.

"What's this?" Emily held up the two small blue boxes, her eyes widening.

"Open them and find out."

"Wait. I have something for you." Emily produced his gift and set it on the coffee table.

"You first."

Emily stared at the smaller box, turning it in her fingers.

"It won't bite, I promise."

"What?" Her head popped up.

"You look freaked out. What do you think is in the …" *Crap.* The smaller of the blue boxes was exactly the right dimension for a ring. The way her wide green eyes reflected a touch of panic caused a wave of anxiety.

She hesitated, then tugged the end of the ribbon, opening the lid to reveal diamond earrings. A swift exhale escaped. "These are gorgeous. Thank you. I love them." She hugged him before setting down the box and opening the second one, which contained a matching diamond pendant. "You shouldn't have, but they're beautiful. Help me put this on."

Aiden brushed her hair aside, fastening the platinum chain before placing a gentle kiss on the nape of her neck. Her body quivered under his touch. "You're welcome."

She fastened the earrings. "How do they look?"

"Perfect." He placed his palms against her face. "They're almost as beautiful as you are."

"Hmm." She reached up to kiss him. "You're sweet."

Before he could respond, she handed him his present, which turned out to be a watch.

"This is great. I can get rid of this." He removed his old one and fastened the new one on his wrist.

"It should hold up to the demands of the ER. I have something else for you."

"Now who's getting spoiled?"

"Get ready for bed, but take your time." She pushed him toward the master bedroom.

He went without argument. When he stepped out of the bathroom a few minutes later, the bedroom had been transformed. Candles flickered on the bedside tables and soft music played, but his focus was drawn to the woman on his bed, barely covered in sexy red satin and lace.

"What took you so long?" Emily asked in a low and seductive voice.

He let a low whistle as he inspected her from head to toe, his pulse racing. "Sorry, but it was worth the wait."

Her soft green eyes lifted to his as he crawled onto the bed. "You like?"

"No, I love." He leaned in, dropping gentle kisses across the bare flesh of her shoulders. Her tiny shiver and soft inhale of breath encouraged him to continue. "Beautiful," he whispered, wrapping her in his arms.

Aiden stroked the velvety softness of her back as they lay entwined on the bed. "Can I ask you something?"

"Hmm, what?" She smiled and brushed her fingertips across his face.

"You were nervous about the gifts. What went through your mind?" This question lingered. He couldn't ignore her obvious relief at finding earrings.

She buried her head against his chest, snuggling closer. "Never mind."

"Uh-uh. Tell me."

"It was nothing."

"I won't be upset." He tipped her chin and looked into her eyes. "Were you worried about what was in it?"

She placed her palm on his cheek and rubbed with her thumb. "It's only been a few months, and I feel like we're on this path, but I don't want to rush it."

"What path do you think we're on?"

She shrugged. "Maybe I'm off base, but we're together all the time. It's comfortable being with you and we have so much in common."

"Comfortable?" That sounded like an old married couple whose passion had settled into a bland friendship, but what they just shared didn't feel anything like friendship or anywhere near resembling bland. That had been pure scorching hot passion.

Emily laughed. "Don't look so concerned. It's amazing because it's easy being with you. There's both a physical and emotional connection and comfort level I've never shared with anyone."

"Phew." He winked. "Did you think there might be a ring in one of those boxes?"

"You noticed?" Her face flushed an adorable pink tone. "I'm way ahead of myself. I'm not expecting or pressuring you into anything, I just thought …" She lifted one shoulder.

He kissed her temple. "I heard you in New York, Em. It's too soon, but is it something you could see happening? Something you might want at some point?"

"Do you want that with me?"

"The old question with a question answer. Tricky." He contemplated her, hoping what he said next wouldn't scare her. Playing mind games wasn't something he enjoyed. He'd dealt with enough women who'd been disingenuous or downright dishonest about their intentions. "I'm ready to commit to one person, but taking it slow is good. Maybe we should start by living together."

Emily's eyes widened. "Do you believe we're ready?"

Aiden cocked his head before sliding from the bed. He strolled to the walk-in closet and peered inside. "Yup. The half-closet rule is fulfilled."

A smile lit her face as her melodic laugh filled the room. "Is that a real thing?"

"Apparently, because your shoes alone have taken over." He flopped onto the bed beside her and propped himself on one elbow. "Do you even have clothes left at your place? If so, we need a bigger closet."

"Touché."

"How do you feel about the idea?"

"It has potential. So I should move here?"

"I own and you lease. And no offense, but my place is nicer and more central. Plus you already have a key."

She entwined their fingers, squeezing gently. "Are you sure?"

"Let's make it official." He sat, taking both of her hands in his. "Emelia Alejandra Anderson, will you move in with me?"

"Yes." She rewarded him with a long, deep kiss.

A sense of peace flooded him, and he knew it was right. His perfect woman. Maybe she'd be the one who stayed.

Chapter 25

Savannah

SAVANNAH SKIPPED FROM HER ROOM, changing her gait to a sedate walk as she moved toward the living room where Justin waited to take her out for the evening. Nervous energy flowed through her, and she took several calming breaths before checking her reflection one last time, happy that her dad had given his blessing on her dating Justin shortly after her birthday. They'd been out several times, but tonight would be special.

Justin stood as she entered, which earned him an approving look from her dad. "You look beautiful, Vanna."

She bestowed a smile on her boyfriend, grateful he made every effort to be social. Maybe it helped that Justin had known her father most of his life. "Thank you." Her heart lightened at the compliment. "I'm ready."

"You two have fun, but have her home before curfew, Justin."

"He knows, Dad." Savannah kissed his cheek before allowing Justin to assist her with her coat. She wished she was allowed to stay out later than ten, but she feared her dad would revoke her privileges if she argued, so she agreed to his rules. "Sorry about that," she muttered as they exited onto the front walk.

Justin linked their fingers as they strolled down the street in silence, sending small nervous glances at each other. It wasn't a long walk to his house, and soon he was unlocking the front door and ushering her into the quiet house.

"How long will your parents be out?" Savannah peered around, her mouth becoming dry.

"They're at an anniversary party, so they won't be back until late." He squeezed her hand. "We have the house to ourselves."

She slung her coat over the bench in the foyer before following Justin down the hallway into his bedroom. Her knees shook as she pushed his door shut.

"Want to watch a movie or something?" He dropped onto his bed and held out his hand.

"Sounds good. At least that part won't be a lie." She allowed him to pull her down beside him.

"Would you like a soda?" he asked a few minutes into the movie. "We could make popcorn."

"Mmmhmm." Savannah nodded, feeling suddenly too shy to speak.

Once they had their snacks, they leaned against the pillows at the head of his bed. Savannah pretended to be engaged in the movie, but she felt the looks as Justin peered at her from the corner of his eye.

She snuggled closer, tipping her head up for a kiss, and Justin wrapped his arms around her, his warm lips covering hers. Whenever they kissed, her heart pounded and a little quiver ran down her spine. This time was no different.

They slid farther down, becoming more involved in making out, the movie now simply background noise.

"You're so beautiful," he murmured against her neck. "Are you …? Do you still want to …?"

Savannah pulled back and stared into his eyes, knowing exactly what he was asking. They hadn't gone further than kissing and making out, but she cared about Justin and they'd known each other for a long time. "Yes, but I'm scared."

"So am I. You know I've never …" He rested his forehead against hers. "What if it's not … good?"

She pressed a fingertip to his lips. "Shh. Let's take it slow and it will be."

"You're sure? We don't have to do it if you don't want to." He cuddled her against him. "I'll wait if you're not ready."

"No. I am," she whispered. "Are you? Did you get protection?"

He nodded and brushed her hair back from her face. "I don't want to hurt you, Vanna."

"You won't." Being cradled in his arms and knowing this boy was sincere gave her comfort. He'd changed and matured over the years, but she realized that underneath, he was the same boy who'd saved her from the bully.

She kissed him again, enjoying the sensations racing through her body at his gentle touch. At her nod, he buried his head against her neck, dropping soft kisses against her skin. It seemed right and she vowed to enjoy this special moment.

Justin kissed her lips, giving her an extra long hug. "Are you okay?" He gazed into her eyes.

"Yeah, I'm good." She offered him a smile. "It was ... good."

"Just good?" A tiny grin appeared.

"Fishing for compliments?" Her giggle brought a wide grin to his face, breaking the tension between them. "How about ... amazing. Especially the second time."

"Now you're exaggerating, but," he snickered, "I'll leave it at amazing." After planting another gentle kiss on her lips, he brushed her hair back from her face. "I love you, Vanna. You'd better get inside before your dad comes out." He waited until she'd unlocked her front door and slipped inside the silent house.

A single light burned as her dad had already retired for the evening. She was grateful she didn't have to rehash her date with him, afraid he might see the change in her now that she'd made love with Justin.

She appreciated how hard her dad tried, but discussing certain topics felt strange and uncomfortable. During these times, she missed her mom even more. Not that she'd have shared tonight's events with her, either.

As she tiptoed down the hall to her room, her phone vibrated, signaling a new text.

Sleep well. I love you.

Her heart sang at his words.

I love you. It really was amazing.

A smile played at her lips as she contemplated the evening's events. At first, the removal of clothing had been a combination of uncomfortable and inelegant fumbling, but once they'd relaxed it had been good.

Justin's sweet and gentle touch had helped, as had knowing he was more nervous than her. His worries proved unjustified.

She'd only half-known what to expect, and the experience was far different from what she'd imagined. Health class had prepared her in general, but the reality of the situation and the feelings it evoked were completely unexpected.

Another text binged on her phone.

So did you?

Instead of texting, she called Leanne. "Yes," she whispered.

"Are. You. Serious?"

"Keep your voice down. Do you want your mom to hear?"

"Sorry, sorry. How was it?"

"Awkward, but nice." She didn't quite know what to say, but it was a relief to confide in someone.

They talked for a while longer before she signed off. After a few moments of thought, she dialed again.

"Savannah?" Emily's sleepy voice carried down the line.

"Sorry. Were you sleeping?"

"It's okay, honey. Do you need to talk to Aiden? He's at work."

"No, I wanted to talk to you." She drummed her fingers against her pillow.

"Sure." Emily's tone became more focused and clearer. "Everything okay?"

"Yeah, but … I needed to talk to someone … like girl stuff. Can you not tell Aiden?"

"I'll be discreet."

Savannah twirled her hair. "I had sex with Justin," she whispered, wincing at the sound of Emily's sharp inhale. "You won't tell, right?"

"Your secret is safe with me." The woman's warm and reassuring voice flowed down the line, soothing her concerns. "That's a huge development in your relationship. You were careful, I hope?"

"We were."

To her relief, Emily talked to her gently, leading her into a conversation, and Savannah found herself relaying her anxieties, fears, and feelings about the night. The words poured out as she confided in a way she couldn't with her friends. Most of them had even less experience with boys than Savannah.

"I'm scared to go to our family doctor. He knows my dad, and he's about the same age." She squirmed, thinking about sitting across from the gray-haired man who'd been her physician since she was a baby.

"I have a wonderful woman's doctor. You're coming to visit soon, so why don't we book you an appointment? She's young and progressive. I believe you'd like her."

"You won't tell Aiden?" Savannah worried about his reaction if he learned about any of this.

"If you want him to know, you can tell him yourself. Should I make you an appointment while Aiden's on shift?"

"Would you?" She stared at her ceiling. "Thanks, Emily. I didn't know who else to call."

"You can talk to me about anything, anytime. You get some sleep, and I'll see you in a few days."

They said good night, and Savannah went about her bedtime ritual. A glance in the mirror showed her the same girl she was earlier in the evening, but despite appearances, she felt different. Like someone who'd never be the same, but that was okay. When she crawled under the covers, she drifted into a contented sleep.

A week later, she was in Chicago. Her dad had agreed to let her spend a few days over the school break, and Aiden had paid for her flights. He'd even authorized her access to his travel account so she could visit anytime and book her tickets directly.

"Morning, Emily." She bounced into the kitchen where the woman was brewing coffee and making breakfast. "Is Aiden at work?"

"Yes, but he'll be done by five." She glanced at her watch. "I was about to wake you. Can you be ready by nine for your appointment?"

"Yes. I'll eat and finish my hair." Savannah picked at a nail, before nibbling at it. "You didn't tell Aiden, right?"

"No, and I won't. He's been clear on the confidentiality issue. Secretly, he'd love it if you talked to him, but he understands why you might be uncomfortable."

Savannah nodded, grateful both Aiden and Emily had kept their word. Aiden hadn't pried into any of the conversations she'd had with Emily, and Emily had kept her confidences.

She definitely didn't want to tell him about her and Justin. Not that he'd judge her, given the circumstances, but she knew he worried about her making the same mistakes. "Thanks, Emily. I'm glad I have you to help."

The woman looked pleased. "I'm happy you trust me enough to discuss your health concerns and talk about things that are important to you." She poured a coffee and placed two plates of food on the counter before sliding onto the stool next to Savannah. "My mom was super strict, so I never talked to her. My sisters and I figured out a lot of this girl stuff ourselves."

"I miss my mom, but I'm not sure I'd have told her about this. Leanne's mom offers to talk to me, but she's strict. She'd freak and spill the details to my dad and then Justin would be in trouble too. Her view is we should wait until we're married."

"Many people hold that belief, but it's a personal decision. To me, it's more important that you're responsible and protect yourself."

"You don't think it was wrong?"

"Of course not. I don't subscribe to the idea of holding out until marriage. You clearly care about Justin, and I suspect it won't be a one-time event with him, but don't be in such a rush to grow up."

"That's what Aiden says. Don't rush, and above all, don't make the same mistakes. It's strange to think he was a father at the same age as I am now. He might flip out if he knew I wasn't his sweet and innocent little girl anymore."

A serious look settled on Emily's face. "I know him well enough to be sure he wouldn't. Don't forget he deals with teenagers every day at work, and he's very understanding. Sex is a normal part of maturing, and even if he'd prefer you'd waited, he'd still be happy to know you acted responsibly."

"You're sure? I'm his daughter, not a patient in the ER."

"True, but even so, he'd accept your choice. No matter how old you get, you will always be his little girl. Aiden will love you forever."

"He never forgot me, either. I think you're right."

Emily patted her knee and grinned. "Trust me, he's seen everything. Being an emergency physician doesn't leave a whole lot to the imagination."

"I suppose." Savannah giggled despite herself. "What things do you see that are so shocking?"

"You don't want to know." Emily shook her head as she took another bite of her breakfast. "I'm sorry I brought it up. Finish eating, and we'll get to your appointment. Then we'll visit Josh. I planned an afternoon of pampering for us. Aiden will meet us for dinner at that little Bistro. Sound good?"

"Perfect." Savannah felt a warm glow inside. The more time she spent with Aiden's girlfriend, the more she loved her.

Chapter 26

Aiden

Aiden tapped the last instructions into his tablet, finishing the handoff on his final patient of the day.

"Dr. Hamilton? A word if we could?" Dana flagged him down as he attempted an escape toward the lounge.

With an impatient glance at his watch, he sighed. He planned to meet Emily and Savannah for dinner in half an hour, and couldn't wait to get out of the ER. "Sure." He followed her into an empty exam room, leaning against the gurney and crossing his arms. "What's up?"

"Administration sent me some paperwork, and I noticed Dr. Anderson has the same address as you. She moved into your place?"

"Is that a problem?"

"It is. From now on, I have to schedule you on separate shifts. It's a hassle, but here's your new schedule." She held out a paper.

"Are you serious? I'm supposed to be off for the next four days." A flicker of anger appeared.

"Dr. Anderson has seniority, so rather than altering her shifts, I have to change yours. I need you in for the next four days to work you onto the new schedule."

"Absolutely not. I have plans, plus I'm your chief, not a first-year. I don't even know what the big deal is. Emily and I are professional about our relationship."

"Before you weren't living together, but if you feel so strongly, I can arrange for you to have eight days off without pay. Your choice." Dana narrowed her eyes. "Suspension or you're in here for your shift tomorrow."

"When you put it that way." He slid off his lab coat. "I'll see you in eight days." No way would he give up his precious time with Savannah. He yanked open the door, leaving Dragon Lady in stunned silence.

"Dr. Hamilton." Dana stalked after him. "Are you sure you know what you're doing?"

"Quit acting like a dictator. My plans can't be changed at your whim. If you want to suspend me, so be it." A hush fell over the normally hectic ER and he was sure the entire staff was taking this in.

"Then make it sixteen days with no pay."

"Fine." Aiden entered the lounge to grab his belongings from his locker.

Tara trailed after him. "McCauley's right ripped about your attitude."

"I don't care." He slammed his locker closed and hurried past Tara. "I'm late."

Once he reached the restaurant, he forced himself to engage in the conversation, trying to hide his irritation at what had happened at work. Perhaps he'd fooled Savannah, but he knew Emily wasn't.

The moment they were alone in their bedroom, she cornered him. "You're in a mood."

He shook his head as he unbuttoned his shirt and tossed it in the hamper, heading into the bathroom to brush his teeth.

Seconds later, Emily wrapped her arms around him, the warmth of her body pressed against his back. "Bad one at work?"

"You could say that. Do you think Vanna noticed?"

"Maybe." She shrugged. "What happened?"

"Dragon Lady noticed your address change and switched my shifts. We'll be working opposite days from now on." He rubbed her hands before turning. "She wanted me to work the next four days to accommodate her arbitrary schedule adjustment. I said no. So she suspended me."

"What." Emily's eyes widened. "She did not."

"For eight days. When I told her she was a dictator, she made it sixteen." He shrugged. "I have a two-week vacation."

"What were you thinking? You want an attending job, yet you say things like that to the boss? Don't be an idiot. You should work."

"Vanna's here. I refuse to give up my time with my daughter. I told Dana I had plans and she didn't care. So now she can search for someone to cover my shifts for sixteen days. I won't get paid, but whatever."

"Must be nice to not worry about being suspended without pay," Emily muttered, shaking her head. "Well, let's get some sleep so we can be up early tomorrow. We have lots of plans for the days she's here. I'll smooth things over with Dragon Lady and get her to relent."

"Uhh, no, you won't. This is between me and her. Don't you dare get involved." Aiden placed his palms on her cheeks, holding her there, trying to let go of his annoyance at her dig about his money. "Promise you'll let me deal with her. If she doesn't want to give me the attending job, so be it, but you're not fighting my battles or putting your position in jeopardy."

"Fine. Do whatever you need." Emily sounded exasperated, but she let it rest.

The next morning, Aiden rose early to make plans for the unexpected days off. First, he called Ross and then his travel agent.

"Morning." He pressed a kiss onto his daughter's cheek.

"You're in a good mood." She smiled before taking another bite of her breakfast. "What are we doing today?"

"We need to pick up a few things." He winked at Emily as she wandered into the kitchen. "Shorts, bathing suit, and anything else you'll need."

"Where are we going?" A grin spread across her face. "Why do I need this stuff? It's too cold for the beach."

"Not if you're in Hawaii." He sneaked a look from the corner of his eye.

Her head popped up and her jaw dropped. "No way. I've always wanted to go there. But … what about Dad?"

"I called him and he's agreed. We'll drop you in Portland on the way home from Maui. If you want to go, that is."

"Are you kidding? Maui." She hopped off the stool, wrapping her arms around him and kissing his cheek. "Emily too?"

"Emily will join us on her next days off. Sound like a plan?" He wound an arm around her waist.

"Yes. This is so exciting." She bounced on her toes. "I have to get dressed. When do we leave?"

The two weeks spent in Hawaii were an amazing consolation for being suspended. Emily even had some banked time. She'd arrived only three days after them and stayed for the duration of the holiday.

Now he was paying for it. Dana had stuck him with a six-to-six night shift, which meant he wouldn't see Emily much for the next four days. He wasn't sure how they'd continue their relationship if they never got to see each other.

He slung his stethoscope around his neck and slammed his locker shut. Ignoring the covert stares, he headed toward the exam room where his patient waited. Surely everyone had heard about the argument with Dana, and they could tell he was in a bad mood. His trek to the admissions desk had been the parting of the Red Sea with everyone scrambling out of his way. That didn't bode well for a day at work.

Emily was nowhere to be seen. Usually, she'd be off shift about now, but he figured she'd been held up with a patient. It wasn't until he was finished several exams that she appeared.

"Aiden." Emily motioned down the hall. "Can I have a minute?"

"Hey, you're here." He followed her into an empty exam room and leaned in to kiss her. "Where have you been?"

Her return kiss seemed hesitant, and she pulled back quicker than usual. "Upstairs." She picked at the corner of the envelope in her hands, finally looking at him. "I got the job."

"Congratulations?" Aiden frowned at her less than excited tone, but he pulled her close.

Emily buried her head against his chest, clinging to him. "Thanks." She peered at him with shimmering eyes.

He studied her for a moment, taking in her downturned mouth and the tears building in the corners of her eyes. "For someone on the receiving end of an amazing promotion that comes with a significant increase in salary, you seem less than thrilled. What's going on?"

She shook her head. "Oh, Aiden. This sucks."

"Why? You got the job of your dreams. You'll be great." He leaned back against the gurney, folding his arms across his chest. "What's up, Em?" He steeled himself for the unpleasant news that was surely coming.

She plucked a letter-sized envelope off the top of her pile, and extended it, her chin tipping downward.

He slit open the envelope, keeping an eye on her expression as he extracted the paper. "Huh. No wonder you can't even look at me."

She brushed the back of her hand over her cheek. "I didn't want to do this here and now, but I only have until the end of the day. Dana would have blindsided you with it. I'm sorry, but they know about us and ..." Her shoulders twitched in a half-shrug as she ducked her head.

"You can't be my boss. Yeah, I get it. Wow, so ..."

"It's not much of a choice. If I take the job, you can't work here. Not because you're bad at your job or did anything wrong, but because you're my boyfriend. Or I turn it down." The dam broke and tears streaked down her face. "I don't know what to do. I can't fire you."

Aiden fought with his emotions as he wrapped his arms around her. This had become a field of landmines. If he told her to take the job, he became unemployed and she'd feel guilty. If he asked her to decline the position, she'd resent him. He released her and sank onto the side of the gurney as her sobs wound down. "What's it going to be?"

Emily shrugged and stared at the floor.

"You already said yes." Aiden rubbed his hands across his face, fighting the overwhelming urge to turn and walk out. A small flicker of anger surfaced, but he sucked in a long breath and pushed it down. The decision had been made without discussion, leaving him with nothing to do but accept it. "It's a terrific opportunity. You deserve the promotion, Em. Everybody knows it." He offered her the tablet in his hands. "I won't hold you back."

She shook her head, taking a step back. "What are you doing?"

"Giving you my patients. I'll resign quietly and make it easy on you."

"We have some leeway. You don't have to leave today."

"Why would I stay and train my replacement? Thanks, but no. I'll clean out my locker and get out of your way." He took out his pen, scratched out the date on the letter, and wrote in the current one. After signing with a flourish, he tucked his pen in his pocket and dropped the signed copy of the letter on her pile. "I've officially resigned. That ought to make Dragon Lady happy."

"Aiden." Emily grasped his arm. "Please don't hate me. When I applied for the job, I had no idea I'd be forced into this position. I'd be your boss. I'd have to evaluate you. How do you expect me to do that? You'll get a good reference from this hospital and department. The reason for leaving will be quoted as personal. You've resigned. I'm not firing you."

"Yeah, you are ... or Dana is ... but I get it. You can't give me fair evaluations. I don't dispute that. It leaves us limited choices. Even if we ended our relationship right now, you still can't be my boss."

"You're breaking up with me?" She blinked hard.

He shook his head. "That's not what I meant, but I'm in a no-win situation. McCauley wants me gone? I'm gone. I'll find another job. Don't worry about it."

"You're angry."

"A little, but not at you. I'm happy you earned the job of your dreams. That's a great thing, but one of us has to give. I refuse to fight over this, especially not here. You've chosen, and now I have to make certain choices. I'll see you at home." Aiden placed the tablet onto her pile, pausing to press a kiss to her temple before he walked out of the exam room.

"Aiden." Tara waved at him.

"Phil has it. Ask one of the others to supervise." He walked into the lounge and yanked his locker open, tossing his personal items into his bag.

Tara poked her head inside and eyed him. "What the hell are you doing? We have a trauma and you're in here spring cleaning your damn locker?"

"There are other doctors on shift." After stuffing the final items into his bag, he peeled his name tag off the front of the metal door.

"What's going on?" Tara stood beside him.

"I resigned. It's effective immediately." He kept his voice flat and unemotional, despite the turmoil inside.

The nurse narrowed her eyes. "From the chief resident position?" She wagged her head. "Wow. I heard a rumor Emily got the promotion. The first thing she does is fire you? What a bitch."

He fixed her with a scathing stare. "I resigned. Emily has done nothing to you, so keep your opinions to yourself."

"It won't be a popular decision with the nurses." The woman folded her arms over her chest.

"It's none of your business, so go back to work." He dodged around her and headed out the door, refusing to look back. His time at this hospital was over. Nothing could change it.

Chapter 27

Savannah

Savannah waved at Leanne as she arrived at school, a smile breaking out as her friend bounded toward her. Spring break had flown by far too fast, and even faster with their trip to Hawaii. It had been an unexpected treat. The longest trips her parents had ever taken her on were excursions into the neighboring states. She'd always been envious when her friends and classmates came back from various tropical vacations, tanned and smiling.

"You are such a lucky girl." Leanne hugged her, and then pulled her toward their lockers. "Maui? I was stuck here where it's too cold to even think about getting within ten feet of the water."

"It was incredible. We spent almost the entire break there." She pulled out her phone, giggling. "Look, me trying to stay up on a surfboard."

"Yeah, yeah. Rub it in." Leanne waved a hand at her. "You sent me so many pictures, it made me crazy. Someone else missed you too." Her gaze cut down the hallway toward the group of boys coming their way.

"Justin." Savannah bounced the few feet toward him, grinning as he swept her into a hug.

He spun her around, laying a passionate kiss on her lips that garnered more than a few wolf whistles from the other students.

"You were gone so long." He kissed her again, earning a stern look and finger wag from a passing teacher.

"Oh, he knows my dad," she whispered, her cheeks heating as she bowed her head.

"Don't worry about it." Justin entwined their fingers, resting his forehead against hers. "I'm so glad you're back. The break was no fun without you."

"I missed you too, but I have to spend time with Aiden. Sorry, I didn't expect a big trip, it was a complete surprise."

"I understand. You're just getting to know him. I wouldn't say no if my long-lost father dropped into my life and offered to take me to Maui either." He grinned. "I'm not mad. It's cool."

"You don't have a long-lost father." She gave him a playful shove. "And it is, right?"

"Ha ha, you know what I mean. Yeah, he's great from what I know about him." He leveled a look at her. "Finding your father has been good for you. I hope it works out and he sticks around. You seem happier."

"I don't think he's going anywhere. It's not like he abandoned me when I was a baby." She placed a hand against his chest. It had been silly to ignore her feelings for the boy for so long. "I am happy, and I'm glad I took the chance. I'm getting to know him, though I still wish my mother felt the same." A pang emerged at the thought, but she pushed it away. "Oh. I brought you something."

"Give it to me later or we'll be late for class. Then you can tell me all about your holiday spent lounging on a tropical beach without me."

The bell rang and they made their way toward the art room. Justin gave her another deep kiss before he gave her a gentle push into the classroom.

"Have fun and I'll see you at lunch. Draw something amazing."

She took her seat, readying herself to start on her next sketch. Aiden had purchased a new book for her before their trip, and she was anxious to use it. Not expecting to be gone from home for so long, she'd left most of her art supplies in Portland.

It was interesting that Aiden knew just where to take her to buy the best art supplies. Even when she thought she'd figured him out, he always managed to reveal another layer, another level, and she wondered if she would ever truly know the enigma who was her father.

After school, Savannah joined Leanne at the Community Center, as was their habit. The girls spent the next two hours reading and supervising the kids on the playground.

On their break, she dug into her bag and pulled out the camera she'd tucked into it.

"Did you rob a camera shop?"

"Silly." Savannah laughed. "Aiden brought it with him to Hawaii and showed me how to use it. At the end of the trip, he gave it to me. He said I have a great eye and I should practice. Apparently, he has many other cameras at home." She ran her fingertips over the top. "I haven't shown my dad yet. He'll only tell me to give it back to Aiden."

"It looks expensive." Leanne stood and struck a pose. "Take a picture."

They spent the next few minutes taking pictures of anything and everything, bursting into laughter at the results.

Savannah finally tucked the camera back in her bag. "Guess I should keep practicing."

"For sure." Leanne giggled.

The two girls headed back inside, ready to finish the last hour with the kids.

The sun shone brightly in the afternoon sky. May had arrived with warm days, lush green grass, and the air was filled with the scent of blossoming flowers. Savannah had begun counting the days until the end of school.

Plans for summer were already at the top of her mind. Leanne had invited her to the Oregon coast with her family for a week to celebrate the Fourth of July, and then she'd fly to Martha's Vineyard for two weeks with Aiden and Emily.

She learned his family owned a summer house, and of course, she'd never been to the small island on the other end of the country. Her dad had made plans to travel with friends, so she could enjoy a guilt-free vacation.

"Bye." Savannah waved at Leanne before continuing down the block toward her own house. Her dad had promised to make his special scorching hot five-alarm chili for dinner. She'd learned to love spicy food, compliments of her mom. She sighed. Missing her mother would never end.

At least she had Emily. Over the past few months, she'd become increasingly close to the woman. They talked often, and Savannah took advantage of having a grown woman to talk to at every opportunity. After Emily moved in with Aiden, Savannah became hopeful about having a stepmother sometime soon.

Her heart twinged at the thought that she'd almost let her father walk out of her life. Aiden couldn't provide all the answers, but he was a precious connection to the missing part of her life.

"Daddy. I'm home." Vanna dropped her backpack to the floor with a clunk. The amount of homework she had tonight was overwhelming. From the weight of her pack, it felt like she had every single one of her textbooks. "Daddy?"

The house was dead silent, and the usual spicy tomato aroma so prevalent on chili nights was absent.

"Did you forget the chili? Dad? I've been looking forward to it all day." She peeked into the kitchen. At first glance, the room appeared empty, but an odd rasping alerted her. A small gasp escaped as she spied the foot, and she rushed around the table.

Her dad sprawled on the floor, the sharp blade of the kitchen knife only a few inches from his outstretched hand. The other hand clutched his chest.

"Daddy?" She sobbed and dropped to her knees beside him, giving him a gentle shake. "Wake up." His face seemed chalky white, and the sound of his breathing was faint as she leaned in, angling her head and listening. She fumbled for the phone and dialed with trembling fingers.

"911, what is your emergency?" the deep male voice asked.

"My dad. He's unconscious and won't wake up. Help me, please."

"I'll send an ambulance. What's your address?"

Savannah managed to choke out the few short words.

"Stay on the phone. Is he bleeding?"

"No, but he's on the kitchen floor. I found him when I came home from school. Hurry."

"Is he breathing?"

Savannah leaned close, and she still heard faint rasps of air. "Yes, but barely."

"The ambulance is on the way. Is the front door unlocked? Can the paramedics get in?"

"No." She pushed to her feet, bounding for the front door and turning the lock with a snap. "It's open now."

The wail of the distant siren grew closer. "I hear them." She stumbled back to where her dad lay on the floor. "Daddy, hang on. I called for help." She swiped her hand across her face as she heard the door and boots thumping across the floor.

"Paramedics. Where are you?"

"In here."

"Miss? Let us get to him." Hands lifted her, guiding her out of the way as the second paramedic placed a device over her dad's face, squeezing in air.

Savannah wrapped her arms around herself, shivering as they completed a hasty exam and prepared him for the ride to the hospital.

"Do you have someone you could call?" The paramedic led her toward the front door.

She shook her head. "I'm alone. Can I come?" She grabbed her small clutch and followed them to the ambulance, crawling after them into the back. Once they'd pulled away from the house, she made the call, sobbing as his voice mail answered. "Aiden? Call me. I need you."

With trembling fingers, she tapped in a text.

daddy's sick. going to hospital. call me.

The ride to the hospital seemed to take forever, the paramedic working over her dad while the siren blared, the ambulance bumping along. When they arrived, they entered into the ambulance bay. She trailed behind the paramedics until they hit the double sliding doors.

"Sorry, you can't go in, honey." A nurse in blue scrubs tucked her arm around Savannah, leading her down the hall. "Let's take you to the family room."

Savannah glanced over her shoulder several times, reluctant to leave, yet knowing there was nothing she could do.

"Can I call someone?" The kind voice cut into her thoughts.

"I called Aiden, but he's in Chicago. Can I borrow a phone?" She held up her device. She'd been texting all day at school, and the battery bar was sinking fast.

"In here." The nurse ushered her into a small room. "Dial nine and the number. I'll check on your dad and be right back. Make as many calls as you need."

Savannah dialed Aiden's number from memory. Voice mail. She hit disconnect and dialed again, trying Emily this time, but reaching her voice mail. After leaving brief messages for both, she paced up and down the small space, glancing at her phone every few seconds.

Her mind spun. Leanne wouldn't be allowed to answer her phone until all her homework was done. Justin was at basketball practice. She didn't know who else to call.

"I need you, Aiden," she mumbled, brushing a fresh set of tears from her eyes. She dialed one more time, hoping he'd pick up.

Chapter 28

Aiden

His phone skittered across the table as a reminder he'd missed several calls and a text. He glanced toward it, longing to flip it over so he could view the screen, but he didn't dare.

"Can you shut that stupid thing off?" Emily huffed out a breath and shot him a scathing look. "Or don't I warrant five minutes of your undivided attention?"

Ever since that unfortunate day at the hospital when he'd resigned, their relationship had been sliding down that slippery slope, drawing ever closer to a final defining moment he feared. The inevitable day he'd come home and find the closet empty of her clothing, nothing but the faint scent of her perfume lingering on her pillow to remind him she'd been here at all.

After the initial tension, things had leveled out, but only briefly. He simply wasn't good at sitting still. Being unemployed made him feel not only useless, but bored and irritable. He'd checked with each and every hospital in Chicago, and at this moment, there was nothing close to what he'd given up. The best offer he'd had so far was picking up the slack at a walk-in clinic that seemed to specialize in minor medical cases. He couldn't picture his future wiping runny noses and telling patients to go home, drink plenty of fluids, and get some rest.

His phone vibrated for at least the fifth time in the same number of minutes. The constant interruption wasn't helping matters when Emily was in this mood, but he still rolled his eyes to relay his extreme annoyance at her sarcastic comment. Only by clenching his jaw shut had he avoided a caustic retort. I

Immediate regret struck him as her eyes narrowed, and he knew he would pay for the attitude. "Relax." He held his hands up in surrender. "It's off."

As he turned it, the name and number caught his eye, as did the text. The blood drained from his face as he stared at it. "It's Savannah. Something's wrong."

Emily's stance softened and some of the tension drained from her body as a look of concern appeared. "Call her," she said in a surprisingly gentle voice. "She needs to come first."

He tapped the redial, pacing back and forth as it rang. "Savannah, what's going on?" Aiden asked without waiting for her to speak.

"It's Daddy." She choked back a sob. "I came home and he was unconscious on the floor. We're at the hospital. What do I do?"

"Can I talk to a doctor or nurse?" He cast a glance toward Emily, giving his head a small shake.

"I'm in a waiting room. They took him and said they'd come for me."

"Which hospital are you at?"

"University Medical." Her voice trembled down the line, broken by the occasional sniffle.

"Keep your phone handy and stay calm. I'll book a flight right away." A sick feeling settled in his stomach. The girl sounded terrified, and he was hours away. "Call one of your friends … maybe Leanne or Justin? Have them come and sit with you."

"I'll try, but my battery's almost dead."

"Ask one of the nurses to borrow a charger. They might keep a few at the nurses' station. Is there a phone I can call you on? I have to call and get a flight."

"Let me see. Yes, it's …" She read the number as he closed his eyes, repeating it in his head.

"Got it. Make sure you ask the nurses for anything you need. I'll call you back in a minute."

"Please hurry."

"Savannah?" He took a deep breath, knowing this was the time for complete calm in order to reduce her anxiety. "It'll be okay. If the doctor or nurse comes back, have them call me or Emily. I'll be there as soon as possible."

Emily pulled her own phone out and frowned at the screen.

"They took Ross to University Medical by ambulance and Savannah is freaking out." Aiden scrolled through his phone, searching for his travel agent's number. "I have to go."

"Is it serious?" Emily rested her hand on his arm.

"They're working on him in the ER. She's alone in the waiting room, and she doesn't know anything. He was unconscious on the floor when she got home from school. Not a good sign. I need to make sure she's okay, but I can't do that from here."

"I'll help you pack."

"Here." He hit dial. "My travel agent is Casey. Can you book the first flight to Portland? Either airport is fine. I won't have time to pick up a rental so ask her to arrange a car to pick me up in Portland."

"Okay." Emily accepted his phone.

Aiden yanked on fresh clothes and packed a small travel bag with everything he'd need for several days. He darted into his office and retrieved a package of documents from his filing cabinet. After tucking his laptop and the last items into his bag, he located his keys and wallet before double-checking he had everything. "Do I have a flight?" he asked as he entered the living room.

"Casey is a miracle worker. She booked you out of O'Hare in two hours and she promised there would be a car waiting at the baggage claim. Do you want me to drive you to the airport?"

"Could you?"

"Uh-huh, if we take your SUV. You know how unreliable my car is these days."

"Perfect, thank you." He added his charger to his bag and tossed Emily his keys before locking the door behind them. As soon as they were on the road he called Savannah again.

"Aiden?" Her frightened voice crackled down the line. "Where are you?"

"On my way to the airport. I have a flight in less than two hours. Any word on your dad?"

"They took him into surgery. There's something wrong with his heart. They said he had a heart attack, and someone will be down soon. Can you talk to them?"

"If they catch me before I get on the plane, but it might be better to have them call Emily. Don't leave the hospital and keep your phone on. Did you call someone? And your phone's charging?"

"Leanne's coming with her mom, and yes, I plugged in my phone so you can call or text me. I'm scared."

"I know, honey. I'll be there as soon as I can. Hey, text me Leanne's number, so if for some reason your phone is off, I have a way to find you."

They pulled into the drop off zone, and Emily leaned across to hug him. "I'll phone when I get home and talk to her until you get checked in."

Their anger had dissipated, both more concerned with Ross and Savannah than what was happening with them. A momentary reprieve at best, he knew they would need to resume their discussion. "Thanks, Em."

"Go. Don't miss your flight." She planted a kiss on his lips.

He dashed through the airport, thankful that he had a first-class ticket. Even with a relatively smooth trip through security queue, the first boarding call had been announced as he reached the gate, so he stepped into line. They ushered him through, and he slid into his seat with a sigh.

As soon as they were in the air, he reclined his seat and closed his eyes. He was exhausted, emotionally drained, and suspected he wouldn't get much rest in Portland.

"Sir?" A warm hand shook him gently. "Dr. Hamilton? We're landing. Please put your seat up."

Forcing open his gritty tired eyes, he realized he'd given in to exhaustion almost immediately. "Thanks," he muttered.

The flight attendant pressed a glass of water into his hand. "You look rough, but water is all I can manage this late in the flight." She gave him an easy smile.

"I'll get something after we land." He sipped the cold liquid gratefully before glancing at the card she'd included along with the refreshment.

The flight attendant glanced over her shoulder as she swayed to her seat and buckled in.

A brief look at the card told him her name was Dani, with a ten digit Chicago number. It seemed he never flew anywhere without someone giving him their phone number. He slid the card into his pocket as the plane touched down on the runway, even though he knew he'd never call her. It would end up in the trash, but right now his mind was occupied with reaching Savannah.

The moment the door opened, he grabbed his carry-on bag and headed for the exit, watching for the signboard with his name, intent on reaching the hospital as soon as possible.

Chapter 29

Savannah

Savannah burst into tears as soon as Aiden opened the waiting room door. She sprang from her seat and bounded across the floor, straight into his welcoming hug. "Aiden." Her shoulders shook as he wrapped her into a secure embrace. "Daddy's really sick."

"Shh. I'm here." His arms tightened as he rocked her.

The scent of his spicy aftershave relaxed her as she cuddled against him, soaking up his warmth. Now she didn't feel so hopeless or alone and she clung to him, allowing the tears to flow down her cheeks.

"It's okay," Aiden murmured against her hair.

"I don't know what's happening."

Leanne's mom stepped forward. "I'm Jane. The doctor was in a few minutes ago and said Ross was moved to recovery. That was," she said as she peered at her watch, "about forty-five minutes ago."

"Can we page the doctor? I'd like to talk to him."

"I have his number." Jane handed the card to him.

"Thanks." Aiden looked into Savannah's eyes. "Don't worry, sweetheart. It's great news that he's in recovery, so let's get some specifics about your dad's condition from the surgeon. Give me a minute." He moved a few feet away, talking into his phone in a low voice.

Leanne's mom slid an arm around her shoulders. "See? It'll work out." She rubbed Vanna's arm with one hand.

"Aiden will stay with me now." Savannah focused on him. "Thank you for sitting with me."

"Are you sure you don't want us to stay?"

She shook her head. "Aiden will know what to do."

Aiden rejoined them and extracted a card from his wallet. "Thank you, Jane. It's late. Leave me your number and I'll update you once we know more." He looped an arm around Vanna. "Until this is sorted, I'll stay in Portland."

Jane's brow wrinkled. "I thought Vanna might like to stay with us—"

The doctor appeared at that moment, striding across the floor and extending a hand to Aiden. "Dr. Kent Morrison, Chief of Cardiology."

"Dr. Aiden Hamilton. I work in the ER in Chicago."

"You're a relative of Ross Phillips?"

"No, but …" He extracted a paper from inside his inner jacket pocket and handed it the surgeon. "What can you tell me about his condition?"

"Let's talk over here." Dr. Morrison motioned to the other side of the room.

Savannah's heart sank at the two doctors' serious expressions. Tears burned behind her eyes, her knees wobbling as she pressed a finger to her lips.

"Savannah, honey?" Leanne's mom tucked an arm around her. "Can we do anything? We don't mind staying."

"I don't need anything," Savannah said, still focused on Aiden and her dad's doctor.

"I just want to make sure you're all right."

"Aiden's staying."

"I'm glad he's here, but the offer to stay with us is open." Jane rubbed her arm. "It's a long trip from Chicago and he might need to go home."

"He won't leave me."

Aiden approached as Dr. Morrison exited the waiting room. "Let's sit." He led Savannah to the chairs and guided her into a seat. A crease developed between his eyes as he sat across from her and grasped her hands.

"What's wrong?" A fresh round of tears built as she clung to his fingers.

"They tried to repair his heart, but the damage was severe."

"Is he going to die?" she whispered as the tears bubbled over.

"He's in critical condition. They put in a pump, which is circulating his blood instead of his heart." Aiden squeezed her hands as Jane offered a box of tissues. "They're evaluating him for the transplant list, but he'd have to wait until a suitable heart becomes available. The device they're using can be kept in long-term if needed."

Savannah's heart ached as she crawled onto Aiden's lap and wrapped her arms around his neck, a fresh torrent of saltiness cascading down her cheeks. The thought of losing her dad was too much to bear.

"I'm sorry, honey," Aiden said. "The doctors are working hard to make him better."

"He's all I have." Her chest hitched as she buried her face against his shoulder. When her mom had died, it had been devastating, but her dad had still been there. Without him, she had no family.

"You'll always have me. I won't leave you, I promise."

Savannah cuddled in his arms, weeping. She couldn't let him go. That would mean facing the truth and leaving the safety of his embrace. "Aiden?" She finally pulled away, rubbing her red, itchy eyes.

"What, sweetie?" He cupped her face in his palms, brushing away a stray tear with his thumb.

"Is he going to die?" She searched for some sign, bracing herself for the answer.

"The doctors are doing everything they can. You need to be strong. I'll take you up to see him when you're ready."

"What do I say?"

"You'll find the words. Be positive, but don't hold back. Talk to him, let him know you love him."

"I might not see him again." She dabbed at her eyes and blew her nose, still sniffling as he offered a tissue.

"He's stable for now."

Vanna nodded. "Okay." She reached for yet another tissue, sucking in a deep breath. "Can I wash my face? I don't want him to see me like this." She brushed at the streak of mascara on the fabric of his shirt. "I ruined it."

"It'll wash."

"Don't leave me." A shiver ran down her spine.

Aiden lifted her to her feet and removed his jacket, draping it around her. "I'm not going anywhere. Freshen up and then we'll visit your dad."

She trudged into the bathroom and splashed icy water on her face. Red, puffy eyes stared back at her, and she leaned on the counter, hauling in several deep breaths. "I'm such a mess."

Leanne trailed behind her and hovered, shifting from one foot to the other. Now she stepped forward, curling an arm around Savannah. "It'll be okay, Vanna. Don't worry about it right now."

As Vanna wrapped Aiden's coat around her tighter, she nodded. "I'm ready."

As promised, Aiden waited for her in the hall, speaking in a low tone to Leanne's mother.

Jane patted his arm and then gave Savannah another long hug. "Hang in there, sweetie. We'll be thinking of you."

"Thank you." She accepted a hug from Leanne.

Leanne threw a sad look over her shoulder along with a small wave as she and her mom walked toward the elevators.

"Ready?" Aiden held out his hand, his grip warm and reassuring.

"I guess so," she said in a small voice.

One of the ICU nurses appeared, motioning them toward the double doors. "You can see Mr. Phillips now."

The walk down the long white hallways took forever, her shoes squeaking on the floor. It was so quiet, the only sounds indistinct murmurs and steady muted beeping from various rooms. So different from being in the ER where everything seemed so loud and furious.

The nurse ushered them into a room, and Savannah clapped her hand over her mouth. His fragility shocked her, his dry, thin skin matching the chalky white sheets. Tubes sprouted from everywhere, and a machine beeped in a dull but steady monotone.

"Daddy?" Savannah whispered. "Can you hear me?" She took her dad's limp hand in hers. "It's me, Savannah."

His eyes opened, but he only stared, a slight frown creasing his brow.

"Daddy, can you hear me?"

"Vanna," he whispered. "You're here."

"Aiden's here too. He said he'd stay until you're better."

"Aiden?" His voice trembled.

Aiden approached the bed, moving in close. "Hi, Ross."

"You came." His gaze drifted back to his daughter. "Let Aiden take care of you," he mumbled.

"You'll be home soon." Her smile wavered. "You need to rest and get better."

"Mmm." Ross bobbed his head. "I love you." The words rasped from his throat.

"I'll visit." She gave him a watery smile, trying not to show him how frightened she was to see him hooked up to so many machines.

The doctor cleared his throat. "We should let Ross rest. You can see him again in a few hours."

"I love you." Savannah planted a kiss on his cheek. Tears burned behind her eyes as she turned and shuffled from the room. Once in the hallway, she slid down the wall into a heap, hugging her knees to her chest.

Not long afterward, Aiden sat beside her and looped his arm over her shoulders. "The doctor suggested we go home and get some rest. We can come back in a few hours for another visit." His soft low voice calmed her, and she nodded. "Do you have a key for the house?"

"Yes, in my clutch." She felt a rush of relief because she knew Aiden wouldn't take her home if he thought her dad wasn't at least stable. Maybe her fears were for nothing.

"Why don't we get out of here? Ross is sleeping again." He stood, holding out his hand and pulling her to her feet. His normally artfully messy hair was sticking up in spots like he'd been continually running his hand through it. His eyes were red-rimmed with fatigue and his shirt wrinkled and streaked from her makeup.

Not that she looked any better. Her eyes were gritty and exhaustion was overtaking her. Hours had slipped by unnoticed, and she had no concept of what time it was or how long they'd been at the hospital.

They retrieved Aiden's bag from the waiting room. Another family had arrived, taking her place as they paced and dabbed their eyes.

Savannah averted her gaze, unable to bear their despair.

Aiden led her to the elevators and then out of the antiseptic smells of the hospital into the fresh air and bright sunlight.

She squinted against the glare of a bright new day. "Should we take the train?" Savannah pointed in the general direction of the station.

"No, we'll take a taxi." They joined the short queue, and moments later he assisted her into the backseat, relaying the address to the driver. "You want something to eat?"

"I'm not hungry." She couldn't remember the last time she ate, but despite that, she had no appetite.

"We'll go home and we can order something later if you like."

Savannah shrugged, though she reached out and took Aiden's hand, needing the comfort and contact. Instead of simply holding it, he wrapped his arm around her and she cuddled against his chest, closing her eyes.

"Hey, we're home." He shook her gently, handing a couple bills across the seat to the driver. After rescuing the keys from her trembling hands, he unlocked the front door. "Why don't you shower or take a hot bath and put on your pajamas?" Aiden said. "You look exhausted."

"Okay." Disheartened, she wandered into the bathroom. An acrid smell hung in the air, and she was sure it was coming from the kitchen, but she wasn't ready to face that room.

Instead, she turned on the taps full blast and dropped in some bath salts before stripping down and sinking into the fragrant, steaming water. She lay back and stared at the wall. Aiden's presence in the next room was comforting. Her worst fear was about to come true, but her father was there, ready to catch her fall.

Aiden tapped softly on the door. "Savannah? Should I order something?"

"Pizza?" She wasn't hungry, but perhaps he was after his long flight from Chicago. He may even have been working, she just didn't know. When she called, her thoughts were all about her dad and how she was clueless about what to do next.

"Sure." He retreated down the hallway, the floorboards squeaking under the worn carpet her dad had been meaning to replace.

With a sigh, she reached for a towel and dragged herself out of the tub, wrapping up in her fluffy robe before shuffling toward her bedroom.

"Hey, which is the best place?" He held up a couple of menus.

"Mario's." She proceeded to her room, pushing the door shut softly. Savannah donned cozy sleep pants and a t-shirt before joining him.

Aiden looked up, his phone pressed against his ear. "We don't know yet, but I'll call you later. Right, I'll let you get back to work." He beckoned to Vanna.

She shook her head and wandered into the kitchen. The unpleasant aroma she'd noticed before was gone, replaced with the light lemony scent of dish soap. The dishwasher hummed and the floor appeared spotless. All traces of the earlier events were gone.

A cup sat on the counter, a wrapped packet of Earl Grey beside it, and a wisp of steam rose from the kettle sitting on the back burner of the old white stove. She cocked her head, listening to the rise and fall of Aiden's voice as she poured the hot water, idly dipping the teabag.

Once silence fell, she joined him on the couch. "Everything okay?"

"Yup, just awesome."

"No, it isn't. Was that your boss?"

"It was Emily. I updated her on your dad's condition. She sends hugs."

"Oh ... I miss her. I wish she was here."

"Yeah, but she's working." His voice sounded sad. "How are you doing?" He held out his arms, cradling her against his chest when she crawled onto the couch beside him.

She shrugged. "I'm worried about Daddy."

"I know."

"Is he in pain?"

"They have him medicated, so it's controlled, and they'll give him something to help him sleep. That's why he was so groggy and unfocused. It's from the anesthetic and the pain management program. It makes it seem worse than it is."

"Oh. It took him a few moments to recognize me."

"Don't let it freak you out. He'd only been moved from the recovery unit into the ICU so it's totally normal." He patted her hand.

She nodded, knowing she could trust him. What he was telling her was the truth, unlike so many adults who tried to cover it, thinking to hide the facts was better than being straightforward.

They watched a movie while Savannah nibbled at a slice of pizza. Then Aiden retired to the guest room and Savannah slid into bed. Two hours later, she was still tossing and turning and her mind wouldn't shut down.

She tiptoed into the guest room where Aiden was sleeping, his head buried in a pillow. "Aiden?" She shook him gently.

"Mmm, what? You okay?" he mumbled sleepily, his eyes half open. "Can't sleep?"

"No." She laid her head on the extra pillow.

"It's been a rough day." He rubbed her arm.

"Yeah." She hesitated, scared to ask, but reluctant to return to her room.

"Do you want to sleep in here?"

"Can I?"

"Sure. Come on in." He gave her a small smile. "No hogging the covers."

"I won't. Thanks, Aiden." She burrowed under the blankets, grateful for the company. As she closed her eyes, she listened to the soft pattern of his breathing, not feeling quite so alone.

Chapter 30

Aiden

The alarm rang far too soon, and Aiden dragged his eyes open, momentarily confused, but it all flooded back in an instant. Losing his job, the fight with Emily, and finally the panicked call from Savannah, along with the frantic trip across the country.

He glanced at Savannah who was curled up in a ball clutching her pillow. She hadn't so much as twitched even when the alarm's shrill beep shattered the silence. It broke his heart seeing her suffer from Ross's sudden illness. He'd let her rest while she could.

After a hot shower, he dressed and placed a call to the hospital. They informed him Ross was resting comfortably with no significant change in his condition.

Time to check on Savannah. "Hey." He gave her shoulder a gentle shake. "Wake up."

It took several more shakes before she finally opened her eyes. The trauma of the recent events dawned, her face crumpling as tears threatened. "Aiden?"

"Everything's good. Your dad's resting comfortably but we should get ready to go." He rubbed her arm, trying hard to keep concern from reflecting in his expression.

Her brow furrowed and she sat, running her fingers through her hair. "He's okay?"

He nodded. "I called a few minutes ago and he's fine. Get dressed, have something to eat, and we'll visit him."

Savannah nodded and crawled from the bed, padding down the hallway to her room.

He sank onto the side of the bed, rubbing his face with both hands. After Savannah had left the room yesterday, Ross had held him back, peering at him through bleary eyes.

"If I don't make it through this, take care of Savannah. Promise. She needs her father."

Now he had to make the dreaded call. *Emily.* Their relationship already sat in a precarious position and adding to it might break them, but he had little choice. As much as he loved the woman, his daughter remained at the top of his list. The promises of one father to another were sacred.

"Hi." She answered immediately. "How are Ross and Vanna?"

"He's stable and she's holding up. We both got a little sleep and freshened up."

"You'll be in Portland for a while."

"I'm sorry, Em," he said softly. "This isn't ideal, but I need to be here." He sighed. "It could be weeks before he's ready to come home, and even then ..." He brushed a hand through his hair. "I hate leaving things this way, with us."

"It's an emergency," she said. "I'm not angry. Just ... do what you need to do. Take care of Ross and Savannah. That's what's important right now."

"Thanks for understanding. I should go. Vanna's almost ready." Aiden inhaled deeply. "I love you, Em. I'm sorry about how things have been between us. This fighting over nothing is stupid." Everything came into sharp focus. He hadn't felt like this about anyone in a long time. "Is there a way we can resolve this?"

"Don't worry about us right now."

He pinched the bridge of his nose, struggling with the emotions that rose to the surface. She hadn't said it back. "Em ..."

"We'll figure it out when you get home."

"I'll phone when I have news." Aiden disconnected the call. He spotted Savannah hovering in the doorway regarding him with sad eyes. Hopefully, she hadn't overheard the conversation. Adding the stress of his tumultuous relationship with Emily wouldn't help her mental state. "Ready to go?"

⁓

Savannah remained virtually silent during the ride, speaking only to give the occasional directions. She hesitated at the entrance, staring up at the building in apprehension. Fear and sadness were written all over her face.

Aiden looped an arm around her, leading her through the sliding glass doors. Once they arrived at Ross's room, he gave her a reassuring squeeze. There wasn't much to say. He didn't want to keep telling her it was okay when it truly wasn't. The best thing would be to give her space for now and encourage her to talk after she'd seen her dad.

Ross barely opened his eyes when they entered his room, but Aiden was sure he knew they were there.

Savannah clapped a hand over her mouth, clearly shocked at his frailty. "Can he hear me?"

"Talk to him, even if he doesn't answer. Do you want a minute?"

She nodded and pulled a chair beside his bed, holding her dad's hand and leaning against his arm.

Aiden stepped into the hallway, watching through the glass.

Dr. Morrison appeared behind him. "He's much better this morning."

He turned. "Thanks for taking such good care of him. What's the prognosis?"

"We're adjusting his meds as he's still retaining fluid, but his numbers are improving. It could be a long wait for a heart, though he's been accepted onto the list."

Aiden let out a long slow breath. "Do you think he'll improve enough to go home?"

"Barring any complications? I believe so, but the ventricular devices carry risk. We prefer to get them out as soon as possible, but there are a number of critical patients waiting for transplants." The doctor patted his shoulder. "We'll do our best."

Aiden nodded. He'd read the statistics, but this was the only option. Further surgery would accomplish nothing. The man's badly damaged heart was beyond repair, but he preferred not to dwell on it. The thought of Savannah losing another person from her life was too much to take. "I appreciate that you're doing the best you can."

Over the next few days, it became a routine. Get up, eat, drive to the hospital, sit at Ross's bedside for as long as the staff allowed, and then return home. As draining as this was, each moment Savannah spent with Ross strengthened the man's resolve to recover.

After a week, Ross had improved, and he and Aiden agreed it was time for Savannah to return to classes. Her grades were suffering as they had when her mother had passed away. Ross was adamant that she not fall into the same predicament of playing catch up.

Aiden wasn't excited about broaching the conversation, but he took the opportunity during dinner. "Time to go back to school. Things need to return to normal."

Savannah stared at him. "Do I have to?"

"It's time. Your dad's doing well. There's nothing you can do, and sitting around the hospital for hours on end isn't good for you."

The doorbell rang, and Savannah hopped up from the table. "I'll get it."

"Don't think we aren't going to finish this conversation, missy." Aiden used his best no-nonsense voice. These words sounded so strange coming from his lips. The *how it could have been* alternate universe if he'd never given her up as a baby.

"Emily."

Aiden's head came up as Savannah's words rang from the hallway.

"Hi, sweetie. How are you doing?" The unmistakable voice of the woman he'd missed so desperately sounded sweet to his ears.

Though he and Emily talked every night, the conversations were brief and they weren't saying much of anything. Her words brought him to his feet and out of the kitchen. She looked so beautiful, and he realized how much he'd missed her.

"Look. It's Emily."

"What are you doing here?" He opened his arms, wanting more than anything to hold her.

"I have a few days off, so I thought I'd surprise you." She responded with a long hug and a kiss before snuggling against his chest. "Maybe you two need some help around here?"

"It's so good to see you," he whispered in her ear, inhaling the familiar scent of her. It was hard to believe she was truly here.

"I've missed you," she whispered back. "I needed this."

"Where are you staying?"

"Here? Would that be okay?"

"Yes." Savannah bounced on her toes. "Please?"

Over the next few days, Aiden's mood improved, but he still hesitated. He loved Emily's presence, yet there were still too many unresolved issues between them.

They'd been preoccupied with getting Savannah back to school and running back and forth to the hospital and hadn't managed the much-needed serious conversation.

"You up for a walk along the river?" Emily asked after they'd dropped Savannah off at school.

Aiden reached for her hand. "I could use some air. We've been sitting around the hospital way too much." Now he could finally breathe and relax about Ross, maybe he could deal with his own life.

They found a parking spot by the river and walked in silence for a distance. It seemed neither knew quite what to say.

"Are you angry with me for taking the job?" Emily glanced at him.

"It's a huge opportunity and a great promotion. I can't say I wouldn't have done the same." Aiden had mixed feelings about the situation but logically, Emily couldn't be his boss. He never wanted to stand in the way of her career and in hindsight, he should have known this was coming when she applied for the job. And as much as he didn't want to hear how things were ticking along without him, he still needed to show his support. "Is it okay?"

"It's been difficult to find a qualified candidate to take over the chief position this late in the year, but given the situation, we'd be looking for someone anyway. I'm betting you'd have quit to be here. Dana would never have allowed you this much leave. She told me I should force you to work the two weeks. Talk about pissed off."

"She wanted my resignation and she got it. She couldn't honestly expect me to stick around and train my replacement."

"Yeah, right." Her expression made him laugh. "She did, you know. Dragon Lady thought she could bully or guilt you into hanging around, which is why she made me do it." Emily pulled him onto a nearby bench in the sun. "I'm sorry I handled it badly."

"You were forced into it. I understand that feeling better than you realize."

"Still, it felt horrible. You're one of the best doctors we have, or had, and losing you hurt everyone. You worked hard to be chief resident, and to have it taken away because of me is so unfair."

"Get used to it. Firing your boyfriend is one of the easiest things you'll face. I won't make a fuss, but I refuse to take it easy on Dragon Lady."

"I don't blame you. I'm not mad anymore either. I hate this. What will you do for work when you get back?"

"Good question. Every available position is either a demotion or won't utilize my skills. I'm Level 1 Trauma. Working at a walk-in clinic ..." Aiden sighed and rubbed his face wearily, forcing out the next words. "If I want to get anywhere with my career, I can't do it in Chicago."

"What?" Emily straightened, her eyes widening. "Where would you go?"

"Hopkins and Mass General both have emergency attending positions posted. I've also considered Portland."

"You can't."

The no-win situation. Take a job he hated in order to stay with Emily, or accept one he wanted and leave her. He'd been mulling a third option ever since she dropped the bomb on him, but he wasn't sure she'd even consider it.

"What would you have me do?" His shoulders slumped. "I've busted my ass for ten years of medical school and residency to work where? Some little clinic where my skills will go to hell? I don't want to move, but ..." He shrugged.

"That's it?" She pulled away as Aiden reached toward her. "Are you leaving me?"

"I haven't taken any jobs yet, but—"

"You were angry about me taking the job without discussion, yet you're looking out of state without talking to me." Her face flushed as her eyes narrowed.

"I have no other choice. It's move or have no career." He took a deep breath. This heated discussion was exactly what he'd dreaded. "Come with me," he whispered.

"What?" Her head snapped up and she stared at him.

"Come with me." His voice became louder and stronger as he committed to the idea. Having Emily with him would make everything perfect. "We'll find a city we like and both get great jobs. Ones that further our careers."

"I've only started this job. How can I give it up?"

"What if there was a position as good or better in another city?"

"Is there?"

"There's one in Boston. Don't believe I haven't thought about what this does to us. I love you. I want to be with you, but if either of us is forced to sacrifice our careers at this early stage, we won't last. But what if we could both have jobs we want, and we could be together?"

"Leave Chicago?" Emily shook her head. "Are you insane?"

His heart dropped. All his efforts in researching jobs and she thought he was crazy. "This relationship means that little? You won't even consider making any sort of sacrifice so we can stay together?"

"We're living together, and you'd leave? Expect me to chase after you? Uproot everything?"

"Inviting you to join me isn't the same thing as you chasing me. What I'm proposing gives us both good jobs that make us happy, and we get to be together. I'm begging you. Please come with me."

"And I'm asking you to stay in Chicago."

"I don't know what you want me to say. That I'll take a job I hate? One where I have no future or possibility of advancing? Is that what you'd have me do?"

"Well, you want me to chase after you to another city."

"I'm not—" Aiden rose from the bench and walked to the railing, staring at the churn of the water as it rushed by. This infuriating and stubborn woman had her mind set and she'd stopped listening. He knew he'd resent giving up his career as much as she seemed to resent him for asking her to leave the hospital and her position.

He glanced over as she touched his arm. "I don't know what to do," he said. "I'll stay in Chicago if something suitable comes up, but I've looked and there's nothing even close to what I gave up. There are positions at exceptional hospitals elsewhere. If I receive an offer, I'll have to accept. I really want you to come with me, but obviously—"

Aiden's phone buzzed and despite the glare from Emily, he pulled it out. He met her gaze. "It's the hospital. Ross's doctor. I have to answer."

Chapter 31

Savannah

Savannah kissed Justin before he slung his arm around her shoulders. They ambled toward the doors.

"Hey you two, wait up." Leanne's voice rang down the hallway behind them. She and Tony caught up with them a few seconds later.

Savannah missed hanging out with her friends and having fun. The overwhelming stress disturbed her sleep, but now her dad was much better and she could relax, catch up on her schoolwork, and be a teenager again.

Her phone buzzed. She extracted it from her pocket with some difficulty, her hip pressing against Justin's as they made their way across the quad to their usual table.

On my way to pick you up. Meet me out front in 15 minutes.

She frowned at the note, a stab of panic hitting.

It's only lunchtime. Everything okay?

See you in a few. I called the office, go sign out.

"Sorry, I have to leave." Savannah sighed. "Aiden's picking me up."

"I've barely seen you." Justin held onto her hand as she stood, and he tried to pull her onto his knee.

"Aiden will be here soon. He wouldn't take me from school unless it's important. I need to get my stuff and sign out at the office. Walk with me?"

Justin nodded. "I hope everything is okay."

"Bye, guys." Savannah waved at Tony and Leanne.

A few minutes later she ran down the stairs to where Aiden waited in his rental car.

"What's going on?" Savannah threw her backpack behind the seat before sliding in and buckling her seatbelt.

Aiden reached over and squeezed her hand before pulling into traffic, heading toward her house. "School okay?" He tapped a finger on the steering wheel.

"It was fine." She shrugged and stared at him. Something was going on, she could feel it. "It was nice to see my friends."

"Good." He continued to tap on the steering wheel, sending an occasional glance her way.

Savannah's hand crept up to rub her heart pendant, before she forced it to her lap. She concentrated on her breathing as a bitter taste appeared on her tongue. In. Out. In. Out. "Aiden?"

They pulled into the driveway and he took her pack as they walked up the walkway. The moment they entered the house he set it aside, taking her hand and motioning for her to sit on the couch.

"Aiden," she whispered as a tremble coursed through her. "What's wrong?"

"I'm sorry, honey." He let out a breath. "Your dad had a stroke. He's gone."

"What?" *What was Aiden even saying?* Her eyes widened. *Gone?* "Daddy died?" The words squeaked out as the tears broke free and streamed down her face. She clung to his shirt, balling it in her fists as she sobbed.

Aiden pulled her into his arms and rocked her against his chest. "I'm so sorry."

Savannah shook her head, the lump in her throat making it impossible to speak. Her whole world was coming apart, a huge weight crushing her as she struggled for air. Her vision narrowed and grew fuzzy. She was trapped in an endless, dark tunnel. "I can't ... I can't breathe."

Aiden rubbed her back and loosened his grip. "Better?"

"No." Spots clouded her eyes as the weight on her chest increased. *Was I dying too?* All she could hear was the hollow sound of her pounding heart as her head spun and her body shook.

"Take slow deep breaths. Relax and breathe. Put your head down." Aiden's deep low voice cut through the confusion.

She dragged in a huge breath and sagged against his chest, struggling to break free of the overwhelming despair gripping her.

"Head down." Aiden shifted her so she leaned on her knees while he rubbed her back. "Breathe, Vanna."

Finally the fog lifted. "Daddy ..." She closed her eyes and clung to Aiden, afraid he'd disappear if she let go. As her sobs slowed, someone pressed a soft tissue into her hand. She looked into Emily's sad eyes.

The woman sat on the couch beside her and Aiden, holding out a glass of water. "Drink. It'll help."

Help what? Nothing could help. Her dad was gone forever.

Savannah accepted the glass and took a few sips. Oddly, she felt better, but just a little. The burn in her throat receded and the weight lifted from her chest.

"Better?" The concern in Aiden's voice made her look up again.

Bobbing her head so he knew she'd heard him, she cuddled against his chest. It felt comfortable and she closed her eyes, inhaling the scent of his familiar aftershave. The steady beat of his heart soothed her and she relaxed.

Aiden said something but it drifted over her, nothing but an unintelligible muffled murmur. She wished to escape this living nightmare where both of her parents were gone from her life. Her eyelids grew heavy and she sought the relief of sleep, wanting to forget or to wake up and find it was all a bad dream.

The light had dimmed by the time she awoke in her own room, fresh tears tracking down her cheeks as she thought of her dad. She missed him already. The only consolations were she'd visited him today and told him she loved him. Now she had to go on without him.

Savannah hugged her pillow to her chest and closed her eyes, trying to will it all away and pretend it was a nightmare. But it didn't go away, and she gave up. She slumped on the side of the bed for several moments before she gathered the energy to pad to the kitchen.

Relief flooded her as Aiden turned and held out his arms. She stepped into his embrace and hugged him tightly without saying a word; none were required.

Her parents had both left her in such a short span of time. Sometimes there were no words.

"I'm sorry, honey." He rubbed her back. "Can I get you anything? Emily and I are making ravioli with tomato sauce. You should eat."

"I'm not hungry." She sniffled and dragged in a long sobbing breath as sadness engulfed her. It was impossible to let go of Aiden, but he seemed to understand and held her until she pulled back to look up at him. "How'd it happen?" she whispered. "And when? I thought he was better. That he was okay. How could he be gone? I saw him right before school."

"The heart pump caused a blood clot. It happened fast, and there was nothing they could do."

"Did it hurt?"

"No. It was quick."

That was what they'd said when her mom died. *Instantaneous death.* That she'd never seen it coming. "What happens now? What about me?" It hit her again and her body began to shake. Aiden surely had to go back to Chicago, and she couldn't live in the house alone.

"Are you sure you're ready to talk about it?"

"I need to know. Please?"

Aiden led her into the living room and sat with her on the couch. "Your dad and I discussed many things over the past few months. He left legal documents. I'm your guardian."

Her breath caught in her chest. *What did that mean?* "I'll live with you?"

"Yes." He squeezed her hand. "Your dad made sure you'd be taken care of, Vanna. You'll always have a home with me."

"In Chicago." That meant leaving Portland along with everything and everyone she knew. She simply wasn't ready to think about it, but at least she had Aiden. She wasn't alone.

―⋖―

The inevitable day of mourning dawned crisp and clear. She straightened her dark dress, struggling with the mind-numbing emptiness. Her gritty red eyes burned from the endless nightly crying.

"Are you ready?" Aiden peeked into her room. "The car's here."

"Yes ... And ... No." Though dressed and ready to leave the house, she wasn't prepared. Today would make it all too real. It wouldn't get any easier. Ignoring reality wouldn't make the pain go away. Saying her final goodbyes was all there was left to do.

Savannah stared blankly out the limo's window as the streets flashed by, clutching Aiden's hand the entire time. He'd kept his arm around her from the moment they'd left the house. Clearly, he knew she wasn't strong enough to do this alone.

All too soon they arrived and she forced her leaden feet to carry her forward, through the glass doors, and into the chapel. There were more people than she expected, and she became overwhelmed. People hugged her in a never-ending blur. Endless tears clouded her vision, and her eyes grew even redder and puffier.

By the time the service finished, and Savannah survived another round of hugs and condolences during the reception, she was exhausted. She longed to escape from all of this sorrow and hide in the peaceful surroundings of her room.

"You alright?" Justin caught her hand.

"No." She shook her head, the tears threatening to bubble up and over again. "I want to go home."

"Ready to go?" Aiden appeared beside them. It seemed he'd been watching her too. "Justin is welcome to join us. Tom and Gramma will join us at the house for dinner."

Vanna nodded, grateful for their attention and relieved the dreaded day was finished.

The minute they arrived at home, she and Justin closed themselves up in her room. She struggled to unzip her dress.

"What are you doing?" Justin frowned.

She waved at the black garment. "It's ... depressing."

"Oh. Let me help with that." He unzipped the back before dropping onto her bed.

Vanna peeled off her dress and slid on a large t-shirt and short before flopping beside him. "I have to tell you something."

"Sounds serious." Justin propped himself on one arm.

"Aiden's invited me to live with him. In Chicago."

"What." He bolted upright. "No. You can't just move."

She linked their fingers. "I don't have any other family."

He shuffled closer, burying his head against her neck. "When are you moving?"

"After final exams in June, so we have some time. We can phone, text and video chat."

"You're never coming back. Are you?"

She shook her head. "I'll finish high school there."

"We have to break up," he whispered. "You'll be on the other side of the country."

"I'm sorry. I love you, so much."

"I don't want you to go. But I understand." Holding her close against his chest, he sighed. "I love you too."

Savannah listened to the steady beat of his heart even as hers broke. Justin was the first boy she'd loved and soon it'd be over. And she still had to break the news to Leanne, although she suspected her friend already knew what was coming.

That night after Justin had left, she couldn't sleep, and loneliness crept in. She padded down the hall to Aiden's room, finding the door open. Right now, she craved the closeness and comfort her father provided. She crawled onto the bed, aiming for the open space between Aiden and Emily.

"Can't sleep?" Aiden handed her a pillow and shifted to make extra room for her. Once she'd settled, he kissed the top of her head. "Try not to wake Emily."

She dropped off to sleep, feeling like they were their own little family. The only one she had left.

~

"Call me if you need anything." Emily hugged Vanna tight.

"I wish you could stay longer."

The woman rested her hands on Savannah's shoulders and gave her a sad smile. "It's back to work for me tomorrow, but I'll see you in Chicago."

The reality of all that had happened made her feel she was drowning. Tears brimmed her eyes as Emily gave Aiden a brief hug and kiss on the cheek and settled in the backseat of the car.

"How are you?" Aiden slipped an arm around her as the sedan disappeared around the corner.

"I dunno." She lifted a shoulder. "I'll miss her."

"You'll see her soon," he said softly.

Her whole life had transformed around her, changing at the speed of light. "I'll miss my friends." In a few short weeks she'd be on a plane, heading into her new life.

"It'll be a huge change, but you can visit them." Aiden sighed. "Why don't we go for ice cream or something?" His smile didn't seem to reach his eyes.

"Yeah, okay." She shot the occasional glance at Aiden as they strolled down the street, trying to read the expressions fleeting across his features. "You must be so thrilled."

"What?" He looked at her. "Why?"

"Well …" She shuffled her feet against the gritty cement of the sidewalk. "You dropped everything to babysit me. Now you have to let me move in with you."

"Hey." He halted and turned her toward him. "Never think that way. I'm sorry about the circumstances, but don't assume I'm being forced. You're my daughter. I love you, and I want you to live with me."

"You do?" She lifted her chin. "I won't be in the way? What about Emily? She doesn't seem too excited about it."

"Emily loves you, Savannah. This has been a stressful time, that's all."

"You've been so preoccupied."

"We have a lot to accomplish before June, and …" He sucked in a breath. "I left my job in Chicago, so chances are we'll end up somewhere else."

"Why'd you leave?" From the tidbits she'd overheard, this news didn't surprise her, but it made her sad they might not live in Chicago. "Where would we go?"

"I've applied at John Hopkins in Baltimore and Mass General in Boston. I checked out Portland, but there's nothing open at the moment."

"You did?" So many questions popped into her mind. Curiosity ate at her about why he'd left the hospital, but his tone told her he wouldn't discuss it. She longed to ask about Emily, but that was a no-go area. Even though his girlfriend had stayed with them for several days and helped with the service, a noticeable strain had developed between her and Aiden.

He nodded. "We'll make the big moves all at once, then we can settle in. We might end up in Chicago for a short time, but it's unlikely. I expect to know within a couple weeks."

"What about our house?"

He tugged her hand to start them moving. "How would you feel about selling it?"

Her shoulders sagged. She wasn't ready to say goodbye to the home she'd grown up in, but she wouldn't be able to live there without her dad. "I'll need the money," she whispered.

"Not right away. The sale proceeds would go into a trust account, along with everything else your dad left you. We'll invest it until you're finished school. Gramma will pay your tuition and I'll take care of everything else."

Relief, sadness, and anticipation, topped with nerves flooded her. Her life here would soon be over.

"Sorry, too many details." Aiden offered a reassuring smile. "You only need to tell me what you want, and I'll make it happen."

"It's better knowing than not knowing." The knowledge that she didn't have to navigate it alone calmed her. "It's overwhelming, but I'm glad you're here."

She'd miss Portland and her friends, but there was a little light inside, fighting to break to the surface. Time to let her fears rest and trust in the father who'd stood by her through these dark times. She sneaked another glance at the man beside her, grateful yet again she'd allowed Aiden into her life.

A few days after she returned to school, Savannah arrived home to find the for sale sign on the front lawn. Aiden had warned her, but she still stared at it for several minutes before entering the house.

The evening routine had been dinner, homework, and then Aiden helped her attack a room of the house. Savannah picked items she couldn't give up and they sorted the rest into donation piles. This process whittled her belongings down to a small, neat stack of boxes.

Despite her growing comfort with her father, a dark spot remained. *Emily.* She'd failed to learn the details of what was happening between Aiden and his girlfriend. Whenever she tried, he brushed it off. Something had gone horribly wrong, or he wouldn't be evading her questions. Tonight was no different.

Savannah picked at her dinner, glancing occasionally across the table, where Aiden was doing the same. "There's a party on the last day of classes. Can I go?" She peered at him. "Aiden?"

"Hmm?" One brow rose as he set his fork on his plate.

"The party? It'll be the last time I go out with my friends."

"Oh. Where is it?"

They got into discussing the details, and it seemed to draw him out of his moodiness. At least for a few minutes.

"You miss Emily, don't you? Is she coming to the Vineyard?"

"Don't worry about that." He pushed his half-finished meal away. "We have plenty of time to figure out our summer plans."

Savannah cleared their plates from the table. "It's almost summer now. Only a couple of weeks and I'm done school. Then we'll go to Boston to find an apartment, right?"

He nodded and then heaved a sigh. "Much homework tonight?"

"Some." She recognized the tactic. Whenever his girlfriend came up in a discussion, he changed the subject. When the opportunity arrived, she'd discuss it with Emily herself.

Chapter 32

Aiden

Aiden moved through the house, taking note of each room as he did. The task that lay before him was daunting, but fortunately Ross had been an organized man.

During school hours, he occupied his mind with sorting and packing the small house, all the while mulling how to approach Emily with the latest developments. Two neat piles sat on the top of the guest room dresser, both great offers, but neither one in Chicago.

After their interrupted conversation by the river, neither had broached the subject of Emily joining him. She'd been wonderful, helping with the service and supporting Savannah in her grief, but by unspoken agreement, they'd avoided discussing the breakdown of their relationship. The last thing Savannah needed was them arguing about their lives while hers was torn apart.

Over the next hour, he sorted paperwork, marked boxes, and stacked them with the items to be shipped, while two of Ross's friends sorted and packed his clothing. Aiden wandered down the hall to the master bedroom. "How are you doing in here?"

"Almost through." Gerald pointed to the boxes and bags piled against one wall. "We'll drop those off at the donation center so there's less to worry about later."

"I'd appreciate it. Did either of you find anything you wish to keep?"

Rich motioned to a box. "We put a few things to the side. Are you sure Savannah won't mind?"

"It was her idea. We'll be happy if friends can enjoy some of the things she can't keep."

"What about selling it to raise funds for Savannah?"

Aiden shook his head. "This is difficult enough without her dealing with the sale of personal belongings," he said. "The money from the house and his savings will remain in trust for her until she turns twenty-one."

Rich nodded. "It's a good thing you're doing for Vanna. Losing both parents so close together is rough."

"It's been difficult, but she's strong," Aiden said. "I appreciate your help."

Not long afterward, they promise to return the next day and help with more packing, exiting with a load of donations.

Savannah arrived home from school an hour later. She wandered through, running a hand over the bare mantel.

"How was your day?" he asked.

She shrugged. "People act weird when I'm around. It's like they're scared of me."

Aiden slipped an arm around her. "They don't know what to say, is all. It'll get easier."

"I guess." She glanced around. "It's so empty."

"Rich and Gerald came by." He pulled her onto the couch. "I received two good job offers. How do you feel about Boston?"

She nibbled on her fingernail. "Where's the other job?"

"Baltimore. What do you think?"

"Definitely Boston if we can't stay in Chicago." She looked thoughtful. "What does Emily think?"

"I wanted to talk to you first."

"She's not coming with us?"

"She has a great job in Chicago." He didn't know what else to say. Until he talked to Emily again, he wouldn't know if she'd reconsidered his offer. He was afraid to find out.

"We should stay with Emily."

"It's not an option. There are no suitable positions available for me."

"Then Boston. I've always wanted to visit."

"My start date would be in September, so it'll give us plenty of time to find a place to live and arrange a new school. Then we'll spend the summer in the Vineyard. How does that sound?"

"Fine." She nodded.

"I'll send the acceptance letter to the hospital tomorrow."

⁓

The next morning Aiden scanned the signed contract, hesitating for only a second before he tapped the send button on his phone.

"Aiden. How are you?" His long-time friend, Will Kavanaugh answered on the first ring. "What did you think of the offer?"

"Amazing, though I'm not looking forward to buying real estate in downtown Boston."

"I hear that." His friend's tone brightened. "You can help me whip these new residents into shape. September?"

"Yeah, but I'll visit soon to find a home. It would be great to go for lunch. A lot's happened over the past few months."

"It must have if you're leaving Chicago." The man sighed. "We didn't receive a resume from Dr. Anderson. Trouble in paradise?"

"I'll let you know once I've booked flights."

"Avoidance. That's a yes."

After Aiden ended his call with Will, he dialed again. He couldn't put it off any longer. Time to make the dreaded call.

"You're at work?" he asked, once the awkward greetings were said.

"I have an hour before my shift. How's Savannah?"

"Holding up." He sank onto the couch, running a hand through his hair. "I received a great offer from Mass General."

"Boston?" Emily sounded … *What?* Disappointed? Irate? Who could tell? "Are you taking it?"

"Mmmhmm. They have other positions posted. You could still send your resume."

"I'll think about it," she said. "You're really doing this."

"I wish I had a choice."

"You do and you're making it."

"Come with us, please?"

Her deep sigh carried down the line. "When are you coming home?"

"As soon as Vanna's finished her final exams we'll spend a few days in Boston for house hunting." He waited for her to say something. Anything. "You could meet us and give your opinion on the new place."

"I need to finish dressing for work."

"Will you at least think about it?"

"I have to go."

"Yeah. Sure. Bye." Aiden hung up and stared at his phone for several minutes before summoning the will to move. He feared their crumbling relationship was beyond rescue. His phone chimed and he sighed before answering. "Hey, Lex."

"Joel, but who's keeping track," the man said. "You have a new nephew."

Aiden pinched the bridge of his nose, blinking hard. "Congrats, man. It went well?"

"Damn, not sure I ever want to see that again." Joel gave a low laugh. "Get down here. Ally wants you to meet Daniel."

"Wish I could, but I'm out of town. I'll visit as soon as I'm back." Missing this moment in his friend's lives saddened him, but there was no way he could leave Vanna. The best he could do was send flowers and a baby gift. "Give them my love."

~

It had been a rough month, and now it was time to leave. The house had sold, the furniture donated to a family in need, and aside from one suitcase, the personal items Savannah wanted to keep were on their way to a storage unit in Boston.

Savannah hugged Leanne, both girls wiping away tears while Justin shuffled from foot to foot. There were more tears and hugs as she said goodbye to her boyfriend, and then they were in the car.

"I can't believe this is it." As they pulled away from the curb, Savannah waved at her friends and sniffled.

"You'll see Leanne soon at their cabin and she's invited to visit the Vineyard."

"I won't be back to this house. Ever."

Aiden reached for her hand. "I'm sorry, honey." He understood on some level, but the only house he had a fondness for was the one in the Vineyard. Even his Chicago condo contained difficult memories.

"Didn't you feel sad when you left home?"

Aiden shook his head. "I never lived anywhere long enough to grow attached. My grandmother's place isn't all that cozy, is it?"

"I suppose not."

The driver unloaded their suitcases, and they checked in for their flight. Aiden led her into the first class lounge where they ordered a light lunch.

"Do you always travel like this?" Savannah looked around. "I didn't come in here when I flew by myself."

"You'll get used to it. Economy is okay for a short trip, but I prefer the comfort of first class." He sipped his drink.

She seemed content to people watch and nibble on her chicken wrap while they waited. When the boarding call was announced, Aiden was both happy and sad. This trip took him one step closer to Emily, but one day closer to the move.

Savannah leaned back in the wide seat and stretched out her legs. A cheeky grin appeared. "I could learn to hate economy."

"A difficult lesson, I'm sure." He patted her knee and relaxed in the soft leather seat.

"What can I get you, Dr. Hamilton?" The flight attendant offered warm towels, flashing perfect white teeth and batting the long lashes framing her sparkling blue eyes.

Aiden avoided her direct gaze while he ordered their drinks. The woman was undeniably attractive with her perky nose and rosy lips, but he wouldn't bite. Especially not while there was any chance of reconciling with Emily.

"Boy, you get good service," Savannah muttered after the willowy and sexy woman had visited several times offering drinks, snacks, and blankets.

"It's the doctor thing, and we're in first class. Didn't you receive good service the times you flew to Chicago?" He looked away as the petite brunette attendant glanced their way.

"Well, better than that crappy flight on the youth trip," Savannah said, snorting as the flight attendant sent a bright smile in Aiden's direction, "but not nearly as good as you get." She eyed the woman as she moved up the aisle toward them, checking on the passengers.

"Anything you need, Dr. Hamilton?"

"Another one of these." He waggled his glass. "Savannah?"

"Can I have a cola?" Vanna smiled but it faded as the woman headed toward the galley. "If she gets any sweeter, I'll barf. She's totally hitting on you."

"Oh, please. She is not." He rolled his eyes for effect, even though Savannah was right. When the woman served his next drink, the expected slip of paper slid into his hand with the glass.

Vanna's eyebrows rose, and a smirk appeared on her face.

He couldn't say, *hey, it happens all the time.* She'd find that out soon enough. Anyway, he'd never take this woman up on her blatant offer.

"She did not just give you her phone number." Disgust infused her tone and she snatched the note from his fingers. "She did. Maaaaaahniiiicaa." She stuck out her tongue and grimaced. "I can't believe it. She hit on you with your daughter sitting beside you."

"Be nice." He slid the paper from her fingers, a grin twitching at his lips. "She probably thinks you're my little sister."

"Ha. Like she even cares who I am." Savannah glowered as the woman served drinks to the couple two rows back. "Emily's way classier. I bet she doesn't hit on the patients either." She cracked the tab on her soda and poured the fizzing drink over ice.

"It's a bit different, Vanna." Aiden sighed at the dark look coming his way. His daughter was relentless. As hard as he tried, he failed to hide the issues between him and his girlfriend. "I wouldn't call her, anyway." He folded the paper into a tiny bundle, tapping it into Vanna's empty soda can with his fingertip.

He turned to stare out the window, sipping his scotch. Even thinking about Emily hurt. The few calls between them had been brief and unproductive. His offer to pay for a flight to Boston met with a noncommittal and cool response. Their relationship had sunk into non-existence, and there was nothing he could do about it.

―∼―

After checking into the hotel and stowing his belongings, Aiden looked at his phone one last time for messages. His heart sank. *Emily wasn't coming.* He missed her so much it had become a physical ache, but he refused to beg. Time to accept the inevitable death of their relationship.

Savannah tapped on the door frame of the adjoining room. "I'm ready."

"Let's go shopping." He tore his gaze from the screen.

At least Savannah seemed excited about apartment hunting. He'd been worried about moving her away from her friends, but the girl had donned a valiant face. Perhaps the few weeks they'd spent in Portland while she finished school had eased the transition, allowing sufficient time for closure.

"The agent will meet us in the lobby. We'll be doing a fair amount of walking, so wear comfortable shoes."

"That's the only kind I own."

In the hotel lobby, a lovely dark-haired woman approached them. "Dr. Hamilton? I'm Melissa."

Aiden introduced Savannah and told the agent to lead the way. He noticed Savannah trailing along, taking in the sights and sounds of Boston as they traveled through Back Bay.

Melissa chattered non-stop, pointing out various historical sites until they arrived at the first apartment and approached the bank of elevators. "This building has excellent security," she said as she held up the key fob and pushed the button for the top floor.

Savannah leaned back as the elevator rose to the top and opened into a small private foyer. Her eyes widened as the agent ushered them upstairs to the expansive private patio. "Wow," she mouthed at him. His daughter's huge grin widened further as she took in the bank of floor to ceiling windows, the shining hardwood, and the kitchen fit for a gourmet chef. She gave him a little nod and thumbs up behind the agent's back as they descended toward the lobby at the end of the tour.

They went through the motions of viewing the other units for sale, but by the end of the afternoon, Aiden decided to take a second look at the first unit they'd viewed.

"You like this one?" He walked through with Savannah while the agent waited patiently by the front doors.

"It's amazing. I love, love, LOVE the gourmet kitchen." She trailed a fingertip along the gleaming counter. "It's perfect."

"We'll see if they accept my offer, but it's ideal. It's close to work and great schools, and it's secure. Bigger than what I wanted, but it has everything on our list."

"You worry about me?"

"It's a city, like Portland or Chicago. I want you in a secure building when I'm on nights."

"I still don't get why we aren't staying in Chicago."

"I needed to make some changes. And Boston has a great selection of colleges for you."

"If I get into a good school."

"The wonderful thing about Boston is there are many great schools. The private ones in the area offer small classes and lots of personal attention. If you work hard, you'll be able to go wherever you want once you graduate."

"Private schools are expensive, right? Will I still be able to go where I want for undergrad?"

"Your job is working hard to get the grades. Paying for school, keeping you safe, and buying clothes are mine."

"You sound like my dad." Tears trickled down her cheeks. "I still miss Daddy."

Aiden slipped an arm around her shoulders. "I can never replace Ross, and I don't want to. I miss him too, but I am your father, Savannah. I want the best for you."

"You two got along so great. I loved that you both tried so hard. You did that for me. And here I am, crying like a big baby again."

He pulled her into a hug. "It's natural to cry and miss him. Never apologize for grieving." He rubbed her arm. "All the changes are overwhelming, but it will get better once we're settled. We'll take care of each other, right?"

"You're an adult, you don't need taking care of." Savannah sniffled.

"Sure I do, but only a little." Aiden gave her a reassuring smile. He loved this girl so much and felt lucky to have her in his life. He vowed never to take it for granted.

Once the offer on the new apartment had been accepted and the visits to the potential schools completed, they returned to Chicago. Aiden let them into the silent apartment, dropping his keys on the tray by the door. It had been months since he'd been home.

"Why don't you get settled, and we'll make dinner?"

Savannah nodded and wheeled her suitcase toward her room while Aiden put his bag away.

A disappointed sigh escaped as he viewed the empty shelves in the fridge. He'd longed to stay in and relax. "Change of plans. We'll have to order in or go out. What are you in the mood for?"

"We're eating out again?" Savannah pouted and batted her eyes at him. "I wanted something homemade."

He laughed and shook his head. "So we need to buy groceries?"

"I'm a weird teenager," she said as she waved a hand, "but we've eaten out so much."

They visited the local market and replenished the cupboards and fridge. Within two hours, they were busy in the kitchen and the savory smells wafted through the air. Savannah chopped vegetables, throwing everything into the wok, the food sizzling as it hit the hot oil.

Emily appeared, setting her bag on the chair near the built-in desk. "I thought you were home tomorrow." She smiled faintly. "Smells wonderful, Savannah."

Vanna skipped over and threw her arms around the woman. "I missed you. I made tons, if you're hungry."

Emily returned the embrace. "I planned to order in." Her gaze briefly met his as she released the girl, then she looked away, crossing her arms and hunching her shoulders.

"Eat with us, please?" Vanna asked.

"I should change, then." Emily skirted around the island, her gaze flitting his way before she headed down the hallway toward the bedrooms.

Aiden set his lips in a flat line as he lowered the heat under the rice.

"Why didn't she come to Boston?" Savannah asked.

"I don't know, but … Hey. Watch the veggies."

"Oh." Savannah jumped into action, turning down the gas flame before seizing the wooden spoon and stirring.

Aiden turned away, pinching the bridge of his nose and closing his eyes for a moment, determined not to let this break him. He forced a smile and set an extra place at the table, even as his appetite faded.

After they'd finished dinner, the three of them worked together to clear the table and tidy the kitchen, Vanna chatting about little things to fill the awkward silence. "I'm beat. I'm heading to bed." Savannah stretched and yawned the moment they were done. "Night, Aiden. Night, Emily." She gave them each a hug and kiss before disappearing toward her bedroom.

Aiden glanced at Emily. "I'm done in and have to unpack."

She nodded and headed toward the bedroom.

Aiden switched off the lights in the kitchen before he followed, retrieving the suitcase he'd left just inside the bedroom door. He unzipped the bag.

Should I even bother unpacking? Based on the furtive glances from the woman propped on the bed, pretending to be immersed in her novel, he wasn't so sure.

What was there to say? Should he express his disappointment that she hadn't bothered to come to Boston, or even respond to his invitation? Tell her he was hurt that her career was more important than him or Savannah? Ask her why she was still here, in his bedroom, when it felt like she'd already left?

"How was Boston?" Emily set her book on the nightstand.

He kept his focus on his task. "We bought an apartment." This statement was met with silence. "Savannah picked a school, so she's set for the fall term." Aiden refused to look at her, dreading what was surely coming next.

"Oh. Good."

The two word answer stung, but Aiden forced himself not to respond. If he opened his mouth, he'd say something he'd regret. After weeks apart, it was difficult to accept she'd only contributed five non-committal, disinterested words to this discussion.

He tossed his dirty clothing into the hamper and lay his suits on the end of the bed, ready to be folded and placed in the dry cleaning bag, formulating a response to the insignificant yet incredibly revealing words she'd offered. He stepped into the closet and tucked his suitcase on the shelf.

"Who's Dani?"

"Huh?"

"Dani." Emily sat crossed-legged with one of his jackets draped across her knees. "Who is she?"

"No idea. Why?"

"Her phone number's in your pocket, so you must know her." She waved a card in the air, directing a scorching look his way.

Aiden squinted. It seemed vaguely familiar. *Dani* ... The hazy memory of that awful flight flitted through his mind. "The flight attendant."

Her eyes narrowed. "You have her number, why?"

"No particular reason. I forgot I even had it."

"I see."

"Do you? I didn't ask for it, she gave it to me."

"I just bet she did," she muttered.

"What the hell is that supposed to mean?" He scoffed. "Don't make a deal out of this, okay? Whatever you're thinking ... what are you thinking?"

"Gee, I don't know. That my boyfriend's been living on the other side of the country for weeks, and when he finally comes home, he has another woman's number in his pocket?" The corners of her mouth turned down as she lifted her eyebrows.

"Really, Emelia?" Annoyance sped through him. "I spent those weeks keeping Vanna together. She lost her father. Are you seriously accusing me of banging some flight attendant?"

Emily bowed her head, hiding her expression.

"I'll only say this once. Nothing happened." He remained rooted to the spot, unable to believe this was really happening. "The lack of trust is—"

"You're leaving me, and I shouldn't be upset? Maybe you've already moved on."

"What's the point of this discussion? You've already decided you're staying. Where does that leave us?"

"How do you know what I've decided?"

He stared at the floor, lowering his voice to barely a whisper. "Am I wrong?"

"No." Emily picked at the corner of the card. "I'll find somewhere else to live. I've got a life and a great job. I refuse to chase after you."

"So that's it?" He rubbed his hands over his face, keeping his voice controlled. "You're moving out?"

"As soon as I can."

Aiden switched to autopilot. Damned if he'd allow her to see his pain. If the feelings were one-sided, he wouldn't allow her further power over his heart. If she'd chosen her job over him, so be it. Her lack of trust made it even worse. "Fine. Do what you need to do. We'll pack before we leave for the Vineyard." He kept his tone flat and expressionless. "I wish …"

"What?"

"Never mind. It no longer matters." He turned away, blinking hard against the burn behind his eyes.

"I'll sleep in the guest room." She bounced off the bed, flipping the card at him as she stalked out, slamming the door behind her.

"Great," he muttered. "Just fucking awesome." He sank onto the side of the bed. Time to lock this away and put it behind him like every other failed relationship. He'd thought she was the one, but as usual, he'd misjudged. He was nothing to her. She certainly wasn't willing to make any concessions so they could be together.

He crawled into bed and closed his eyes. He'd been so close to happiness, and now it was over.

Chapter 33

Savannah

Savannah leaned against the wall, cringing as their raised voices carried down the hall. Eavesdropping was wrong, but she'd been on her way back from the kitchen with a glass of water and curiosity had gotten the better of her.

She ducked into her room at the rattle of a knob, the tears trickling freely down her cheeks as a door slammed, followed by footsteps and the soft click from the direction of the guest room.

Vanna pressed her back against the door, brushing at her damp cheeks, smothering her sniffles. Dinner had been excruciating, with Aiden and Emily barely saying a word as she chattered on about anything that came to mind. Her worst fears were confirmed.

After a several minutes, she crept from her room and tiptoed to the master bedroom. She tapped on the door.

"Come in."

She padded across the dark room and crawled into the massive bed beside Aiden.

"You okay, Vanna?" he asked in a low voice.

"Can I sleep in here with you?"

"Of course." His voice was soft and sad which had become the recent normal.

It hadn't escaped her how discouraged he seemed when Emily hadn't shown in Boston or that he hadn't been himself the past few days. She'd noticed the constant checks on his phone and how his smiles had lacked their usual brightness. Emily's refusal to join them said it all. The relationship had fallen apart.

He rolled onto his side to face her. "You can talk to me."

Better to admit her worries. Aiden had a way of seeing through her that was most unsettling. "Emily's not moving, is she?"

"No," he said in a flat tone. "She's not coming to the Vineyard either."

"You're breaking up? Why?"

"It's complicated, but Boston is the right choice for us, with or without her."

"Did you do something? Or did she? Or is it me? Did I cause this?"

"No, nothing like that. It's not that kind of breakup. You can talk to her whenever you like, but she and I won't be together as a couple."

"You should marry her."

"Stop."

She should leave it alone, but she just couldn't. "Emily makes you happy. If you marry her, she'll move."

Aiden sighed and turned onto his back. "Go to sleep, Savannah."

Now he sounded like a dad and not the cool big brother she thought of him as when they first met. Maybe that wasn't such a bad thing. "Goodnight, Dad." She leaned over and kissed his cheek before settling down on her pillow.

"Goodnight, my sweet girl. Get some rest." He ran a hand across her hair and ruffled it before he kissed her cheek in return.

Savannah let the tiniest of smiles cross her face. The thought of losing Emily saddened her, but she loved his acceptance of his new title. Maybe things would be okay. Maybe Emily would see he loved her and change her mind.

When Savannah woke up the next morning it was almost nine and her dad was gone. She showered and dressed before heading into the kitchen.

Emily sat at the table sipping a steaming cup of coffee. The woman looked tired, her eyes red and a touch puffy, but she smiled as Savannah entered the room. "Good morning. Sleep well?"

"Where's my dad?"

"He had some errands. What do you think about a girls' day out?"

Savannah frowned. Was this to ease the transition and allow Emily to make excuses?

"Don't look so concerned. He had legal papers to deal with for the Boston apartment and some banking to complete before you go away for the summer. If you're not up for shopping with me, Aiden will take you tomorrow."

"No. I'd like to go."

"It'll be fun." Emily extended two envelopes along with a stack of cash and a shopping list. "Aiden had some clothing suggestions."

Savannah flipped through the pile. Her eyes widened as she counted the substantial stack of bills. Then she turned her attention to the envelopes, both of which had been opened. Inside the first one, she found a credit card with her name on it. She bounced on her toes. "Aiden got me a credit card."

"You can use it for anything you need." Emily glanced at her watch. "Why don't we go out for breakfast?"

Savannah nodded and hurried back to her room to organize her wallet with her new card before meeting Emily at the front door.

They walked in silence for the two short blocks to the small café.

Once seated, Savannah fiddled with her napkin. How would Emily react to her questions? "Why aren't you moving to Boston with us?"

Emily dragged her fingers through her curls, leaning one elbow on the table. "Haven't you discussed this with Aiden?"

Savannah studied her, unsure how far she dared push the issue. The woman's lips set in a firm line as she returned the scrutiny without any outward sign of emotion. Finally, Vanna shrugged. "He asked you to move. Why won't you?"

"It's not so easy, sweetie." Emily sighed. "I have a job, and Aiden needs to move to further his career."

"I don't understand why he left the hospital. If he'd stayed, we could all be together. You won't come to Boston for me?" Savannah almost missed the tiny rise in Emily's brow. "Or help him get his job back?"

"He didn't tell you why he left?"

"Just that he needed a change, and he can't find anything in Chicago. Why?"

Emily dropped her credit card on the table and waved down the server. "We have a lot of shopping to do before your appointment with Josh this afternoon."

Savannah studied her. The way Emily avoided looking at her made the woman seem guilty. Whatever the case, the subject was closed.

They spent the morning buying summer clothes and then visited Josh for a trim and some pampering. She'd miss this closeness and having Emily in her life on a daily basis. Soon she'd be on a plane to Oregon to visit Leanne, and then she'd fly to the Vineyard to meet up with Aiden. She needed to find a way to include Emily.

After they returned to the apartment, Emily helped her pack two bags. One for her time with Leanne, and one for Aiden to take with him to the Vineyard.

Savannah nibbled at her lip before she finally blurted out the question at the top of her mind. "Do you love him?"

"Who? Aiden?"

She frowned. "Who else would I be talking about?"

"I care about him a great deal."

"Oh." Savannah gnawed on her lip. Is that why she'd allow him to move so far away and decline his invitation? Didn't she see a future?

"I can tell what you're thinking, but the situation is complicated."

"Why do adults always say that? You love him or you don't. What's so complicated about that? Why are you choosing a job over us? He needs you, Emily. Why can't you see that?" Savannah's eyes burned with fresh tears.

"Savannah." Emily reached toward her.

She shoved Emily's hands away. "You care a great deal? And you asked who I meant? Are you seeing someone else?"

Emily's eyes widened. "No. I wouldn't do that."

"Then why? Is it me? You don't want to be with someone who has a kid?"

"This is between me and Aiden. It has nothing to do with you. I promise."

"I can finish by myself." Savannah inhaled a long shaky breath. "Can you leave me alone?"

"We can't talk about this?"

"I don't want to talk. You're leaving me just like everyone else. You don't love him. Why did you move in here?" The anger flashed from nowhere, and she couldn't hold it in. Another person was abandoning her. It wasn't fair. "Just go away and leave me alone."

Emily held up her hands. "It's hard to understand—"

"Get out of my room. I hate you. Get out." Savannah burst into tears.

Aiden appeared in the doorway. "What the hell is going on in here?"

Savannah didn't understand any of this. Why couldn't either of them see it? Aiden loved Emily, yet she couldn't see what she'd done to him.

Emily seemed frozen and helpless, but then she let out a choked sob, brushing by Aiden as she dashed from the room.

"Em?" Aiden hesitated for only a moment before he opened his arms to Savannah, wrapping her into his embrace. "Calm down." He rocked her against his chest. "Shh. Don't cry."

She struggled to breathe as the horrible and familiar feeling overtook her. A crushing weight descended onto her chest. It all crashed down around her. Losing her parents, her mother's rejection, the refusal of her grandparents to meet her, leaving her friends, and now, Emily too. She'd just lost the closest thing she'd had to a mother in a long time.

Unable to speak, she burrowed against Aiden and clung to him. "Don't leave me. Don't go away too."

Chapter 34

Aiden

Aiden tucked Savannah into her bed, cradling her and rubbing her back until she fell asleep. His presence had calmed her down, but it brought a fact into clear focus. He'd misjudged the damage this breakup had done to his daughter.

He returned to the bedroom, finding Emily gathering the last of her things from the bedside table. Her rapid exit from the master bedroom made it far too real. The unfathomable had happened. How had things gone so wrong in such a short time?

"Is she okay?" She turned her red-rimmed, puffy eyes toward him.

Aiden sank onto the side of the bed. "She had another panic attack. This situation is hard for her, and us fighting isn't helping. What did you say to her?"

"Nothing. She freaked out. What did you say?"

"Only that you're not moving with us to Boston." He rubbed his hands across his face. "It's my fault. This move was a huge mistake. She needs her friends."

"Or you could stay in Chicago."

"I signed a contract, so I couldn't stay even if the most amazing job appeared tomorrow. I should have stayed in Portland and found something there. Savannah needs a little stability in her life."

"So you would've taken a job you hated to stay there?"

"For my daughter? Yeah, Emily, I would. That little girl has lost pretty much everything at this point." He lifted his gaze to hers. "What did she say to you? What caused her to lose it?"

The silence stretched out forever before Emily sat beside him, head bowed. "She asked why I wasn't moving to Boston. Then she freaked out on me. I guess she didn't like the answer."

"Oh. I'll talk to her when she gets up."

"That's it?"

"What do you expect from me?" The answer to the question, of learning what Emily had said to Savannah was something he wasn't ready to hear. Maybe she'd admitted what they had wasn't enough, and she didn't love him. "You don't want to move and I can't stay. You believe we'll make this work long distance? See each other when we can fit it in between shifts? This is hard on everyone. I wish I hadn't let her get so damn attached to you. It's done more harm than good."

"So I should get the hell out?" Emily shoved off the bed, stalking away from him.

"That's not what I said. I'm not throwing you onto the street. I can't believe you'd even think I would." He closed his eyes, drawing in a long breath, concentrating on keeping his tone level. "Take as long as you need to find a place. We'll be gone by Friday."

"You're running off for the summer?"

"I'm taking the vacation we planned with my daughter. You're choosing not to come. Don't blame your decisions on me, Emelia."

Emily brushed at her eyes. "You're choosing to leave me."

"You think I want this?" He threw his hands up. "I hate this. All of this. I'm doing what I need to do, for me and for Savannah. She's my daughter and it's better for her to be away from her mother, and I need a job. If one of us is forced to give up our career, we'll only resent it."

She burst into tears, covering the few feet between them and wrapping her arms around him. "This is it? We're over just like that?"

"Yeah, I guess we are." He pressed his cheek against her hair, forcing back the 'I love you' he longed to say. "I wish things were different." He sighed. "Can we keep it civil?"

"You're right. I don't want our relationship to end like that. Do you think I can make it up to Vanna? I don't want her to believe I'm abandoning her."

"She won't think that."

"She hates me."

"That's not true. Once she wakes up, you two can talk." He placed a kiss on her forehead. "You'll find she doesn't hate you at all."

Emily wiggled free of his grasp and hurried from the room, and he let her go.

There was nothing to gain by chasing her. He needed to process the painful reality and let her go.

Aiden let his daughter sleep, occupying himself with packing and moving his clothing into the wardrobes delivered by the moving company. Once most of his clothing and personal items had been stowed away, he tapped on Savannah's door. "Vanna?"

She said nothing, but he could tell she was awake by the tiny movement as she curled up under the covers.

"Why don't you come out? It's past dinner time. You must be hungry."

"I want to stay here."

Aiden sighed. "Oh, sweetie, you can't hide forever. At least come out from under all those blankets before you suffocate." He sat on the side of the bed and folded back the covers.

She opened her puffy red-rimmed eyes and stared at him. "I can't come out. Ever. I'm a horrible person. Emily hates me."

"Emily will never hate you. This is my fault, and I'm sorry. You've had too many changes in such a short time. I should have tried harder to find something in Portland."

"It's not your fault, it's hers. She's leaving."

"She and I are breaking up, but she's not leaving you. She hopes the two of you can still be friends. Even though we won't be together as a couple, we still care about each other. Don't write off the relationship you've built with her."

"You were fighting over me, so it's my fault. Just admit it."

"No, Savannah. It wasn't over you." He shook his head. "It was over us. Nothing you say or do can change what's happening between me and Emily."

She picked at a nail, nibbling at it before she finally looked at him. "I'm sorry for losing it. It won't happen again."

"It might, but don't be so hard on yourself." He held out his hand, happy when she reached out to take it and allowed him to pull her in for a hug. "I love you."

"You can forgive me just like that?"

"Of course. Part of truly loving someone is accepting they'll make mistakes. Being able to forgive is part of real love. Now come out and talk to Emily, please? She's upset about what happened, and you two need to talk."

"Okay." Savannah seemed reluctant, but she slid off the bed. "I'll be out in a minute."

Their last day in Chicago arrived all too soon. As awkward as it had been with Emily flitting in and out of the apartment, Aiden wasn't quite ready for it to end.

"Sweetie." Emily rounded the counter and wrapped Savannah in a hug. "I wanted to see you before you left for Portland."

Before they left forever. He wished Emily would come to the Vineyard, but their goodbyes had already been said. Stretching out the relationship any longer would lead to nothing but misery and pain.

"I'll miss you." She clung to the woman, her eyes shimmering with unshed tears.

"Oh, honey, please don't." Emily brushed at her own eyes. "I'll miss you so much." She stepped back, keeping her head down as she retrieved her purse.

Aiden didn't want to watch her leave, but he kept his expression impassive, wrapping an arm around his daughter.

And then Emily was gone without a backward glance.

"We should finish getting ready. You have a flight, and I'm heading to Boston to take possession of the apartment."

"You going to be okay?" she whispered.

He dropped a kiss on her hair. "Don't you worry about me. You'll have a good time with Leanne. I loaded the bags, so get your things."

Savannah said little during the ride to the airport. Once she'd been checked in, he walked her to the security screening area. "Bye, Aiden."

"Have fun in Portland." Aiden pulled her in for one more hug. "Check in with me after you land."

"I will." She stretched and planted a kiss on his cheek, giving him a last hug before she joined the security queue.

He waited for a few minutes before he sent the text.

Love you, Vanna. See you soon.

Her sweet reply came only moments later.

Love you too, Dad. I can't wait to visit the Vineyard.

With a sigh, he exited the airport and slid behind the wheel of his car. Today was the end of something amazing, but also a beginning as he started his journey as a full-time father. That would have to be enough.

Aiden tossed the last item into his shopping cart before making his way toward the cashier.

"Hey, Aiden."

"Joel." He pushed his cart to the side. "I didn't know you were here. How's Alex? And Daniel?"

"Fine. She'd be better if you'd tried harder to be there when our son was born."

"Sorry. It couldn't be helped." He forced a smile. "Did she like the flowers and baby gifts?"

"Duh. She classed it all as either extra-cute or extremely thoughtful." Joel's eyes rolled skyward. "Throw money at it and all is forgiven. She can't shut up about that spa voucher."

Aiden sighed. He had considered the gifts carefully and visited Alex and their new son the day after he'd returned to Chicago, but apparently that wasn't enough. "Well, at least one of you appreciated it."

"You're an asshole, but we've been friends forever and for some reason, I miss you."

"Well, thanks. I've missed you too." Aiden controlled the urge to roll his eyes.

"The lovely Emily with you?"

"We broke up."

"What did you do this time?"

"That's a very long story I'm not ready to tell." His friend's assumption of wrongdoing was upsetting, but if he accepted the blame, it might shut down the inevitable questions. Even thinking about her hurt. He wasn't ready to discuss it quite yet. "You know me. I can never keep it together long before it all goes to shit."

"Could it have something to do with a certain leggy, blue-eyed blonde that you've been running into with alarming frequency?" Joel raised a brow.

"Not a chance." A short harsh laugh burst free at Joel's smug grin. "I thought you'd gotten the picture. Quit bringing it up."

"Hmmm. You're here alone?"

"Yup. Licking my wounds after yet another brutal dumping."

"Don't even pretend. You liked this one." His friend tilted his head.

"What's not to like? She's intelligent, gorgeous, sweet, and kind. Some guy will be very lucky someday."

"Just not you."

"Nope."

"Maybe it's for the best. Emily is fantastic, but it's not fair to either of you to force yourself to love her."

"She deserves better, right? I'm destined to be alone because every woman warrants more than I can give."

"Oh boy, you're in rough shape. Come over tonight for our famous fish tacos. We'll have a couple cold ones."

There was no point in arguing. If he didn't go to them, Joel and Alexis were sure to appear at his door. "Let me take this stuff home."

Two hours later, Aiden headed down the beach.

"How are you?" Alexis hugged him and planted a big kiss on his cheek. "I've missed you, honey."

"He told you about Emily."

"Mmm." She nodded. "Are you okay?"

"As okay as I ever am. Where's that baby boy of yours?"

"On the patio with his daddy. Why don't you join them? Beer?"

"I'll get it." He fished one from the fridge and cracked it open, taking a long swallow. "Can I help with anything?"

"I've got it all under control." She steered him toward the patio doors. "Relax."

"Joel." He peered at the tiny boy in his friend's arms before dropping into a deck chair. Seeing this domestic scene made his heart ached for the baby girl he never held as an infant.

"You made it. Could you hold the little man for a minute? I should light the grill."

"Absolutely." Aiden took Daniel, expecting fresh baby smell, but wrinkling his nose as the odor hit him. "Whew, was that a trick?"

"What?" A guilty grin appeared.

"You need to get your nose checked. Where's the change table?"

"Ally will do it."

"You'll never win points by making her change all the diapers." Aiden headed toward the house, shaking his head.

"Uh, you sure you know how to change one?"

"It's hardly a novelty for me."

Joel laughed and Daniel started to whimper. "Right. I guess a nasty diaper is nothing, doctor."

"You've got that right."

Aiden had the baby changed and into a fresh outfit within five minutes. "That's better, huh Daniel?" He cradled the tiny boy in one arm and retraced his steps to the patio, almost walking into the blonde woman as she rounded the corner. "What are you doing here?" He glared at Joel.

"I could ask you the same thing." Tiffany eyed the baby nestled against Aiden's chest.

"I'm staying at my house for the summer."

"Hmmm. Daniel looks comfy with you."

Joel disappeared into the house, throwing a surreptitious glance over his shoulder.

Aiden narrowed his eyes at his friend's back, cursing the man's cowardice. "We get along great."

Tiffany peered toward the house. "Are you still seeing her?" she whispered.

Aiden sighed. "Her adoptive dad died about a month ago, so she's moving to Boston with me."

"What the hell are you thinking?" Her eyes looked stormy, like icy daggers digging into him.

"You don't need to be involved. Marry Harrison and live in your little dream world." He scoffed, her apparent lack of concern about Ross's death and how it affected Savannah causing a flicker of anger.

"What about Emily? Is she moving to Boston?"

"No."

"I'm sorry to hear it didn't work out." She sounded anything but sorry to Aiden. "She knows everything?"

"Yes."

"You're sure she won't talk?"

"Positive." Aiden kept his voice level.

"You're angry with me."

"Maybe I'm disappointed." He bounced Daniel gently, lowering his voice even further. "If he loves you, he'll understand."

"Sure, because everyone will be so accepting." She swept her hair back over her shoulder, her chin tilting upward. "They'll judge me. Maybe you're fine with that? But I'm not." Anger dripped from her words. "They'll be all boys will be boys about you, while I'll be branded a cheap slut."

"Oh, please." He snorted at her dramatic tone. "Everyone who? Anyway, it was years ago. Things have changed."

"That's why you're still with Emily. Why'd you break up?"

"Not because of Savannah."

"You can't keep a relationship together, so how can you know what I'm dealing with?"

Aiden rolled his eyes. "At least I don't run to Daddy to fix my problems. Why is it so hard to acknowledge your daughter's existence?"

"Any hint of impropriety and Harrison won't get elected."

"Good to know you're a warm and caring individual."

"Don't be an asshole. If you mess things up between me and Harrison, I'll never forgive you."

"Once I move you won't have to be concerned. You can keep on being a selfish bitch. Were you always this two-faced? Guess you had me fooled for all those years. Makes me wish we'd never met."

Joel came out carrying a tray of vegetables. "You two look serious. Everything okay?"

"Aiden is moving to Boston."

Joel spun, fumbling with the tray. "What? Why in the hell would you move to Boston?"

"I have a job offer. I start mid-September."

"When were you going to share this big news?"

"I'll check if Alex needs help." Tiffany smirked, a triumphant expression on her face as she stalked into the house.

"What the fuck, man? Why didn't you tell me she'd be here?"

"Uh …"

"I bet you and Lex have some big reconciliation planned, but it's not happening. Get it out of your head. I'm leaving." Aiden held out the baby.

"At least stay for dinner. You don't have to talk to her."

"That'll work. We can sit in awkward silence." Aiden shook his head. "If I'd known about your house guest, I'd have declined. Just accept that we'll never get back together."

"Ally refuses to give up after all that matchmaking in our teen years." Joel held his arms out for Daniel. "What the hell is up between you? It's like you want to kill each other."

"Give my apologies to Alex." Aiden strode away. He'd looked forward to a relaxing evening with his friends, but their unbelievable crap had ruined it. He was done with Tiffany, and he had no intention of ever looking back.

Aiden answered the call, thinking it was Joel. He'd avoided the phone since the run-in with Tiffany, opting for a day on his sailboat rather than chance having to deal with any of them. He wasn't sure Joel or Alex would let it go.

A shrieking baby obliterated his greeting. He winced at the harsh sound and hit the speaker button.

"He won't stop crying." She sobbed into the phone. "I don't know what to do."

"Tiffany? Is that Daniel?"

"He's screaming his head off."

"I got that part." He rubbed his ringing ear. "Does he have a fever?"

"I don't know. He's been like this for almost an hour. Should I take him into emergency?"

"No, I'll look at him. Hang tight, and I'll be there as soon as I can." Aiden pulled out the small fully-stocked medical bag he kept in the closet.

Five minutes later he pulled out of his driveway. Tiffany let her emotions get away from her too often, and despite the fact she'd had a baby, he didn't think she had much experience with their care. The poor little guy needed immediate rescue.

"Thank goodness you're here." Tiffany shoved the shrieking infant at him the moment he stepped inside the house. "What took you so long?"

"Excuse me for not having a transporter." Aiden rolled his eyes. "Come here, little man. What's the matter?" He unwrapped the screeching baby from his fuzzy blanket. Aiden draped the baby over his shoulder and bounced him while giving him gentle pats on his back which only made Daniel scream louder. He laid the baby on top of the blanket and did a quick exam.

"What's wrong with him?" Tiffany paced, and then halted to peer down at them. "Should I call Joel and Alex?"

"Geez, relax. His belly is fine, as are his ears and eyes, and there's no fever. Sometimes babies fuss." Aiden checked Daniel's diaper, leaving the sleeper undone. "Did he eat?"

"He took a full bottle. I tried giving him more, but …" She shrugged.

"How big was the bottle?" Aiden nodded as she held up the empty. "Not hungry then." He rested Daniel against his shoulder, rocking the baby, swaying back and forth, constantly changing the baby's position as he rubbed his back. "What's the matter, Daniel?" He wandered into the kitchen and turned on the fan, still swaying with the baby, using the white noise to soothe him with no effect.

He kept moving and changing the baby's position, stepping out on the patio, and pacing back and forth. After a time, Daniel lost steam, his cries becoming small hiccuping sobs. Aiden offered his pinky finger, and Daniel latched onto it, his tiny digits wrapping around Aiden's.

"He'll get cold." Tiffany held out the heavy blanket.

Aiden gave his head a small shake, keeping his attention focused on the baby. "That's better, huh?" He kissed the top of Daniel's head, cuddling the little boy close, still rocking him.

"It's working," Tiffany whispered. "I'll get his soother. He wouldn't take it earlier."

"No need. We're going to relax. Right, little man?"

"You're great with babies. I wouldn't have thought to bring him outside." Tiffany ran a fingertip over Daniel's head. "He's so little, I panicked. Sorry for dragging you over here. I should've just handled it."

"He's only a few months old, so having a doctor check him isn't a bad idea. I suspect he overheated. It's summertime and babies' temperatures change rapidly. It's easy for them to get too hot or too cold."

"Oh. That simple? I feel like an idiot."

"Now you know." Aiden kissed the baby's head again.

"He's asleep. Like magic."

"I'll put him to bed."

She followed him upstairs, hovering over the bassinet as he settled the baby inside. Tiffany gazed down at the sleeping infant, the tears coming unbidden and without warning. She let out a sob and pressed the back of her hand against her mouth.

"He's fine. No need to cry."

She turned and buried her head against his chest, the tears falling freely. They stood there for some time, his arms wrapped around her as she soaked his shirt, and he rocked on his feet, allowing her to cry. He rested his cheek against her hair and shut his eyes, wondering at this change. He hadn't seen this side of her in a long time; a side he didn't know still existed.

"It should've been like this for us with our baby girl. We never had a chance."

The tears weren't about Daniel. They were about him and his failures. He had tried to keep them together, but his efforts had been futile. "You blamed me for not being stronger."

This made Tiffany cry harder. "I never blamed you, Aiden."

His thoughts traveled to the acrimonious fights, the stony silences, and the inevitable and devastating end of their marriage. "Could've fooled me."

"Stop, Aiden. Please stop it." Tiffany pushed away, pausing halfway to the door. "You should go. Leave me alone." With those final dismissive words, she bolted from the room.

"And the bitch is back." He ran his fingertip over the baby's soft cheek. "She's impossible, Daniel. Do yourself a favor and avoid women. They're trouble."

Tiffany's sudden flare of temper reminded him of the final volatile months of their marriage. Her denial of how badly she'd damaged their relationship with her betrayal. Those last weeks combined with the loss of a close friend had him bailing, desperate to save what little sanity he had left.

Aiden stared down at the tiny boy who looked so peaceful, his chest rising and falling regularly. Would he ever have the chance for another child? It might not happen and he longed for all he'd missed with Savannah.

After some time, he let himself out the front door. There was nothing left to say. He'd never persuade Tiffany to see her daughter, and he didn't want to put any of them through it. She'd made her choice and now they'd live with it.

Aiden stared over the azure blue water, shielding his eyes against the sun glinting off the flat expanse, white sails dotting the horizon. All the good times they'd had, running wild during those carefree summers flashed through his mind. The memories of her and how it used to be.

It made him nostalgic. Or idiotic. Who could tell? Last night he'd felt … *What?* The echoes of faded love? Compassion? Or simply regret? For an instant, he'd felt close to her but then the feeling vanished along with the glimpse of sweet Tiffany.

The hot, sunny day beckoned and the patio burned under his bare feet, making him itch to be on the water. He longed for a taste of how it used to be, but could never be again. There was nobody to even join him.

The hell with it. Aiden tucked the necessities into a waterproof bag and loped down the stairs, heading to the kitchen to pack a cooler. A day on the water might make him feel less alone. Less hopeless.

He'd only boarded his boat and gone below when a thump on deck alerted him.

"Permission to come aboard?"

"Ryan?"

"Who else?" The tall man swung down the steps and dragged Aiden into a bone-crushing squeeze. "What do you think you're doing? Were you going sailing without me?"

"Never." Aiden returned the embrace, the edge of sadness evaporating at the unexpected appearance of his childhood friend. "What are you doing here?"

Ryan released him and stepped back a pace, a sly grin appearing. "I had a few extra vacation days coming." He shrugged. "Here I am."

"Damn that Alex." He narrowed his eyes, gauging his friend's reaction.

"Only because she cares … Crap." Ryan snickered. "You and your sixth sense."

"No surprise she called for reinforcements. What took you so long?"

"It's quite a haul from California, but well worth it." The man rubbed a hand through his artfully messy blond hair. "She'd be down here whipping your ass into shape herself if she didn't have that cranky little dude keeping her busy." He snickered. "New babies are a ton of work too. And she had to go back to Chicago for the week."

"Ha ha." Aiden pushed him toward the stairs. "No matter how you got here, I'm happy to see you."

"Good, because I'm staying in your guest room."

"Then earn your keep. It's time to cast off."

Ryan gave a mock salute but moved easily across the deck, hauling in the bumpers. "I hear you rescued Daniel last night. Imagine, Sharkie in tears?"

"I don't know who was fussing more, her or the baby. She had him bundled tighter than a burrito." Aiden shoved lightly against the dock. "Did she confess?"

"Nah. Alex found incriminating evidence."

"Oh?"

"You left your thermometer." He sighed. "Call Alex. She wants to thank you for the house call."

"Not necessary. I was happy to help." Aiden hoisted the sail and they were soon skimming along the water. "This was a great idea."

"Call her, Aiden."

"Why? So she can pull some more of that match-making shit? Thanks, but no."

"Hey, I get it, but they never will unless you out Sharkie. For fuck's sake, man. The woman ripped a chunk out of you, and you still protect her? Alex deserves the truth."

A touch of the joy of seeing his friend left him. "Can't we just sail and have a good day without discussing ... that?"

"Sorry." Ryan patted his shoulder. "Sailing it is."

The sun was high in the sky by the time they stopped for a break, anchoring not far from shore. Aiden cracked open a cold beer, offering a bottle to Ryan before setting out lunch.

The man examined the spread. "Crab rolls?"

"I threw a few meals together." Aiden cut open two crisp buns before handing one to Ryan.

The other man scooped out a heaping portion of the crab mix and added a generous spoonful of potato salad to his plate. "Hmm." He took a large bite, chewing slowly before taking a long pull from his beer. "What's really going on? Boston? Breaking up with Emily? This continuing feud with Tiffany?"

Aiden set his plate aside and sat on the side of the boat to dip his feet into the cool water. "It's ... a long story." He glanced at his friend before guzzling half of his beer.

"I have all damn day." Ryan brushed the crumbs from his shorts and lowered himself to the deck beside Aiden. "Start with Emily. Or Boston. Or Sharkie. Just throw it out there."

"It's big, Ryan." He heaved a sigh. "Life altering. For all of us."

"I'm listening."

He closed his eyes. *Just say it.* "The daughter we put up for adoption fifteen years ago found me and—"

"Whoa. Full stop." Ryan's waved in a time-out motion. "Daughter? And who the fuck is we?" His eyes widened. "You and ... Tiffany?"

Aiden lifted a shoulder and swallowed another mouthful of his drink.

"I'm ... speechless." Ryan scrubbed his hands over his face. "Your daughter's fifteen? You met her?"

Aiden fished out his phone and found a recent photo. "Her name's Savannah."

"Damn, Aiden. She's a darlin'. When does she get to meet her Uncle Ryan?" The man frowned. "I get to meet her, right?"

"Yeah. I bet she'll love you." He sucked in a breath. "Her adoptive parents are both gone. Savannah is moving with me to Boston."

Ryan waggled his head as his eyes widened. "Gone ... as in ... they died?"

Aiden pinched the bridge of his nose, swallowing hard as the events of the past several months overwhelmed him.

His friend squeezed his shoulder. "Take a breath." He rose, returning moments later with two bottles of water, handing one to Aiden. "Drink."

He drained half of the bottle and blew out a long breath. Already he felt better just by sharing with one more person. "You must have a thousand questions," he said finally.

"Millions, but not until you're ready. Just know I'm here to help in any way I can." He grinned. "I can't wait to meet my darlin' little niece."

Chapter 35

Savannah

The tiny airport wasn't at all what Savannah expected. It didn't compare to the ones she'd been in before. The building seemed almost quaint, but she supposed the island was relatively tiny and they didn't need anything bigger.

"Savannah." Aiden's voice came from behind her.

"Aiden." She threw herself into his arms, kissing him on the cheek as he swung her around. "I missed you."

"I'm so happy you're here." Aiden tucked his arm around her and led her to the small baggage carousel. Her suitcase was already there and he scooped it up before leading her to the car.

"Can we put the top down?" She eyed the older, but pristine, Mercedes convertible.

"We sure can." Aiden hit a button after stowing her bag in the trunk, and the dark canvas opened.

Savannah grinned as they left the parking lot, enjoying the light swash of air sweeping over them. "This is great, I love it already."

"Glad you like it." He reached over and squeezed her hand before placing his back on the wheel. "My … our place is right on the beach, so the boat is docked there."

"You have a boat?" Her eyes widened. Despite his tales of days on the ocean, he'd never mentioned he owned a sailboat.

"I'd love to teach you to sail over the summer." He cast a glance at her. "I swim just after sunrise most mornings if you ever want to join me. It's the best time of the day." He turned the car into a wide gravel lane.

"Sunrise might be too early for me. We'll see." Savannah gasped as the house came into view. She'd expected a cozy beach cabin much like Leanne's family owned, but this took her breath away. It sat on a lush green space surrounded by trees with two massive decks off the back. She imagined the view of the ocean would be spectacular. "That's yours?" Vanna pointed at the craft moored at the dock.

"Mmhm. Her name is Maya." Aiden parked at the side of the house. "Let's get you settled." He retrieved her bag and led her across a flagstone patio.

"This is beautiful," Savannah said as she followed him into the large open space, immediately drawn to the chef's kitchen. The place didn't seem big from the outside, but inside it was spacious and luxurious. She opened the fridge and her eyes lit up. "All my favorites. This is great."

"Want to see your room?" He led her upstairs and turned left. "This used to be mine, but it's been updated a bit since then." Aiden put her suitcase aside and sat on the edge of the bed, patting the mattress.

She sat beside him, curling one leg beneath her. "What?"

"Your Uncle Ryan is here and he'll join us for dinner tonight."

Nerves but also excitement quivered through her. "Uncle … like Tom is my uncle?"

"Exactly." Aiden looped an arm around her. "He'll be back soon, so unpack and come downstairs."

Once Aiden left the room, she explored her new surroundings. The spacious room felt cool and comfortable despite the heat of the day, courtesy of the light sea breeze wafting through the open window. She peered out, taking in the large tree to the side that blocked the bright rays of sun while leaving a stunning view of the beach and glittering ocean beyond it.

A figure appeared below. A tall, tanned, solidly built man with short blond hair. He paused, shielding his eyes as he looked toward their house. The man ran a hand through his hair, before waving at someone unseen and continuing his journey across the sparkling sand.

Savannah watched his progress until he disappeared from her sight and the rumble of low masculine voices drifted from the main floor. She ran a brush through her waves and straightened her sundress.

Aiden smiled as he caught sight of her hovering at the base of the stairs. "Vanna, this is Ryan Hartmann."

She bowed her head, suddenly shy in the presence of this imposing man who seemed to fill the entire space. When she dared raise her gaze, she met inquisitive blue eyes and offered Ryan a small hesitant smile.

"Hello, my darlin'." His wide grin was followed by her engulfment in his muscular arms as he scooped her into a gentle hug and planted a light kiss to her cheek. He set her on her feet and stepped back a pace.

She craned her neck upward, fighting her own grin. Ryan towered over her, but despite his size and apparent strength, he projected a gentle kindness that immediately drew her to him.

"Don't mind him." Aiden gave a low laugh. "He goes overboard with his greetings."

"Nah." Ryan waved a hand at his friend. "I believe Savannah and I will get along just fine, won't we darlin'?"

Savannah nodded. Despite all her losses over the past months, she'd also gained an entirely new family who so far, had provided a warm welcome. That gave her an unexpected sense of comfort.

Savannah hummed as she chopped vegetables and swayed to the music playing on the sound system. After a full week, she felt completely at home, especially after the time spent with not only Aiden, but her Uncle Ryan. She'd been sad when the man left, but the promise of his return the next weekend made her smile.

She popped a crispy bit of red pepper into her mouth before rinsing a second one and setting it on the cutting board.

"Tiffany? What are you doing here? Harrison won't be too pleased about you hanging out with your ex—"

Savannah spun and froze at the sight of the dark-haired woman in the doorway.

"You're not Tiffany." The woman's eyes widened as she scanned Vanna from head to toe.

Savannah's heart pounded. *Tiffany*. The beautiful blonde who rescued Aiden's credit card when it was in danger of being hacked to bits. Her mouth dried as she eyed the intruder. "Who are you?"

"Alexis Nichols." The woman's gaze never faltered as she stepped closer, one hand cradling the tiny bump in the wrap wound around her. "What's your name?"

Savannah's breath caught in her chest as the woman advanced. *Tiffany Baxter*. The pieces clicked. "Savannah Phillips."

Alex's eyebrows went up as her head tilted. "I'd ask if Aiden knows you're here, but I suspect he does." She motioned to the knife in Savannah's hand. "We're not dangerous."

Savannah offered the woman a small smile as she lowered the knife and set it on the counter. "Sorry. He'll be back any minute."

"My, you're just like her ... except for your eyes. That hair ..." Alexis stared at her.

I look like the woman who'd run the other direction? "Tiffany is Aiden's ex."

"Mmhm." Alexis blinked. "Haven't you ...? How old are you?"

"Fifteen."

"Uh-huh." Alexis set her bag onto one of the stools at the counter and unwrapped a squirming baby, nestling him in one arm. "This is Daniel."

"How old is he?" Savannah tensed, still confused as to why this woman had walked into Aiden's house and made herself comfortable. She contemplated the tiny boy in the woman's arms, searching for some resemblance.

"Two months. We thought we'd surprise Uncle Aiden with a visit." She rubbed her son's back. "Joel and I own a house up the beach."

Savannah relaxed. "Joel. Your husband?"

Alexis nodded. "I didn't mean to frighten you, but you took me by surprise. Aiden's car is in the driveway and Maya is at the dock, so I figured he was home."

"We have two cars."

"Right, Aiden doesn't drive his fancy sports car on these roads. So tell me ..." Alexis raised a brow. "Where's home? How long are you visiting Aiden?"

"I live with him." Savannah looked down, picking at a nail. "Home used to be Portland, but we're moving to Boston." She dared to peek at the woman.

"Portland," Alexis whispered, her eyes shimmering. "You're—"

The front door opened and closed. "Hey, I'm back. Guess what ...?" Aiden froze in his tracks. "Lex. What are you doing here?"

"I'm having a nice chat with"—Alex looked at Aiden, her eyes narrowing before her gaze traveled to Savannah, and then back to Aiden—"Savannah."

"Ahh. Where's Joel?"

"In Chicago for work, but he'll be back on the weekend." She shifted the little boy in her arms.

"How is our little man?" Aiden placed two large bags on the side counter and scooped the baby from Alex's arms. He kissed the baby's downy head and a tiny fist came up and tapped his cheek. Aiden nibbled at the fingers, coaxing a coo out of the baby. "You should join us for dinner. Tonight's menu is seafood chowder, along with grilled chicken and shrimp."

"Sounds delicious." Alexis smiled and pressed a kiss to his cheek. "If you hold Daniel, I'll put away the groceries. It'll be nice to have a little break. With Joel gone, Daniel's on me 24/7."

Aiden draped the baby over his shoulder and rubbed his back. "Hear that, Daniel? Mommy needs a break."

Savannah peeked out of the corner of her eye, marveling at how comfortable he was with the tiny baby.

"Make yourself useful and light the grill." Alex fluttered a hand at Aiden, who tucked Daniel into the crook of his arm and headed toward the deck.

"I wish he'd settle down and have a family." Alex gave Savannah a sideways glance. "He'd be a great dad."

"He should marry Emily." The words came out before she could stop them.

The pause in Alex's movements was brief and subtle, but it was there. "You know Emily?"

Savannah nodded.

The woman blinked hard as she flattened her palms against the granite counter, her face crumpling as a tear trickled down her cheek.

"You know who I am." Savannah's heart dropped. She'd gotten between Aiden and another woman who was clearly important in his life. "Please don't be angry with him because of me."

"I'm not." Alexis sniffled and brushed her fingertips under her eyes. "Aiden tried to talk to me a while back."

"About me?"

"I think so, but I was so preoccupied."

"You're close to him."

"We've been friends since we were kids." Alexis sighed. "Things have been weird for the last while. Now I know why."

Savannah bowed her head.

"It's okay." The woman patted her hand. "This explains a lot."

"It does?"

"Mmhmm, but it's amazing." A smile crept across the woman's face. "You should call me Aunt Alex." Alexis pulled her into a hug, but let go as Vanna stiffened. "Sorry. You must think I'm some crazy woman, but you're ... Aiden's daughter. That makes you family."

Vanna stared at the woman for only a second before she threw her arms around her. The total acceptance by this woman stunned her. *Aunt Alex.*

"I'm sorry about Tiffany." Alex rubbed her back. "I don't get what she's thinking. She's said nothing about any of this."

Savannah released Alex. "She's ashamed of me. Emily and I saw her when we were shopping, but she ran away." The tears burned behind her eyes.

A warm hand landed on her shoulder, and she realized Aiden had come inside without her noticing.

"Hey, let me take Daniel and feed him before we eat." Alex relieved him of the baby and scooped up the diaper bag before heading upstairs.

"I'm sorry, Savannah. I didn't want you to find out like this, but now you know." He slid an arm around her shoulders.

"Tiffany. She's my mother?"

"Yes. Emily told me what happened that day."

"Emily knew it was her, didn't she?"

"It's hard to hide the resemblance. It's been difficult keeping it a secret from everyone, and I wanted to tell Alex a while ago. Tiffany and I have our differences, so it's been tough."

"You don't get along because of me."

"No, Vanna. We both made choices, and that's on us. It's not your fault. Don't ever think you caused our issues."

"She'll never want me, will she?"

"Maybe one day she'll come to her senses, but until then," he said as his embraced tightened, "you have a whole family."

Savannah sniffled. The hard facts settled over her. Her mother would never want her, but Aiden did, and that had to be enough. "Tiffany's engaged to some guy who wants to be Governor. I've seen it in the news."

"That's right."

"Does she love him?"

Aiden shrugged. "It's not my business. She and I were over long ago, and we've barely spoken in the past eight years."

"If he loves her and she loves him, wouldn't it just be okay? Emily stayed even after you told her."

"Different situation. I don't know if I can explain it, but with politicians, some of them are good people, but it changes people too. Tiffany wasn't always like this, but she grew up in politics and she sees it a certain way."

"It hurts that she doesn't want me." She leaned in, letting Aiden hug her.

"I know, but we can't change it. We can only live with it."

"Emily lied to me. How could she do that?"

"That's my fault. I asked her not to say anything." Aiden rubbed her arm. "Don't let my actions affect your relationship with Emily, it'll just make everything worse. Don't do that to any of us."

Savannah didn't understand how he could be so forgiving of the woman who'd broken his heart, but if he wasn't angry, maybe there was still hope they'd get back together.

"Shall we get Alex and finish making dinner?"

"She wants me to call her Aunt Alex."

"You can. She's great, Vanna. I've known her forever."

Savannah wiped away her tears and nodded. "I'd like that."

Aiden pressed a kiss to her hair. "I'm sure she'll love it."

Chapter 36

Aiden

A SOFT GLOW EMANATED FROM THE fire pit as the last of the flames died out. Aiden stretched out his legs, one arm wrapped around his daughter, who leaned heavily against him.

Savannah rubbed her eyes and smothered a yawn. "I'm exhausted." She planted a kiss on Aiden's cheek. "I'm headed to bed." After only a second of hesitation, the girl leaned in and embraced Alex. "Night, Aunt Alex."

"Sweet dreams, Savannah." The woman gave Aiden a teary smile over Vanna's shoulder as she hugged the girl. "We're here for the rest of the summer, so be sure to visit."

"I will." Vanna waved before stepping inside the house.

"She's beautiful. I love her already." Alex joined him on the wicker sofa, linking her arm through his. "You tried to tell me, didn't you?"

He placed his hand over hers. "There were so many times I wanted to, Alex, but I couldn't."

"I don't understand," she said softly, staring out over the darkened waters. "Tiffany did this to you? To her daughter?"

Aiden took a long deep breath, ready to let it all out without holding anything back. "It gets worse. We divorced because she cheated and I walked in on her with the guy." He took a long gulp of his beer. "I tried to forgive her but—"

"Shh." She peered at him. "You don't need to explain, except … Why did you allow her to get away with so much crap? You let us blame you. Why?"

He scrubbed his hands over his face. There were many things about those dark days he'd never tell. "I couldn't let people take sides. It was my fault as much as hers."

"You, my sweet man, are a better person than I could ever be. If Joel cheated I'd string him up by the balls." She sighed. "We did choose sides, in a way." Her voice was sad, and she snuggled closer. "I'm sorry, Aiden, for every time we've pushed you two together. I'm especially sorry that it didn't work out with Emily."

He shrugged. Pain lanced through him at the thought of the woman who'd broken his heart.

"Is Savannah why you were out of town? Why you missed Daniel's birth?"

"She needed me, Lex. Can you forgive me for not being there for you?"

"Oh, honey, you're already forgiven. Never doubt you did the right thing. Your daughter has to come first in everything." She smiled. "What did Ryan say? You told him, right?"

"He adores her already." He grinned. "People look at Ryan and assume he's a shallow playboy, but he's never been that guy. He was incredible with Savannah. Tom too. I still have to tell Jenna. She's going to slay me."

"A tangled web of lies, huh." Alex rubbed his arm.

"Something like that. Tiffany will freak when she realizes everybody knows. I doubt Harrison even realizes she's been married before. I'm the dirty little secret she never tells." He picked at the label on his bottle. Their whole relationship had been one huge mistake. He'd lived under its cloud for years, and the repercussions were never-ending.

"You shouldn't feel that way." Alex slid her arms around him, wrapping him in a hug. "You're an amazing guy and any woman would be lucky to have you."

"Yeah, right," he said under his breath. "That's why they always leave. Emily's been the most serious relationship since Tiffany and even she's choosing her career over me. I asked her to move to Boston and she said no."

"Any chance she'll change her mind? Maybe you should ask her again."

He shook his head, looking away to hide his sadness. The harsh lessons learned during his first marriage stuck with him relentlessly. "I'll call Tom tomorrow and see if they're coming for the weekend, or if I should take Vanna to Chicago. It's time Jenna met Savannah."

Two days later, Aiden headed along the beach toward his friends' house, preparing himself for the difficult conversation to come. *Time's up.* He sighed heavily as the woman approached.

Jenna waved and gave him a bright smile as she skipped across the sand. "I'm glad you called." Her long hug and kiss reminded him of what he loved about this sweet and caring woman. Jenna Maxwell was the sister he'd always wished for. "How are you?" She studied him. "I'm sorry about Emily."

"I'll survive."

They headed down to the sand, meandering along the stretch of waterfront. She caught his hand. "Something's up. Tell me." At his silence, she sighed. "How long have we been friends?"

"Forever?"

"Exactly. I'm worried about you."

"I'm really okay, Jenn, even if my life is a complicated mess." He sucked in a long breath of the salty air. The time had come to confess, no matter the consequences. "It's not only about me anymore."

"What do you mean?" Jenna frowned.

Aiden found a picture of Savannah and extended his phone.

Jenna squinted at the screen. "You're … getting back together with Tiffany?" Her brows shot up. "I don't understand." She shaded the phone from the sun's glare and studied the image again. "That's … not Tiffany … but … who is this?"

"Savannah," he said. "My fifteen-year-old daughter."

"Your … What?" Jenna pressed a hand to her mouth. "A daughter who looks like—"

"Her mother."

"Wait. Are you telling me that this"—she shoved the phone in his face, waving it inches from his nose—"this girl is your child, and Tiffany is her damn mother? You two had a … a …" Jenna's eyes filled with tears, and she emitted a choked sob. "You have a fifteen-year-old daughter? And you never told me?"

"Jenn, I—"

"You asshole." The woman dealt him a resounding slap across the face. "You've hidden a secret child for all these years?" She spun and stalked down the beach, still clutching his phone.

"Damn." He rubbed his stinging cheek as he jogged across the hot sand after her. "Jenn. Please let me explain."

"Explain? Two people I thought were my friends, and you've kept your child a secret? What's to explain?" She sank onto the nearby log and stared at his phone. "Why didn't Tiffany say something? When was she born, and how …?" Her gaze rose to meet his. "Portland?"

Aiden nodded. "Our families threatened us into silence. We told no one."

"Tom didn't know?"

"Not until," Aiden said and cringed, "recently."

Jenna's pursed lips accompanied a sideways glower. "Who else knows?"

Aiden sat and slipped an arm around her waist, avoiding her gaze. "Well …"

"I'm the last to find out? Even Ryan knows?" She smacked his arm with the back of her hand. "How long has Tom known? Just wait until I get my hands on that man."

"I swore him to secrecy, so blame me. Everyone else is only finding out now."

She scoffed but then graced him with a small smile. "A daughter, huh?" Her grin widened as she slapped his shoulder. "Jerk."

"Ouch." He rubbed his arm but returned her smile. "Are you done hitting me?"

"For now," she said. "Savannah. Pretty. She was adopted?"

"They took her the moment she was born. I never even got to see her."

Jenna's eyes shimmered and she turned, wrapping her arms around him. "I'm so sorry. I can't imagine how that felt." She drew back and patted his cheek. "Can I meet her? Tell me everything."

⁓

Aiden glanced over as Tom tapped his shoulder and offered him a frosty bottle.

Tom motioned toward Savannah as she scooped a handful of water and flung it at her Uncle Ryan. "She looks happy."

"Things have turned out pretty well, considering." Aiden grinned as his daughter shrieked, dashing through the waves washing onto the stretch of sand. His happiness faded a touch as Savannah turned, flipping her hair over her shoulder in that particular way, reminding him of another teenage girl playing on this very beach.

That Tiffany had disappeared entirely from the island concerned and saddened him. Despite the differences between them, the girl needed her mother. Or maybe just *a* mother. He closed his eyes, struggling to banish the images of the green-eyed dark-haired woman who'd abandoned him when he needed her most.

A gentle touch against his back brought him to the present.

"Have you heard from her?" Jenna asked.

Was he so transparent? Aiden shook his head and swallowed a mouthful of beer. "That's over."

"Is it?" A soft smile appeared. "Those two," she said and jutted her chin toward Joel and Alex who were ensconced on loungers a few feet away, "were completely off base. It's been obvious all along who your heart belongs to."

Aiden scoffed and looked away. "The woman doesn't feel the same."

"I'm not sure that's a fair assessment. Emily kept a huge secret for you for months and Savannah adores her. She made an effort to bond with your daughter. No woman does that for a man unless deep feelings are involved."

Tom sighed. "Leave it, Jenn. Aiden has enough to deal with right now."

Jenna shook her head. "He needs to hear this. I've spent a fair amount of time with Emily over the past months, and she doesn't strike me as a careless, thoughtless woman. There has to be a reason she won't move."

"She's amazing, but that doesn't mean our relationship can survive. Emily needs to focus on her career, not deal with my messed-up life and confused teenage daughter." Aiden tucked his arm around Jenna. "I appreciate your concern, but I'm fine." A smile twitched at the corners of his mouth. "I get to be Savannah's dad. How great is that?"

"Your daughter is wonderful, but wouldn't life be even better with the right lady?"

"Sure. Maybe one day I'll meet this mythical woman who will make my life absolutely perfect." Aiden squinted at her, noting her sly grin. "Whatever you're thinking, don't."

The grin widened, her eyes sparkling as she laughed. "Whatever do you mean?"

Aiden understood Jenna wanted him to be happy, but she had to accept him moving on without Emily just like Alex and Joel had accepted his future without Tiffany.

Happiness didn't have to revolve around the convoluted dynamics involved in romantic relationships and marriage. He'd tried that and failed in spectacular fashion. True joy could be about being reunited with his daughter and appreciating the amazing friends surrounding him. And for now, that would be enough.

Continue with The Hamilton Series with Everything For Love, Book 2.

Share the Love

If you enjoyed this story please consider leaving a review at the retailer where you purchased the book, on Goodreads, or even give it a mention on social media. The best compliment an author can receive is positive recognition of their work.

The Hamilton Series

Purchase links for these book may be found at: KateSmithAuthor.ca

Everything we Lost

Everything for Love

Never let you Fall

Everything left Unsaid

Everything we Dream

Everything we Promised

Chapter 1

Emily

EMILY STROLLED DOWN THE BOARDWALK, gazing at the expanse of water. Maybe he was doing the exact same thing, even if it was a different ocean on the opposite side of the country. How was he managing as a full-time parent? Was Savannah settling into her new life?

Shame touched her. She'd avoided contacting Aiden and Savannah. She wasn't oblivious to the damage she'd done but …

"Aunt Emily." Her niece skipped toward her, balancing a precarious scoop of ice cream, a rivulet of sticky caramel trickling down her wrist in the hot California sun. "Look what Mommy got me."

Natalia arrived seconds later. She fished a napkin from her pocket and dabbed at the girl's arm. "Eat it before it melts." Her rueful look at Emily said it all. "I couldn't say no."

Emily smiled gently. Her sister was compensating for Isabella's absent father. Again. Yet how could she judge after witnessing Savannah's devastation when she lost Ross? Sometimes a steady stream of love and indulgence was what it took to dull the pain.

"Emelia?" Nat nudged her with an elbow. "You're thinking about him again, aren't you?"

Isabella bounced across the sand, a seagull hopping away from the energetic girl.

"You are so good with her, Nat. How do you manage?"

"What else can I do?" Her sister glanced at the dark-haired angel as she dropped to her knees, examining something buried in the sand while taking the occasional swipe at her ice cream with her tongue. "It would be easier with a partner."

She avoided the knowing look coming her way. "He'll be fine," she said under her breath.

"Will you?" Nat arched her brow.

"Ha, no. Jenna is adamant about my part in the wedding." The recent text from Jenna conveyed irritation about the secret Emily had kept from her, oddly followed by a phone call an hour later. The warm thank you for being there for Aiden and for keeping said secrets been a pleasant surprise. "That means the grand combination of pissed off man and his bitchy ex-wife."

"She's still the maid of honor?" A horrified look appeared.

"Apparently. Jenna is sweet and gentle and she hates hurting anyone's feelings. She's keeping the peace in hopes Tiffany will come to her senses."

Nat smirked. "You and Jenna are soul sisters."

Emily sighed. Natalia was right. She'd paste on a smile and attend each and every wedding-related event without a single complaint, even if being near her ex-boyfriend was awkward and painful. Over the months of dating Aiden she'd grown close to his friends, especially Jenna, and the woman made it clear that the break-up was no excuse to abandon her bridesmaid duties.

"Let me suggest an easy solution to the pissed off man part of the equation, Emelia."

She squinted at Nat, shaking her head.

"What have you got to lose? You have the vacation time booked, and you know he has room. If he doesn't, Jenna would let you stay with her and Tom."

"I have to leave some space. Let him adjust to being a single parent."

Nat scoffed. "I love you, Emelia, but you're completely insane to let an eligible guy like Aiden go."

"There's more to a relationship than—"

"Uh-huh. Don't pretend this thing between you and Aiden doesn't encompass everything a woman could possibly need." Nat pointed her index finger. "One. He's that perfect combination of adorably sweet and impossibly sexy."

"Right, which means fighting off more flight attendants and supermodels."

"Yet the fictional Dani and legendary Jazlyn are in his rearview mirror." Nat wrinkled her nose. "Two." A second finger came up. "He's got a great career."

"So he works long hours." She cringed at Nat's glare.

"Three." She held up her hand, waggling her extended fingers. "He's an involved and caring dad with the bonus that he makes beautiful babies."

"And he has a bonus crazy-ass ex-wife who hates me."

"Really, Emelia?" Nat glowered. "Four. He's financially stable."

"I don't need a rich guy to take care of me."

"Five." Her sister splayed her fingers, fanning them in Emily's face. "You're in love with him."

Emily clamped her teeth onto her lower lip.

"Ahh." She grinned. "Six." Nat lifted her other hand. "He's in love with you."

"Not anymore. Besides, the minute crazy-ex comes to her senses, she'll want her husband back."

Her sister tapped her pursed lips. "How many years ago was that divorce?" Natalia raised another finger. "Seven. You lov—"

"Stop." Emily clapped her hands over her ears, but her sister tugged them away.

"Unless you want to hear the rest of my many reasons, then get on a plane. Take a chance. He's worth it."

Emily shook her head. Tomorrow she'd board her flight to Chicago and get on with her life. No matter how many reasons her sister thought of or how much her heart ached, the relationship was too complicated. Too messy. Definitely over.

―※―

"Bye." Isabella wrapped her arms around Emily and kissed her cheek. "Do you have to go?"

"Sorry, cariño." Emily hugged the girl tight, pressing her face into her soft fragrant hair. A familiar ache built as it always did when she left. "I'll miss you, but I'll visit again soon." She released the girl and turned to her sister. "Love you, Nat."

Her sister embraced her and whispered, "Thank you, Emelia. I found the envelope. One day I'll repay you."

She gave her sister a squeeze. "No need."

"You help Mama and Jules too, and you have medical loans. How can you afford it?"

Emily blinked hard. "I do pretty well as a doctor and you're family."

"You're an angel."

After a last hug, Emily slid into the back of the taxi and waved, sinking into the seat and closing her eyes as the car merged into traffic. Soon she'd be unable to help her sister and niece. The only reason she could now was because Aiden waved off every attempt to contribute to the monthly bills. Not that she could admit that tidbit and provide her sister more ammunition.

As they drew closer to the airport, Emily dug into her bag for taxi fare and pulled out the boarding pass for her flight to Chicago. "Thanks." She smiled and accepted her bag from the driver. She weaved her way through the crowded concourse, spying the check-in.

Emily joined the queue, staring at the pass in her hand. *To jump or not?* When she finally reached the agent she asked, "How do you get from LAX to Martha's Vineyard?"

"Generally through Boston." The agent held out her hand.

"Can I exchange my ticket for a flight to Boston?" She clenched the paper between her fingers.

The woman sighed.

"It's important. There's this guy …" Emily bowed her head and set her paperwork on the counter as the woman curled her lip.

"Honey, there always is." The keys clacked as the woman slammed her fingers against them. "One seat left on the next flight." Her lips twitched as she glanced at the economy booking in front of her. "First class. The last minute fare is … much, much more, Dr. Anderson. The Chicago ticket is non-refundable."

Emily peered at the number on the screen and shook her head. How could she swing it after giving Nat half of her last pay check and knowing she'd soon have to pay a damage deposit and rent for a new apartment?

The agent's smile widened. "The next flight isn't for seven hours. I have economy on that one. Care to wait?"

Emily shook her head again. Aiden wouldn't be that happy to see her anyway. Maybe fate was telling her to forget the entire ridiculous idea.

"So we'll just check you in for your Chicago flight, then?"

The ache built. She had no choice if she wanted to see Aiden. "Let me find my credit card." Emily tugged her wallet free from her bag, pausing. Maybe this was a bad idea. "Never mind, I'll just—"

"Upgrade her ticket and get her on the first Boston flight, please." A large hand came into view. One holding a platinum card. "Book the connecting flight for the Vineyard too."

Emily lifted her chin, peering up at the owner of the deep voice, taking in the broad shoulders and solid muscular chest straining under a dark button-down shirt.

"My treat." He winked. "I believe in paying it forward."

"Thank you, sir." The woman behind the counter directed a smile at the man, batting her big blue eyes before she checked Emily's bag and issued a boarding pass and an itinerary with details on her connecting flight. "Have a nice flight, sir."

Emily slung her bag over her shoulder and snatched the papers from the agent's hand, turning away with a scoff. "How is it the men always get the good service?"

"Don't take it personally. I'm a frequent flyer." The man fell into step beside Emily as they headed toward the security line.

"Yeah, that's it, I bet." She laughed as she took in the guy's tall muscular frame, strong jaw, and sparkling blue eyes. "It has nothing to do with the fact you're tall, blond, and handsome. She practically launched over the counter and tackled you to the floor."

"Aww, darlin', I'm flattered." He grinned and motioned for her to precede him into the queue.

"I don't know how to thank you. If you give me your address, I'll repay you."

"No need." He handed her a gray bin for her belongings and opened his bag, separating his electronics into his own bin and adding his shoes and carry-on bag to a second tray. "You're a doctor?"

"Mmhmm. Emergency medicine." Emily eyed the man before handing her boarding pass to the uniformed security officer and stepping through the metal detector.

Once the man joined her, she extended her hand. "My flight will be called soon … I don't even know your name."

"Our flight. I'm also headed to Boston." He gathered his belongings. "We should go."

Emily glanced his way, unsure of what to say. Had this man bought her ticket because he expected a hook up? She raised her chin and straightened. "I'm involved with someone. I'm sorry if you thought …" She arched a brow at his low chuckle.

He held up his hands. "I'm not hitting on you, I swear." His grin widened as they continued toward the departure gate. "I heard the part about the guy and I'm a sucker for a grand gesture of love."

Her cheeks reddened, heat burning her ears. "Why waste your time on someone who's taken?"

"Since when is making a new friend a waste of time?" He guided her into the priority boarding line. They presented their passes and he followed her onto the plane. "Look at that. We're neighbors." He winked as he settled into the plush seat beside hers.

"How did you manage that?"

"You really are a suspicious woman, Dr. Anderson. Relax. I'm an investment advisor, not a weirdo stalker."

Emily laughed. "Sorry. It's just that guys usually …"

"Want to get laid?" He shook his head. "I'd never interfere between you and your man. Some things are sacred."

The flight attendant appeared. "Would you like a warm towel? Something to drink while we board the rest of the passengers?"

Emily sighed in contentment as she accepted the delightfully warm square of smooth cotton, the gentle heat relaxing her as she brushed her fingers across it. She only experienced the little luxuries of first class when she traveled with Aiden. The difference from economy still amazed her.

The man ordered a scotch and his meal before motioning to Emily. "What would you like, darlin'?"

"Vodka and cranberry." After she'd selected her meal, she stared out the window, idly tracking the movements of the ground crew as they loaded the baggage. What to say to Aiden when she appeared with no warning? She feared a cooler welcome than on her last surprise Vineyard visit.

"How about you and this guy?" The blond man asked once the flight attendant had served their drinks.

"It's stupid, really." She gulped a large mouthful of tart cranberry. "We broke up, so I doubt he'll want to see me." Emily drummed her fingers on the arm rest. "You wasted your money on a first class ticket."

"Yet you're on this plane. That means hope." The man leaned back and crossed an ankle over his knee, taking a leisurely sip of the amber liquid in his glass. "How long since you broke up?"

"Five weeks. Plenty of time for him to hook up."

"Do you always have so little faith in men?"

She drained the cold liquid, swallowing hard. "I've dated a series of cheaters and liars." Even her own father had joined the love 'em and leave 'em club when she was young. Her broken-hearted mother struggled as a single parent, leaving Emily with zero tolerance for infidelity.

"Which one is this guy?"

"Neither." Emily closed her eyes. "He's just … complicated."

The flight attendant worked her way up the aisle. "We're ready for departure …"

The routine words drifted over Emily as she adjusted her seat into the upright position and forced herself to breathe while they bumped across the tarmac. The engines roared and her stomach did the familiar flip as the aircraft sped down the runway and lifted from the ground. She clenched her hands in her lap until they leveled off and the seatbelt light went out.

"Anything I can get you?" The flight attendant asked.

"Another vodka-cranberry, please." Emily drummed her fingers on the arm rest. This flight would pass quicker and easier once she took the edge off.

The man across from her ordered another scotch, studying her silently until they had fresh drinks in hand. "Explain complicated."

A nervous laugh escaped. How to even begin? "I've known him for years. We worked together and he's an amazing doctor." She glanced at the man.

"Yeah, bad idea to get involved with a colleague, right?" She sucked back half of her drink. "Especially a guy like him. He can have anyone, but he chose me."

The man smiled and nodded. "And?"

"One day he asked me to dinner. We'd gone out for drinks after a crap shift many times, mostly with a group, but this invitation had a different vibe." Emily shifted in her chair, taking another sip. "Somehow he managed tickets to a sold out play I'd been dying to see. Brought flowers. Picked me up in a limo. Took me to an expensive restaurant." She sneaked a look at him, noting the wide grin. "Yes, the date ended with mind-blowing sex." A flush crept up her neck. "Did I really did just say that to a total stranger?"

"Ahh, darlin'. I'm not judging."

She ran a finger around the rim of the glass, blinking rapidly. If this man only knew how she judged after that passionate night. How secure it felt being in Aiden's arms, the sweet way he'd treated her, but then allowing insecurity to creep in. How could a man like Aiden value a simple woman like her, raised on the wrong side of town? "He's so perfect."

"What's the problem then?"

She focused on her drink. "He has a teenage daughter and he's moving to Boston."

"Hmm. Is it the teenager or Boston that's the issue?"

"His daughter is lovely and he's an amazing dad. I grew attached to her really quickly."

"So it's Boston?"

"It's so … fast. What if he regrets it? I'll have left my job and followed him and then he's stuck with me. He's sweet and generous and … it's confusing." Emily sighed. "And then there's the ex-wife. What if he can never love me like he loved her?"

"You're worried about Shar—" The man shifted and cleared his throat. "I wouldn't worry, Emelia. She's the ex-wife for a reason."

"Maybe." Confusion rushed in and she shot him a look. "How do you know my name?"

"Uhh, I saw it on your ticket?" He scrubbed a hand through his short, artfully messy hair. "Maybe you need to tell … this guy … to slow it down. Chicago isn't so far from Boston. If you love him, then it's worth the complications. So the question is, do you?"

Emily contemplated him. "How do you know I live in Chicago?"

He shrugged. "You aren't tanned enough to be a resident of L.A. and you were heading to Chicago, so I assumed. Do you live there?"

She narrowed her eyes, but nodded. "Where are you from?"

"Chicago originally, but I went to Stanford and ended up with a job in L.A. Once my contract is up, I plan to move so I can spend more time with my niece and nephew. I miss my friends."

"And your family?"

"Sure, though my parents are divorced and I'm not close to my older sister. I consider my friends as family."

This man reminded her of Aiden. "Funny, he says the same thing. He's not close to his parents, which should be a huge red flag but oddly isn't. He's an only child but his friends are amazing people."

He rewarded her with a warm smile. "Maybe you're overthinking this. Why not take the chance?"

"He seems too good to be true."

"What if he's the real deal?" The man turned serious blue eyes her way. "How does he make you feel," he said, tapping his chest with his index finger, "in here? Can you picture a future?"

She pressed a hand to her chest, wishing she could stop the ache inside. Aiden made her feel so incredibly special all the time, and like Nat, she could easily identify what she loved about him. His generosity. His smile. The wonderful way he had with kids, especially his love and patience with Savannah. How sweet he'd been with her family. The list was endless. "I do, you know."

The man turned her way. "What?"

"I love him and want babies and the ring and ... just everything with him. Even when I hate him, I love him. When he's infuriating and stubborn and so damn impossible, I love him even more." She cupped her hands over her face. "I'm terrified of what he'll say if I show up on his doorstep. What if he's with someone else? What if he doesn't feel the same?"

"He's not and I'm sure he does." The man rose. "I'll be back in a minute."

"How do you know?" Emily whispered. This man either had remarkable powers of deduction or he knew something she didn't. Once he'd entered the tiny bathroom at the front of their section, she snagged his briefcase from the floor and searched the front pockets, smothering a sob as she came up with a pack of business cards. "Ryan Hartmann." The familiar name brought tears to her eyes. She tucked the cards away and set his bag in its place, a shiver running through her.

"You cold?"

The voice startled her and she turned her burning tear-filled eyes his way.

"Hey." Ryan crouched beside her seat. "Don't cry, darlin'. It'll all work out with your guy."

"How would you know?" Emily scoffed and dashed the back of her hand over her eyes. "Is it because you and Aiden talk about me? Do you, Ryan?" She sniffled. "You've known all along who I am. Nobody calls me Emelia besides Aiden."

"Sorry," he said, placing a hand over hers, "but it's not what you think."

"You're not spying on me so you can report back to him?" She pulled away. "Sucker for love, my ass. What a dickhead move. You did this for Aiden."

"Yeah, but I also did it for you." Ryan sank into his seat. "You clearly have regrets and you're in love with him."

Emily turned away, brushing at the tears flowing down her cheeks. "Which you know because you tricked me into telling you everything. Now you can all laugh over what an idiot I am for trusting you."

"Nobody would ever laugh at you for loving Aiden. He's one of my best friends. I want him to be happy." Ryan sighed. "When we get there, I'll take Vanna to Tom's so you two can sort things out."

Emily turned away and closed her eyes. Any intention of visiting the Vineyard faded. Every wish and thought had been exposed, including her stupid comment about having Aiden's babies. All revealed to a supposed stranger she thought she'd never see again. What if Aiden never wanted any of those things?

"I'm sorry. I never meant to hurt or embarrass you," Ryan said softly. "Aiden will fucking annihilate me for that."

"Good," she muttered. "You deserve it. Now leave me the hell alone." She didn't know who to be angrier with; Ryan for luring her into divulging the information or herself for trusting some random guy. Hot tears scalded her cheeks as she curled up facing away from him. That would teach her to trust men.

Hours later they landed in Boston. Emily averted her gritty, red-rimmed eyes from Ryan and exited the moment the crew opened the door. She longed to be home, except she had no true home. The penthouse belonged to Aiden. Going there meant facing the memories. Not going there meant the guest room at her mother's tiny apartment and endless explanations.

"Emily." Ryan caught up with her on the concourse. "Where are you going? The gate is that way." He motioned and then glanced at his expensive gold watch. "Our flight leaves in twenty minutes."

"It's not *our* flight, Ryan. My flight goes to Chicago." She glared at him. "What you did was low."

Ryan scrubbed a hand over his face. "Why are you so angry?"

"I told you things thinking I'd never see you again. Aiden doesn't even know half of it, yet you do? I feel so"—she wrapped her arms around herself—"stupid." *Vulnerable.* Trusting a man with her heart was hard enough, and his friend holding power over intimate information scared her. This man could destroy everything.

"I swear I'll never breathe a word of our conversation to anyone. You tell him what you want when you want."

"Assuming I can trust you. Which I clearly can't."

"When I saw you, and heard what you said, I knew." He tugged her out of the flow of passengers. "Aiden is like a brother to me. I needed to help you get to the Vineyard because he does, Emily."

"Does what?"

"Love you, you beautiful, crazy, stubborn woman." Ryan tugged on her hand. "Please get on the plane. I promise you won't regret it."

"I already regret this."

"Aiden will be pissed if I ever tell him. That would involve confessing to screwing up his chances with the woman he loves. He'd never speak to me again."

"Ahh. It's about saving your own ass."

"You get a free trip to the Vineyard out of it." He widened his eyes. "Do I have to beg?" The man dropped to his knees, clinging to her hand. "Emelia Anderson, would you please take pity on a stupid man, forgive his grievous errors, and save his friendship?"

"Get up." Her cheeks burned as odd looks came their way.

"Not until you say yes." His grip on her hand tightened. "I'm not lying about how he feels. He'll want to see you."

She stared into his hopeful face. Even though this was the first time she'd met Ryan in person, the man had been mentioned many times. *Aiden confided his innermost secrets to Ryan almost as often as he did to Tom.* Emily nodded.

"Let's go." Ryan bounded to his feet and hauled her toward the gate and they arrived just as the last of the passengers disappeared down the jetway.

"Cutting it close." The attendant checked their tickets and ushered them through the gate.

Ryan held her hand tightly until they reached the plane, allowing her to precede him onto the small aircraft. They barely got seated before the door clunked closed and the safety demonstration began.

"Thank you, Emily. This is the right choice."

"I sure hope so." She closed her eyes, preparing for the inevitable stomach flip. Now she had to figure out what to do when she arrived.

Thank you for reading!

I always love to hear from readers. I can be contacted at http://katesmithauthor.ca

Follow me on social media:

https://www.instagram.com/katesmithauthor/

https://twitter.com/KateSmithAuthor/

https://www.facebook.com/katesmithauthor/

www.ingramcontent.com/pod-product-compliance
Lightning Source LLC
Chambersburg PA
CBHW030230100526
44583CB00013BA/677